Francis Bacon
and the
Style of Science

Francis Bacon and the Style of Science

James Stephens

The University of Chicago Press

Chicago and London

James Stephens is associate professor of English
at Marquette University.

The University of Chicago Press, Chicago 60637
The University of Chicago Press, Ltd., London

Library of Congress Cataloging in Publication Data

Stephens, James.
    Francis Bacon and the style of science.

    Includes bibliographical references and index.
    1. Bacon, Francis, Viscount St. Albans, 1561–1626—
Style. 2. Rhetoric—1500–1800.   3. Scientific litera-
ture. I. Title.
PR2208.S8   192   74-33514
ISBN 0-226-77260-8

Contents

For Pat, Cass, and Alice

Preface

The subject of communication among intellectuals was a primary one for Francis Bacon. We find him deeply concerned in *The Masculine Birth of Time*, a very early work in his career as a philosopher, about how science is to develop "any art or precepts" for the exchange of information. What is needed, he says, is a philosophy of the higher communication which will allow science to use its style of presentation both to "select her followers" and to restore the high standards of honor and duty which should prevail among scholars (*Works*, III, 528-29). Because he has found little in the rhetorical tradition and less in the philosophical tradition to guide him in this search, Bacon grapples with the problem of delivery for the next two decades. In the *New Atlantis*, which was revised just before he died, the transmission and ornamentation of the new philosophy, the "second Scripture," is still under discussion, and Bacon continues there to make telling points about the kind of audience qualified to receive what he has to deliver.

This study, then, is an effort to follow Bacon's mind as it moves through "progressive stages of certainty" to a clear and defensible theory of the philosophical style. What emerges from his works is a complete and sophisticated theory which tells us almost all we need to know in order to understand and appreciate Bacon's goals and achievements as a writer. Moreover, it helps to resolve a good many difficulties which always arise in discussions of Bacon. The failure of his own philosophy, and especially its incompleteness, for example, is explained by the fact that he has no particular philosophy—"I do not pronounce upon anything" (*Works*, V, 210)—and sees himself as a "wit" with skills of recording which will make the first steps to a new philosophy easier to take than they might have been. A wit, in Bacon's mind, is one who uses his intellectual faculties constructively and creatively to clarify, teach, persuade, or entertain.

Bacon begins his program for a new delivery by recognizing that two obstacles must be overcome by the modern philosopher: the nature of the human mind and its weaknesses; and the traditions of logic and rhetoric which continue to encourage those weaknesses by catering to them. The first chapter of this study, "The Philosopher, His Audience, and Popular Rhetoric," deals generally with all the problems which faced the philosopher who would communicate in Bacon's time. Since his discussions of discourse in general and of the rhetorical tradition provide the seeds for a new theory of style, they are primary background for the theory itself. Rather than cover material which has been dealt with fully by such scholars as Morris W. Croll, George Williamson, and Brian Vickers, I refer readers to their work and concentrate on Bacon's debts to Aristotle. It is certain that Bacon went back to Aristotle for guidelines to a new delivery and found much in him that he sought, despite his distaste as a philosopher for the Greek and his work. Bacon's final break with the rhetorical tradition is made with the assistance of Aristotle, who was, ironically, the father of rhetoric, and it is made in the interests of Bacon's new audience and new material.

Bacon thought style should provide a kind of intellectual therapy by playing two roles in his Great Instauration: preparing the mind for the new induction and at the same time engaging it by haunting the imagination. Because the new science needs both converts and qualified practitioners, its spokesman is forced to become more than a reporter. He must also become a fine rhetorician. Chapter 2 of this study outlines what I take to be the three doctrines of Bacon's theory which do most to unite science and style in practical experience: the psychology of discovery; the union of method and manner; and invention by literate experience (or literary invention). The gradual development of these principles is followed as Bacon recorded them between 1603 and 1623; special attention is given to important early works that now are seldom read.

Chapters 3 and 4 turn to Bacon's own style and its achievements in the major works. It is apparent that the aphoristic manner, which I treat in chapter 3, evolved through trial and error and is passed on to us in preliminary form. Bacon holds it up as an ideal form of delivery, one which he himself is incapable of mastering because he never comes to the stage of certainty at which it is the only appropriate means of communication. Bacon's use of the aphorism, fortunately perhaps, is highly rhetorical and persuasive; it rarely comes without the examples, illustrations, testimonies, and similitudes that he knows are essential in the early stages of his work. Yet all these forms of amplification are justified in new ways by Bacon's theory of scientific writing as outlined in the "Plan of the Work," *Parasceve*, and other places.

In chapter 4, "Fable-making as a Strategy of Style," another of Bacon's philosophical methods is examined, the acroamatic. This Bacon perfected to obtain the "quiet entry" into the minds of his readers which he discovered to be essential. Even when the intended receivers are the "sons of science," rather than the "crowd of learners," the author must conspire to enchant them with emotional and imaginative appeals designed to satisfy certain psychological needs. Though he seldom admits it, Bacon too has these requirements, and he delights in the divine mysteries of fable and prophecy. From the late 1590s until his death, in fact, he plays intellectual games with the acroamatic method of delivery, formulating ciphers and secret alphabets, hieroglyphs, codes and tables of all kinds, and attempting to unite them into one large fable for the new world and a new audience of responsible men of vision. The games are serious ones, for Bacon regards the acroamatic method in modernized form as the one sure way of giving science the power to "select her followers" and thus preserve itself from the vulgar minds who would (and sometimes have) debased it. Quite early in his career, then, Bacon decides to work on the problem of granting philosophical authority to figurative language. He wants the success for his project that poets and prophets have earned for theirs, and he is willing to imitate their methods up to a point, especially in the preliminary stages when the "hard" sciences are unperfected.

I naturally hope that this treatment of Bacon's style from the perspective of his own "plan" for science will prove a coherent guide to the works as a whole. Since mine is not an exhaustive analysis, however, it is offered in the Baconian spirit of inquiry, with the wish to stimulate more research and interpretation along these lines. Though Bacon has not, in the worn phrase of literary criticism, "been curiously neglected," he has been approached, I believe, from the wrong angles. If his work is not looked at and evaluated from the modern point of view on science and style, it is almost invariably treated as an extension of or reaction from some traditional figure's work, usually the Greek philosophers, the Stoic writers, or Ramus. These approaches, though sometimes illuminating, create exactly the kind of foliage and overgrowth that Bacon dedicated himself to clearing away. He deserves to be taken on his own terms and to stand or fall by them.

It is difficult to record all my debts for various kinds of help on this project. I cannot name all the librarians—at the University of Wisconsin, Marquette University, the British Museum, and the Folger Shakespeare Library—who were cooperative and patient when I needed assistance. My typist, Mrs. Charlene Lorch, and my students and colleagues who have listened to and discussed much of this material deserve more than thanks. So do my professors at the University of Wisconsin-Madison, Mark Eccles and Lloyd F. Bitzer, who encouraged my work on Bacon when it started in 1967 and 1968. Professor Eccles gave me invaluable direction on my dissertation in 1968 and has been encouraging ever since. I am grateful to Fritz Grunwald, my research assistant, for careful proofreading, and to Joseph Schwartz, my chairman, for reduced teaching loads and other considerations. To *Speech Monographs*, for permission to reprint, in revised form, my article "Bacon's New English Rhetoric and the Debt to Aristotle," *SM* 39 (1972), 248-59, I extend thanks. I also thank *Studies in English Literature* for allowing me to reprint portions of my article "Bacon's Fable-making," in *SEL* 14 (1974), 111-27. I must acknowledge here my gratitude for grants from the Marquette University Graduate School, in 1970 and 1972, for a 1972 Summer Stipend from the National Endowment for the Humanities, and for a travel grant from the American Philosophical Society in 1973. To the members and fellows of The Institute for Research in the Humanities at the University of Wisconsin-Madison, I am grateful for a year in their congenial company. Finally, I thank my family for its cheerful and tolerant presence throughout the preparation of this work.

A Note on Primary Sources

The edition of Bacon's works which is cited throughout is *The Works of Francis Bacon*, 14 volumes, edited by James
Spedding, Robert L. Ellis, and Douglas D. Heath (1857-74; fac-
simile rpt. Stuttgart-Bad Cannstatt: Friedrich Frommann Verlag
Günther Holzboog, 1963). This edition is the one most readily
available in American libraries. To save space, I have provided
internal documentation from this edition, referred to as *Works*.
Volume and page numbers are not always cited for the *De augmentis*, the *New Organon*, and other works which are organized into
brief sections, aphorisms, or chapters, since passages are easily
located in any edition by the number Bacon gives them.

1   The Philosopher,
       His Audience,
       and Popular Rhetoric

> For what is glory, but the blaze of fame,
> The people's praise, if always praise unmixt?
> And what the people, but a herd confus'd,
> A miscellaneous rabble, who extol
> Things vulgar, and well weigh'd, scarce worth the
>   praise?
>   Christ in *Paradise Regained*, III, 47–51.

Francis Bacon might well have said what Milton, a
Senecan and a Baconian of a later era, allows Christ to say of the
masses he hopes one day to lead to glory. Bacon enjoyed drawing
overt comparisons between himself and Christ. He saw the obstacles
to his success in terms of those which Christ faced, and he was not
embarrassed to call the work of the new scientist a "second Scripture." Like Milton's Christ, Bacon the philosopher sincerely did not
seek to bask in the "blaze of fame," not simply because he saw glory
as a hollow motive, but because he accounted the praise of the "herd
confus'd" as no praise at all. No other man of his time knew as well
as he the compromises, the temporizing, and the loss of self-esteem
which the search for public approval seems always to entail. While
he pitied the common man and sought against great odds to relieve
his existence of unnecessary burdens, Bacon devoted his career as a
philosopher to the preservation of essential knowledge from the
masses. He spent his energies in the meticulous analysis of the
human intellect for the benefit of fellow scientists, and he gave up
much of his time to devising strategies of communication which
would weed out unqualified readers without alienating the potential
"sons of science." The modest assessment which he made of his own
talents led him to conclude that his primary powers lay in a certain
"wit" and in skills of expression which could be exploited in the
interests of philosophical reform. He hoped to make a "beginning"
by using his talents to seduce the intellectual community into the

1

movement on behalf of the advancement of learning. So entirely does this concern inform his major works that we can say with no exaggeration that communication is the primary and most difficult question Bacon treats as a philosopher. Since it was not until late in his career that he recognized his own limited potential as a scientist, however, we are forced to piece together from fragments and lesser works the picture of his early struggles to perfect the manner and method most appropriate to philosophical discourse. Though they dictate the form and style of his great works, Bacon's ideas on communication seemed secondary to him in the face of early setbacks, and he does not take the time to explain in detail how he arrived at his most original suggestions for the reform of communication among intellectuals. But it fortunately takes very little sleuthing to uncover in Bacon's works a theory of the philosophical style, one which grew naturally from his struggles to improve learning itself. It is this theory which is the subject of the present study.

In the most general sense, it is his audience and its education which combine to present the most daunting obstacles to the Renaissance philosopher who would communicate. Bacon sought to divide his potential audiences into the "crowd of learners" and the "sons of science," but he discovered very early in his career that men of science would actually have to be created from an audience of students, molded by the new scientist from the common clay produced by the English educational tradition. He never forgot, even after he gave up his efforts to reform pedagogy, that the elite in Europe's universities are as human as those for whom they teach and write, that their passions are as low, their self-satisfaction as pronounced, as anyone's. To preserve philosophy from the abuses of human error, Bacon perfected for his own use a program for the gradual redevelopment and augmentation of knowledge, beginning with the most fundamental of sense perceptions and moving upward through "progressive stages of certainty." In this manner he hoped to provide for the qualified reader a form of intellectual therapy which would cure the ills of the human understanding, restoring it to the workable machine it was meant to be, and at the same time eliminate along the way anyone among the crowd of learners who could not make the whole journey to the noble heights of pure knowledge. This became for Bacon a rhetorical problem, of course, for he began to see that the greatest obstructions to intellectual therapy were not inherent weaknesses of the human mind but rather the traditions of logic and rhetoric which catered so shamelessly to those weaknesses. By 1605 Bacon is denouncing those traditions as the first diseases of learning and beginning the first in a series of studied attempts to reform the "arts of arts" for the benefit of the new philosophy. Like Milton's Christ he rejects the false arts of persuasion and paradox, claiming that truth and knowledge are to be communicated plainly. The "majestic unaffected style" for which Christ praises the prophets is what Bacon seeks when he calls, in the *Advancement of Learning*, for a masculine, unadorned form of discourse which will do philosophy credit, even with the common man who may not understand it. All the details of his theory of the philosophical style, which we will examine in later chapters, seem to have developed as responses to these two most pressing problems: the nature of the human intellect and the corruption of its training in modern schools. A brief look at Bacon's views on the audiences he addressed, followed by a survey of his responses to the chief figures in the rhetorical tradition, will provide the necessary background for a study of that theory.

The Audience

Bacon's fear of the common man informs all his works. Whether he is writing for his "sons," the men of science, for his fellow counselors at Court, or for posterity, the theme of inherent human weakness is never far from the center of his argument. Even when he is charming the public with pious little "grains of salt" from the moral and civil sciences and delighting it with ingenious mythological interpretations, the irony and cynicism of his philosophy of human nature inform each point he develops. If his contempt for the vulgar often dictates the content of his writing, it has no less profound an effect on its style or manner, for "the common people understand not many excellent virtues" (*Of Praise*), and it will do philosophy no good to be exposed nakedly to them. Remarks of this kind invite charges of arrogance and pretentiousness; and it is true that Bacon's exasperation with the frailties of mankind, with its willful refusal to seek correction and help, makes itself felt in the strides which his prose style takes. His irritable glances at the common man reveal less tolerance than pity, nor does he flinch from the scientist's duty to see things plainly and to describe them candidly. The failure of his program for learning to gain the stature which religion enjoyed, the lingering power of superstition and false idols to grip men's souls, the corruption and sycophancy tolerated in the business of life, lead him at one point or another to speak despairingly not only of butchers and bakers but of philosophers, monarchs, and the teachers of youth. Not least among the failures were Bacon's fellow scientists, who disappointed him until he died.

The bitter lesson which he learned very soon in his career as a writer—that even men of learning are afflicted by the vices of passion and blindness—affected him deeply. Even the wise will force the man with a message to appeal to their weaknesses by flattering their sense of self-importance and by engaging their imaginations with flights of fancy. As Bacon admits, poets and prophets possess the most formidable weapons for the forces of good—vision and expressive powers—and it is to further development of these that he turns after the initial failure of his program for the advancement and reform of learning. The lack of enthusiasm for his proposals was a blow both to his ego and to his masterplan for reform, because it forced him, he thought, to entice and stimulate the intellectual community as he would the mob. In the end, however, it allowed him to come as close as perhaps anyone yet has done to preserving the ideals of science in poise with the values of the common man. Forced to argue for the new organon as a poet or an orator would, he developed a style of communicating which preserved content in its discovered form and delivered it with charm and persuasive force. This difficult feat is to the modern mind Bacon's greatest achievement. It obscures and minimizes his plagiarism, his inaccuracies, his occasional and astonishing lack of information, and even his apparent arrogance. We are engaged fully even today by his zeal and by the sense we have of being ushered into the secret chambers of true learning. The effects are strategically planned to convert us to his religion.

At the same time we are made to feel superior, by virtue of our special understanding, to the crowd of learners, not comprehending that we fall prey to many of the same devices of argument and demonstration which served the medieval and ancient philosophers Bacon asks us to patronize. Distaste for the lower ranks of mankind is an apparent virtue of the philosophical style, and the Attic pose of possessing supreme wisdom to be shared with the fortunate few is struck by Bacon with great success. His self-knowledge and his instinctive distrust of us all serve Bacon well in his role as philosopher. He sees in us perhaps larger versions of his own nearly ruinous flaws of character. It is in his analysis of human nature that we find the first important keys to the development in Bacon of a new style for philosophers.

His own fate with the popularizers of science, with the mystics, and with so many others supporting special causes has demonstrated the validity of Bacon's fear for the future of the new learning should it ever come into the hands of the common people. He knew that the ordinary man had allowed what was most valuable in the philosophical tradition to sink in the river of time, and that only the lightest and most easily understood material had survived. His works reveal the shrewd conclusion that, while reforming the human intellect was a project worth continuing, the wise philosopher would seek as well to insure his own survival with those who matter in the world of philosophy. His Preface to the Great Instauration is his most powerful plea for the preservation of science from just such unhappy experiences as he has suffered. It outlines clearly the problems he had faced for years, and it makes a new bid to enlist the proper kind of audience for the ventures into reform that he envisions. It is beautifully written and clear; it speaks figuratively when it can, and it invites all readers to enter the special circle where few can go.

As Bacon puts it in the Preface, the ordinary man possesses neither the desire nor the skills to penetrate to the inner meanings of things. Though he may have the potential to do anything he likes, he is content with his "store" of knowledge and underestimates his power to increase it. What is an even more serious obstacle to progress in philosophy is man's inability to question the value of what he already possesses, much less "frankly and without circumlocution to strip it away and enter the kingdom of knowledge as a child, naked and innocent of preconceptions." Bacon tells us in several places that the state of learning, like Scylla, has a beautiful face which leads man's thoughts away from the foul and barren womb, the now deadened seat of creation. Because the professors and tutors possess no more insight than their charges, because both scholars and students worship the present state of things as they would a statue, little chance for the advancement of knowledge and less for its reform exists in the schools. Among the masses, of course, the prospects for learning are bleaker still, for the populace love only what is "contentious and pugnacious, or specious and empty," and the effect of popular demand on would-be scholars is to pressure them into research which promises to reward the reputation, not by leading anywhere, but by allowing researchers to bow once again to "the judgment of the time and the multitude." The leaders in the sciences tend therefore to be limited men. Not only are they apt to "exempt ignorance from ignominy" by blaming the condition of man and his inherent weakness as a species for their inadequacies, they also tend to complain of nature's built-in protection of her secrets and of the impossibility of attaining ultimate knowledge. Such hollow arguments have brought the sciences down to the level of the common man and, as a result, they are in a state of atrophy:

> Now for those things which are delivered and received, this is their condition: barren of works, full of questions; in point of enlargement slow and languid; carrying a show of perfection in the whole but in the parts ill filled up; in selection popular, and unsatisfactory even to those who propound them; and therefore fenced round and set forth with sundry artifices. (*Works*, IV, 16.)

Though some few philosophers have wisely sought to solve problems presented by the ordinary human intellect by turning to logical method and making that the foundation of their procedure, not many know that the received logics are designed to simplify knowledge and flatter the common understanding. Logicians do see clearly that "the human intellect left to its own course is not to be trusted," but they are blind to the fact that available methods lack the power to remedy the natural condition and are in a sense symptoms of what they seek to cure. "The logic which is received ... is not nearly subtle enough to deal with nature; and in offering at what it cannot master, has done more to establish and perpetuate error than to open the way to truth." While the ancients were no doubt excellent in "everything that turns on wit and abstract meditation," we must see that "before we can reach the remoter and more hidden parts of nature, it is necessary that a more perfect use and application of the human mind and intellect be introduced." It is method, which he equates with style, that becomes the primary object of Bacon's search for new modes of communication for the learned.

The remainder of the Preface to the incomplete work called the Great Instauration is given up to a prayer and a series of admonitions, both of which emphasize the common weaknesses in all men and the urgent need for the new philosopher to recognize them in himself and take steps to conquer them. Bacon begs to be preserved from failure in his quest because of the ordinary flaws of "fancies and vanity." He hopes not to be swayed too much by the senses and not to presume, as others have done, that things human may interfere with things divine, or that the mysteries are susceptible to the arrogant probing of the merely curious. That which belongs to faith ought to be preserved for faith, he says, increasing his credit with readers without in any specific ways limiting the province of scientific inquiry. He concludes the Preface by asking that the scientist, when he succeeds in purging philosophy of "that venom which the serpent infused into it," be not "wise above measure and sobriety, but cultivate truth in charity." The admonitions which follow this prayer are directed at the most predictable causes of the collapse of science: ordinary men are, on the one hand, likely to deny altogether the existence of anything which the senses may not verify, and this Bacon rejects as a sure way to seal up heaven entirely. More serious and likely a stance, though, is that of the righteous, who take moral law into their own hands, as Adam eventually did, and who respond to the original sin by denying man's right to investigate nature fully. Both common errors are inimical to the rights of scientists. Having compared himself to Columbus naming reasons to risk a dangerous voyage, Bacon makes this point again by demonstrating how the modern naturalist resembles the prelapsarian Adam on the question of man's right to probe his world. "For it was not that pure and uncorrupted natural knowledge whereby Adam gave names to the creatures according to their propriety, which gave occasion to the fall. It was the ambitious and proud desire of moral knowledge to judge of good and evil, to the end that man may revolt from God and give laws to himself, which was the form and manner of the temptation." To man's lust for power and unattainable knowledge, then, Bacon adds the vulgar motives of fame, pleasure, contention, superiority, and profit to his list of passions which may exempt one from participation in the "inquisition of nature." Finally, he asks that the spirit of inquiry be preserved, that judgment of his doctrines be suspended by the average reader. "I cannot be fairly asked to abide by the decision of a tribunal which is itself on its trial," he concludes.

The danger posed by the ordinary man to the Baconian plan for the reform of learning is stressed throughout the philosophical works. The first book of the *New Organon*, for instance, contains a large number of aphorisms, brought forth from earlier works and amplified, on the theme of the common intellect and its weaknesses. Man's intellect, Bacon says, continually searches for satisfying generalities because it soon "wearies of experiment" (Aph. XX), and this is a fact to which scientists who would communicate must yield without sacrificing accuracy. The four idols of the mind have taken such deep root in the human intellect that "truth can hardly find entrance," and these are conditions with which the scientist must also contend (Aph. XXXVIII). Among the idols the worst, in one sense, are the idols of the tribe, for they "have their foundation in human nature itself." Man's understanding, like a false mirror, "receiving rays irregularly, distorts and discolours the nature of things by mingling its own nature with it" (Aph. XLI). Combined with idols of the cave, man's individual errors of perception, and idols of the marketplace, which arise from man's communication with other men, and then further enhanced by idols of the theater, "play-books" and "stage-plays" of philosophy and demonstration, those of the tribe make the human mind the most formidable obstacle to its own growth and achievement.

In Aphorisms XLV–LXIX of Book I, Bacon analyzes brilliantly the human understanding and suggests the difficulty of the scientist's task if he is to overcome its weaknesses. Six primary qualities of the intellect which are treated in that section seem to have special bearing on his formulation of a philosophical style.

First, Bacon claims that "the human understanding is of its own nature prone to suppose the existence of more order and regularity in the world than it finds" (Aph. XLV). In other works, as well as here in the *New Organon*, he blames traditional methods of teaching logic and rhetoric for the perpetuation among intelligent adults of this common error. A truly philosophical style will imitate nature, Bacon believes, in all its disarray, and will avoid producing in the minds of others the fancies and dreams of both common logical demonstrations and rhetorical artifice. Though demanded by the common man in normal situations where communication is required, such fancies and dreams are vicious and "affect not dogmas only, but simple notions also." Bacon's major law for a workable philosophical style is that knowledge be delivered in the same way in which it was discovered.

A more specific point is made in the next aphorism, where the author notes that "the human understanding, when it has once adopted an opinion . . . , draws all things else to support and agree with it." No philosopher or scientist worth the name will knowingly fail to introduce negative evidence as part of his demonstrations. The principle that information should be delivered as it was invented would ideally include the introduction of all negative evidence which turned up along the way. Though not particularly interested here in persuasion, Bacon does say that the use of negative material will work to the philosopher's advantage. Common men may prefer affirmatives and such vanities as dreams and omens to the truth; but the scientist knows that "in the establishment of any true axiom, the negative instance is the more forcible."

A third important reminder to the writer is that "the human understanding is no dry light, but receives an infusion from the will and affections; whence proceed sciences which may be called 'sciences as one would'" (Aph. XLIX). Since human passions color the understanding in many ways and thus affect both belief and action, the scientist who would communicate must become a psychologist. His charge is to perfect a method of managing the wills of men which does not also compromise either the nature or the arrangement of his material. As we shall see, Bacon's understanding of the psychology of discovery and persuasion is sophisticated and practical. His conception of the philosophical style, unlike that of the Stoics, whom he criticized, recognizes fully the writer's obligation to provide imaginative appeal and satisfaction to the human passions. He gives sound advice on how to manage these faculties of the mind without sacrificing anything significant to them.

As Bacon says, "The human understanding is of its own nature prone to abstractions and gives a substance and reality to things which are fleeting" (Aph. LI). Since the objective of the new science is to dissect nature, not "to resolve nature into abstractions," communication among scholars will adhere to the principle that "matter rather than forms should be the object of our attention." Always concerned with how to make nature and its secrets as stimulating to the imagination as unnatural fancies and abstractions can be, Bacon concentrates on giving life and form to things which are true.

A fifth important point to be kept in mind by the writer is that "contemplations of nature and of bodies in their simple form break up and distract the understanding, while contemplations of nature and bodies in their composition and configuration overpower and dissolve the understanding" (Aph. LVII). For this reason, the wise scientist will alternate particles and structures in his demonstrations, so as to give at every step a view which is "at once penetrating and comprehensive." A good philosophical style will avoid presenting masses of material or information without summaries of hypotheses or potential conclusions. This is a rule to which Bacon adheres even in the most advanced steps of his progress to axioms—the histories and aphorisms.

Finally, Bacon tells the philosopher or scientist that the most forbidding and uncontrollable of his tools will prove to be words. "Now words, being commonly framed and applied according to the capacity of the vulgar, follow those lines of division which are most obvious to the vulgar understanding" (Aph. LIX). An understanding of greater powers and "more diligent observation" than average will confront the impenetrable roadblock which words present each time it attempts to change others' comprehension of things to suit the demands of nature and the truth. Though Bacon dreamed of a new language, with new words and a new alphabet, for philosophical discourse, he wisely focused instead on how to use precisely the words available, cautioning all scientists to avoid words when pictures or symbols will serve. Words, he reminds us in Aphorism LIX, are merely symbols of notions.

Thus communication among scientists, to use the most general guidelines, will avoid unnatural arrangements of data and will employ negative data just as it does other true forms of experience. At the same time, it will somehow control the human will with appeals to its native urges and will do so without resorting to the common forms which have warped the human understanding in the past. Moreover, it will contrive to satisfy simultaneously the need for resolution and the need for penetration by alternating details with up-to-date summaries of achievement. This, of course, it will do without flying to abstractions. Finally, the philosophical style will treat words as enemies and will employ near-substitutes for them whenever possible. It is to the very challenging task of creating both a style and a theory of discourse for scientists that Bacon dedicates himself after the initial failure of his plan for reform.

Seeing as clearly as he does the obstacles to be overcome by the new leaders, Bacon is careful and detailed in his introductory outline of what must be done to make way for the advancement of learning. Specific flaws of human nature have worked to defeat this purpose, so that "the true way is not merely deserted, but shut out and stopped up," as he says in Book I, Aphorism LXXXIII, of the *New Organon*. The list of these failings and obstacles is endless and, Bacon realizes, once compiled, apt to cause despair in even the most ambitious and resourceful of scientists. It is a major function of a philosophical style to inspire hope, without failing in its duty to draw clear pictures of things as they are. Bacon names as the first enemy of hope the apparent lack of interest which the human race shows in discovery or progress, but he cautions those who hold science in true affection to disdain popularity anyway. If the new scientist recognizes that most of the gallery of revered thinkers are "professorial and much given to disputations," that most have sought parade, applause, and timeliness, he can take hope from his lack of a large following. Even the Greeks were like boys, "prompt to prattle" and full of the wisdom which "abounds in words but is barren of works" (Aph. LXXI). Among other philosophers, the School of Night is denounced for propounding forms and dogmas which invite despair, while the logicians are attacked for their use of forms which flatter the common understanding by "proving" its own faulty opinions. The alchemists and magicians, who fascinated Bacon, are nevertheless seen by him as curious examples of the effects which innocence and unwarranted optimism produce in research. Because of the average man's "littleness of spirit," lack of ambition, superstition, and "blind and immoderate zeal of religion," the world of philosophy as Bacon found it seemed entirely given over to the pseudo-scientists and professors, men who tend to talk and dream more than they inquire, men who make their livings by bringing abstruse and important knowledge down to the level of the vulgar understanding. The public notion of a scientist was therefore apt to be that of the inventor of an aphrodisiac or a fountain of youth—a man full of promises which nature cannot echo. Even in the schools, Bacon laments, one finds that "everything is adverse to the progress of science."

> For the lectures and exercises there are so ordered, that to think or speculate on anything out of the common way can hardly occur to any man. And if one or two have the boldness to use any liberty of judgment, they must undertake the task all by themselves; they can have no advantage from the company of others. And if they can endure this also, they will find their industry and largeness of mind no slight hindrance to their fortune. For the studies of men

in these places are confined and as it were imprisoned in the
writings of certain authors, from whom if any man dissent he is
straightway arraigned as a turbulent person and an innovator.
(Aph. XC.)

It is no surprise to learn that, while Bacon in later years was
willing to bow to popular habits of mind in order to gain entry, he
was never willing to allow science to do the same. In his Preface to
the *New Organon* the method he will follow is outlined clearly. The
principal goal will be to avoid overhasty generalization by establishing "progressive stages of certainty." While retaining the evidence
of the senses as a forceful way to truth, he will reject "the mental
operation which follows the act of sense." Instead, "I open and lay
out a new and certain path for the mind to proceed in, starting
directly from the simple sensuous impression." The old logic is
indicted in the same passage for coming too late to man's rescue and
and for failing to restore the human understanding to a workable,
machinelike faculty of the mind. Like rhetoric it does little more
than haunt the mind with vain dreams and perceptions which may
not be verified. Beginning with a simple sensuous illustration, Bacon
explains the need for complete reform of the mental operations:

There remains but one course for the recovery of a sound and
healthy condition,—namely, that the entire work of the
understanding be commenced afresh, and the mind itself be from
the very outset not left to take its own course, but guided at every
step; and the business be done as if by machinery. Certainly if in
things mechanical men had set to work with their naked hands,
without help or force of instruments, just as in things intellectual
they have set to work with little else than the naked forces of the
understanding, very small would the matters have been which,
even with their best efforts applied in conjunction, they would
have attempted or accomplished. (*Works*, IV, 40.)

The analogy is developed further, revealing Bacon's mastery of
simple descriptive logic with its emphasis on what he calls the
"concordances" in nature and experience. He asks us to suppose
that "some vast obelisk were . . . to be removed from its place" and
to look at the alternatives which present themselves to the men who
must accomplish the task. We would think them mad if they were to
attempt to do it with their naked hands, yet "in matters intellectual," we still tend to proceed with "the same kind of mad effort and

useless combination of forces," hoping for great things somehow "either from the number and cooperation or from the excellency and acuteness of individual wits." Similarly, we would look with alarm on the movers of the obelisk if they were to "call in aid the art of athletics," requiring "all their men to come with hands, arms, and sinews well-anointed and medicated according to the rules of art." Would not any sensible man "cry out that they were only taking pains to show a kind of method and discretion in their madness?" Yet this is exactly what men are doing with their minds "when they endeavour by Logic (which may be considered as a kind of athletic art) to strengthen the sinews of the understanding." No amount of decoration or pomposity can disguise the fact that our logics do little more than apply the "naked intellect" to the problems at hand. Bacon concludes that all great works require "instruments and machinery, either for the strength of each to be exerted or the strength of all to be united" (*Works*, IV, 40-41).

The point, of course, is that the reform of the intellect and the advancement of learning will not be accomplished until a new system of disseminating information is developed. As part of his own program for the growth of the arts and sciences, Bacon insists that the new system be a dual one. It should allow both for discovery and for communication, for research and teaching:

> Let there be therefore (and may it be for the benefit of both) two streams and two dispensations of knowledge; and in like manner two tribes or kindreds of students in philosophy—tribes not hostile or alien to each other, but bound together by mutual services;—let there in short be one method for the cultivation, another for the invention, of knowledge. (*Works*, IV, 42.)

Having distinguished between the creators or discoverers and the users of knowledge, Bacon is then able to present his case for a new method of philosophical demonstration to a special audience, those men who aspire to invention and creative research. In reviving for the Renaissance Aristotle's doctrine of audience accommodation, he makes it possible to relate rhetoric to the larger aims of science. Philosophical rhetoric is designed for two purposes: teaching students and stimulating fellow scientists. The former rhetoric, as we shall see, is markedly different in most respects from the popular manuals which held sway in English schools, yet Bacon is able to modernize and employ many of the principles of Aristotle, Cicero, and Quintilian for the pedagogical purposes of scientists. (He was, of course, the student of all three ancients in his own speeches and occasional pieces.) Moreover, he makes the distinction sharply when he describes the method which the scientist uses in teaching as "literary," while his method for colleagues in great works of invention is always "philosophical." Remarks of this kind in the *Advancement* and *De augmentis*, works designed to teach by taking the audience to the first stop in the "progressive stages of certainty," make it clear that Bacon is using rhetoric to separate his audience into discrete groups. He concludes his Preface to the *New Organon* by inviting us all to participate in the new adventure. If he wishes good luck to the busy men who have no time for it and to the lazy or ignorant, he also hopes that a strong call to action will be answered by many readers:

> But if any man there be who, not content to rest in and use the knowledge which has already been discovered, aspires to penetrate further; to overcome, not an adversary in argument, but nature in action; to seek not pretty and probable conjectures, but certain and demonstrable knowledge;—I invite all such to join themselves, as true sons of knowledge, with me, that passing by the outer courts of nature, which numbers have trodden, we may find a way at length into her inner chambers. (*Works*, IV, 42.)

The appeal is irresistible to become one of the chosen, and the distinction between rhetorical strategies could not be clearer. The new breed of inquirer will look for answers, not premises; he will challenge nature directly, using the tools of science, not the principles of debate.

Bacon's final words in the Preface constitute a promise to his reader. He will propound nothing but what is true, and yet he will undertake to present everything "in a manner not harsh or unpleasant." These lines describe the goals of a philosophical style as Bacon conceived it, and it is to these purposes that he directs himself from the earliest *Essays* to the last great works of philosophy. If he holds unfailingly to the truth, regardless of how confusing and unpleasant it proves to be, he will accomplish the intellectual therapy which men of learning and purpose so desperately need. Though not addressing himself to the common audience, he does bow to the needs of the "sons of science" by promising a manner of delivery which is pleasing and which will entice them to proceed without fear of discomfort. Finding a method and style of communication which would echo truth and still enchant the mind proved for Bacon no easy matter.

The Rhetorical Tradition

Emperor Marcus Aurelius, in his *Meditations*, thanks the gods for preserving him from logic and rhetoric. He regards it as a sign from heaven that he was soon freed from the youthful urge to make poetry or to use his manner of communication as he would a suit of clothes. He thinks his success in life may largely be due to his inability to waste time tracing syllogisms or applying artificial modes of reasoning to speculative questions. Like the active men who have been attracted to the *Meditations* over the centuries, Marcus Aurelius looks for the truth—undisguised and clear—in discourse. Common sense tells him that the arts of persuasion are obstacles to the discovery of truth, that they confuse the mind and force it to settle for something less than what it naturally seeks. Rhetoric, especially, he says is a womanly art. It works against reason and against philosophy, which he thinks are the two things capable of giving man a successful existence and a happy soul.

Bacon, who says much the same thing repeatedly in his works of philosophy, makes a fine distinction between logic and rhetoric as they are in the schools and as they ought to be. Just as he inspected the philosophical tradition, drawing from it whatever deserved to survive, he went over thè rhetorical tradition with a sharp eye for clues to solutions to his own rhetorical problems as a scientist. In the Preface to Book II of the *De augmentis* he tells King James just how much he respects the arts of communication, giving his own views of their scope and significance. He looks on logic and rhetoric as more meaningful arts than those which pass for logic and rhetoric in the schools. Objecting primarily to the use of ancient texts, untried in the contemporary context, he explains that an effective monarch will follow James's own maxim and adjust the curriculum in universities to suit both the demands and the accomplishments of the present time. Logic and rhetoric, being the "gravest of sciences" and the "arts of arts," provide the most conspicuous examples in a series of studies derived entirely from ages "more obscure and ignorant than our own." At the very least, he suggests, the presentation of so important a discipline as communication should be reexamined. It will be discovered that logic and rhetoric are being taught at so elementary a level as to invalidate their traditional roles in education. Not only is it the custom to teach them to novices—that is, to men without the "stuff" or "furniture" which fills the mind of knowledgeable people—but the condition of pedagogy in these fields has deteriorated to the point where professors hold forth in a manner which is "unprofitable" and suited only to "the capacity of children." These remarks are delivered by Bacon to the King in a manner which he hopes will illustrate a new kind of style. The most acceptable science of ornamentation will emphasize a manner of delivery which is "active and masculine, without digressing or dilating." It will work as an example of what can be achieved without the conventional but dated methods of teaching rhetoric in the schools. Instead of the "premature and untimely learning of these arts," which most students experience, moreover, the new scientist will cultivate them only after compiling the necessary knowledge which defines true education.

It is not surprising, after reading this Preface and other passages like it, to learn that Bacon has very little to say for the rhetorical tradition. For the philosopher's purposes, the "excellently well-laboured" art of arts has not much to offer. Studies of Bacon's style in relation to that tradition yield little more than a few concrete illustrations of his thorough knowledge of what the inventors of rhetoric, as the Renaissance knew it, had to say. For his own information and use in public situations, Bacon invariably depends on Cicero, Tacitus, Seneca, the Greek writers, and a few modern political theorists, rather than on the Elizabethan stylists. His references to them all are frequent and learned, but they do not, when taken in the aggregate, suggest that he is committed to any one school of thought. It is only in common life and in normal rhetorical situations that he can recommend any of the great rhetoricians other than Aristotle, and his hostile remarks about the *Rhetoric* and other works make it appear that even Aristotle fails to meet Bacon's standards. It is nevertheless true that his conception of a rhetoric for philosophers owes many debts, mainly for stimulation and suggestion, to the major figures in the tradition. Without repeating too much of the scholarship available on the nature of these debts, the present section of this study attempts to provide a broad view of how they relate in specific ways to Bacon's theory of the philosophical style.

Bacon begins his career as a philosopher with an attack on the

Ciceronians of his time. The fine old art of the classical rhetoricians, men with admirable if outdated cultural ideals and great learning, had been reduced by the Renaissance stylists to a theory of ornamentation. The new rhetoric of adornment ignored the knowledge to be delivered and turned the language into a tool for trickery in the marketplace and pedantic specializing in the classroom.[1] It left the man who had new things to say without a reliable modern guide to the art of expression. Bacon's memorable summary of the abuses of Ciceronianism and Euphuism is one key to the rhetoric which he would propose; it was the vogue with too many writers, he says,

> to hunt more after words than matter; more after the choiceness of the phrase, and the round and clean composition of the sentence, and the sweet falling of the clauses, and the varying and illustration of their works with tropes and figures, than after the weight of matter, worth of subject, soundness of argument, life of invention, or depth of judgment. (*Advancement,* I, in *Works*, III, 283.)

Another key to reform is provided by the addition Bacon makes to this passage under rhetoric in the *De augmentis*, VI, 3. That work, the *Advancement*'s Latin translation, published eighteen years later, often reflects changes in Bacon's judgments, especially about rhetoric. There he rejects any style which fails to appeal to the imaginative powers of the receiver. The plain manner of Stoic philosophers, by refusing to direct itself to man's will, the agent of action, through his imagination, neglected the essential function of the communication process. If the Ciceronian manner is "the first distemper of learning," the Stoic manner of pregnant brevity must be ranked with it as a primary offender against the rights of men to receive and comprehend the truth. If "it is accompanied by a taste for mere words and their concinnity," the brief, plain manner can obstruct communication just as surely as the florid, copious one of the Ciceronians can. "For the method of the Stoics, who thought to thrust virtue upon men by concise and sharp maxims and conclusions, which have little sympathy with the imagination and will of man, has been justly ridiculed by Cicero" (*De augmentis*, VI, 3).

Though he admits frankly in the *Advancement* that "to clothe and adorn the obscurity even of philosophy itself with sensible and plausible elocution" is not a thing "hastily to be condemned,"

Bacon finds that all schools of rhetoric put the emphasis on manner rather than on matter. If the Ciceronians stressed diction and rhythms, the Stoics gave too much consideration to the rhetorical devices of subtlety and paradox (*Works*, III, 284). Bacon is forced, he thinks, to make a very strong effort to shift the focus in rhetoric from copy to weight, from style to substance. He puts rhetoric, which he calls the "illustration of discourse," in his scheme of learning under logic; and he makes it clear, as we shall see, that the major function of this science is to employ reason to work on the imagination in order to move the will. As a sub-subheading under logic, rhetoric is treated as if it were a science to be mastered and, though "inferior to wisdom," an important one. The conflict between Stoic and Ciceronian philosophies of style, greatly simplified both by the Renaissance and by modern critics of its literature, is resolved for Bacon's purposes by his claim that there must be two modes of discourse and two theories of style or method of delivery. These theories must be dependent on the audiences addressed, not merely on the occasions or purposes of address. The chief function of any style will be to engage the imagination, and though "mere words" would accomplish that, a philosophical style will take the second major step in the communication process by moving the will to act on the dictates of reason. How seriously Bacon takes the need for reform is reflected in his list of philosophers who succeed as stylists: Cicero, Seneca, Plutarch, Plato, and Xenophon. It is significant that no one of his own time is named.

Because style should grow naturally from a cultural goal or from an urge to communicate something specific, the Renaissance manuals of elocution fail badly in their purpose. They offer theories of adornment, reducing all the elements of grammar, logic, and rhetoric to stylistic devices.[2] Even those philosophers whom Bacon names as successful stylists, moreover, offer no models suited to the goals of modern thinkers. They employ manners of delivery appropriate only to "civil occasions, of conference, counsel, persuasion, or the like." Even their styles are full of "delicacies and affectations" which render them useless to the new scientist. And the most serious failure of the new philosophers is that they quench "the desire of further search, before we come to a just period," and encourage us to study their words, not their ideas. In short, the styles of even the finest of philosophical writers are appropriate only to the use of knowledge already discovered and to its cultivation, and not to the "severe inquisition of truth and the deep progress into philosophy" (*Works*, III, 284). The irony is that, while both modes of delivery popular with Bacon's contemporaries are suited only to audiences of little cultivation, both serve at the same time to "discredit learning, even with vulgar capacities." The first disease of learning, the study of words and not matter, has had a more serious effect on intelligent men, the audiences of the philosophers, so that there are more followers of Adonis, a false divinity, than of Hercules among men who would inquire.

Bacon believes that he can explain why the arts of delivery are in so serious a condition of decay among scholars of his own time. Though the ancients had dealt perceptively and almost to excess with the subject of rhetoric, Bacon's contemporaries had occupied themselves primarily with further efforts to do what Richard Sherry, author of *A Treatise of Schemes and Tropes*, had hoped to accomplish in 1550: that is, to make the schemes and tropes speak English. As Bacon explains it, the revival of classical works seems to have begun with Martin Luther and the reformers, who sought to "awake all antiquity . . . to make a party against the present time." This led to a great frenzy of feverish and meticulous scholarship and to "exquisite travail in the languages original," the result of which was that educated men, in their writing, soon sought to imitate the manners of the ancients. Moreover, the movement to an English classicism provided a desirable corrective to the styles of the hated Schoolmen, who showed no regard in their writing "for the pureness, pleasantness, and . . . lawfulness of the phrase or word." In response to the Schoolmen and their ways of communicating— ways filled with objections, distinctions, and "vermiculate ques- tions"—leading reformers in the Renaissance placed heavy empha- sis on the development of a style which would allow scholars to communicate directly with the people. The necessity for enlarging and engaging an audience for intellectual works, and at the same time for advancing the educational opportunities open to the common man, offers, then, still another explanation for the emerging preoccupation with style among scholars: "For the winning and persuading of them, there grew of necessity in chief price and request eloquence and variety of discourse, as the fittest and forciblest access into the capacity of the vulgar sort." The result was that "an affectionate study of eloquence and copie of speech . . . began to flourish," and men like Ascham began almost to "deify

Cicero and Demosthenes, and allure all young men that were studious unto that delicate and polished kind of learning" (*Works*, III, 283-84). So serious a threat had the new style become to progress in philosophy that Bacon undertakes to guide the reform of rhetoric for scholarly purposes, a task he resists until 1605.

Though it is Bacon's style rather than his expressed opinions which tells us most about his reforms, we have enough from him to construct an outline of his rhetorical ideals. There is not much information to be gained from a study of the tradition in its relation to Bacon's work, for we find very little beyond the obvious and expected in his remarks on the major ancients. His criticisms of the Stoics and Ciceronians do tell us, however, that, besides appealing to the imagination on reason's behalf, an effective manner of delivery will encourage interest in the content by stimulating interest in the author or his manner. Neither a man nor his style should be the primary object of the audience's concentration, because "doctrines should be such as should make men in love with the lesson, and not with the teacher; being directed to the auditor's benefit, and not to the author's commendation" (*Advancement*, II, in *Works*, III, 418). Moreover, a good scholarly style will avoid both the unnecessary subtlety of the Stoic manner and the leisurely pace of the grand Ciceronian manner. "To write at leisure what is to be read at leisure," he says in a letter, "does not interest me" (*Works*, XI, 146). Nor does he seek to spin the useless cobwebs of learning which the spacious style encourages. That manner represents no less than a disease of learning, one which erupts "when men study words and not matter." It causes philosophy to decline in prestige even with common men because "words are but the images of matter; and except they have life of reason and invention, to fall in love with them is all one as to fall in love with a picture" (*Advancement*, I, in *Works*, III, 284).

The abuses of the plainer manner, of course, are similarly offensive to Bacon. Renaissance imitators of the Senecans too often make their material appear impossibly difficult. They imply that only readers of great penetration may "pierce the veil." Some of them like to "coin and frame new terms of art," as the Schoolmen do, "to express their own sense, and to avoid circuit of speech." One of their favorite and most annoying devices of style is an imitation of Senecan "nicety": that is, the fragmenting of knowledge into "sticks." Such techniques for obscurity are attacked by Bacon as affectations of would-be philosophers:

And such is their method, that rests not so much upon evidence of truth . . . , as upon particular confutations and solutions of every scruple, cavillation, and objection, breeding for the most part one question as fast as it solveth another. (Ibid., p. 286.)

Such a form of delivery repels all readers, for the people are "apt to condemn truth upon occasion of controversies and altercations," especially when these break out over "matter of no use nor moment."

It is possible to follow Bacon from his earliest fragments of philosophical writing up to the *De augmentis* and *New Atlantis* as he discusses the problems raised by the failure of those in charge of the communication arts to provide any hints for a manner suited to learned discourse. In 1597 he published the essay *Of Discourse*, in which he notes the faults of what then seemed the model for a popular conversational style among educated people. He sees clearly that some in their discourse seek a reputation for cleverness rather than for wisdom, "as if it were a praise to know what might be said, and not what should be thought." And in *Valerius Terminus*, Cap. 18, probably written in 1603, he speaks quite emotionally of the obstacles to a scientist's communication. It is "not a thing so easy as is conceived to convey the conceit of one man's mind into the mind of another without loss or mistaking, specially in notions new and differing from those that are received." It is clear that he has given careful study to many alternatives, for in the same passage he gives a thorough survey of most forms of the popular style which a philosopher might emulate, and he rejects them all. It is his conclusion

that the very styles and forms of utterance are so many characters of imposture, some choosing a style of pugnacity and contention, some of satire and reprehension, some of plausible and tempting similitudes and examples, some of great words and high discourse, some of short and dark sentences, some of exactness of method, all of positive affirmation, without disclosing the true motives and proofs of their opinions, or free confessing their ignorance or doubts, except it be now and then for a grace, and in cunning to win the more credit in the rest, and not in good faith. (*Works*, III, 247-48.)

We know from this passage and a number of similar ones in the early works that Bacon had learned to reject the popular style, in all its variations, for the delivery of knowledge. He had tried a number of the methods he condemns in *Valerius Terminus* and found them unworkable. By the time the essay *Of Seeming Wise* is published in 1612, he is also expressing very serious doubts about the manner of those philosophers he most admires, the Senecans and their disciples. Most writers who affect the plain manner rather than witty or oratorical styles are flawed as well. "Some are so close and reserved, as they will not shew their wares but by a dark light, and seem always to keep back somewhat; and when they know within themselves they speak of that they do not well know, would nevertheless seem to others to know of that which they may not well speak" (*Works*, VI, 436). Other common affectations which obscure their manners are the profession of distaste for whatever they do not understand, the use of portentous signs or a "great word" to signify the importance of the writer, the employment of an amusing subtlety to disguise ignorance at a given point. More serious than these flaws, for Bacon's purposes, is the tendency of the plain style and those who employ it to dampen hope by constant quibbling about things of no significance. Men who use this trick of delivery find it simpler to be "of the negative side." We should not overlook the obvious need on Bacon's part to create a new kind of style for a new kind of content. Most of his attacks on both Senecan and Ciceronian rhetoricians are but small battles in the great war being waged against the cultural ideals, the educational structures, and the philosophical methods which those figures defend and represent.

Bacon did not, on the other hand, write or think about communication in a self-created vacuum. While he criticizes Aristotle and Plato for both idealism and hypocrisy, he is greatly indebted to those philosophers. While he rejects Cicero's and Quintilian's rhetoric for its lack of philosophical justification and moral authority, and for its inflated view of its own standing among the arts and sciences, there are many small obligations to them both which he is willing to record. And, though Ramus and most of the moderns are found by Bacon to be lightweights, worthy of being called neither philosophers nor rhetoricians, he sees that their intentions were good and he frequently tries to succeed where they failed. Most rhetoricians, he feels, entirely overlook the audience in their debates over style, and this error is what forces him to return in the end to Aristotle's *Rhetoric* and its sound guidance for the thoughtful writer. Though many versions of the philosophical rhetoric subordinate style to logic and dialectic, as Bacon would have it, they all seem to lack vitality, and no thinker successfully explains the science of *pathos* and appeal to the imagination which is central to the philosopher's success.

In fact, the nature of a philosophical style was, in Bacon's time, difficult to describe. The tradition provided so many contradictory and perplexing versions of learned discourse that Bacon himself, after careful study, concluded in 1603 that no satisfactory alternative to popular rhetoric had yet been formulated. Indeed, Bacon was among the first to see how few clear distinctions could be made, in the final analysis, between what passed in his time for a high-minded rhetoric for intellectuals and what was being taught to prospective lawyers and poets in the schools. A brief survey of the development of a body of literature on the philosophical style will underscore both the assets and the liabilities of what the ancients had to offer Bacon, revealing at the same time why he found himself in the end back at Aristotle's door, forced to revise the work of the modern philosopher's worst enemy in order to develop standards that were his own.

The English Renaissance, by reviving major classical works on style and rhetoric, gave new life to the quarrels and confusions which had marked the works of Aristotle's and Plato's Roman disciples. The supreme authorities on communication were challenged in Bacon's time as often as they were praised and imitated, mainly because Greek and Roman ideals were not easily translated into modern English ones and were never brought intact to the rhetorical manuals of the sixteenth century. Too often, the authors of those guides to successful speech and writing simply altered the doctrines of Cicero and Quintilian to suit the goals of essentially style-conscious and pedestrian men uninterested in theory. The ancient controversy between philosophy and rhetoric was certain to gain new intensity under such conditions. Having begun with conflicts between Plato and the Sophists, the argument continued in Cicero's battles, first with the Atticists and then with the Stoics. Many other figures of importance—Aristotle, Tacitus, and Quintilian among them—added their weight to one side or the other in the controversy, and all parties, with the exception of the most rigid of Stoic thinkers, attempted to offer ways to heal the wounds which both sides had sustained, the goal being to effect a reunion of philosophy and rhetoric. Bacon's role in helping to resolve this conflict for the philosophers of a new age is of some significance. He sees that the great figures in the rhetorical tradition forced the arts of communication to conform to some cultural ideal and to reflect through their achievements the larger objectives of all men. He understands that the works of Aristotle and Cicero can be evaluated only in terms of their own cultures and the goals they hoped to reach. Though Bacon's personal objectives in the development of a style for philosophers may vary greatly from those of ancient writers, then, he is capable of both building on and transforming for a new set of goals the worthy contributions of those who preceded him. His concern as a writer is not just with the "excellency of learning and knowledge," but also and primarily with the "augmentation and propagation thereof" (*Works*, III, 263). Bacon may seem to agree that rhetoric, as it is defined by both the ancients and the moderns, is inimical to philosophy, but this understanding does not prevent him from seeing as well that it may be possible to retrieve from the "excellently well-laboured" art of rhetoric some strong suggestions for the development of a science of communication to which modern thinkers may turn for guidance.

The plain style, as Cicero describes it, is appropriate to occasions which require an unadorned treatment of a serious matter. It should not evince the characteristics of the grand style. Structure will be loosened and rhythm disguised to allow the speaker to "seem to move freely but not to wander without restraint." Sentences will not be balanced with any great care; words will not appear to have cemented together. In general, the plain manner will affect "a not unpleasant carelessness on the part of a man who is paying more attention to thought than to words" (*Orator*, XXIII).[3] With the exception of "an abundance of apposite maxims," which is his stock-in-trade, the creator of a plain style will avoid all the rhetorical furniture in his productions. His manner will be restrained, designed to give those who hear him confidence that they, under the same circumstances and with the same material, could perform just as well as the man before them.

> Consequently the orator of the plain style, provided he is elegant and finished, will not be bold in coining words, and in metaphor will be modest, sparing in the use of archaisms, and somewhat subdued in using the other embellishments of language and of thought. Metaphor he may possibly employ more frequently

because it is of the commonest occurrence in the language of townsman and rustic alike. (Ibid., XXIII–XXIV.)

Bacon certainly took no exception to any of these remarks from Cicero on the manner most appropriate to serious discourse. He praises the Roman frequently for his useful advice to lawyers and businessmen on how to conduct their affairs with the public.[4] His letters, prefaces, and speeches reveal how closely he followed Cicero's rule about maintaining a "wise adaptability" in rhetorical situations, and his sections on the sciences of "negotiation" and "advancement in life" depend more on the Roman than on any source other than Solomon for quotable suggestions. From Bacon's biographer, Dr. Rawley, and from Ben Jonson, we know that his speeches were models of the plain style. Always advising intelligently, he never engaged "in any precipitate or grievous courses, but in moderate and fair proceedings."[5] And, as Jonson says, "No man ever spake more neatly, more precisely, more weightily, or suffer'd lesse emptiness, lesse idlenesse, in what he utter'd." The structure of his speeches, even in delivery, revealed no concessions to the demands of the grand style. "His hearers could not cough, or look aside from him, without losse."[6]

Since Bacon attempts to turn nearly all the branches of learning into sciences, the advice of Cicero on the arts of business and persuasion had some effect on his developing understanding of how the philosophical style may work in sciences where opinion rather than knowledge counts for most. He has no difficulty in seeing that the maxim and the metaphor, abused as they may be by Renaissance stylists, could serve scholarly discourse as devices for clarity and coherence. He gives them both a kind of scientific authority to operate in philosophical works, agreeing with Cicero that they call attention to content in a way that enhances it and the communication process in general. When employed properly, they preclude the need for endless repetition, explanation, and amplification.

In particular, the metaphor is praised by Bacon as a means of communicating new material to a reluctant audience. It stimulates the imagination and shifts the reader's focus from abstractions to concrete pictures. It is a major rule for scientific method, he says, *"That whatsoever science is not consonant to presuppositions, must pray in aid of similitudes"* (*Advancement*, II, in *Works*, III, 407). Even when not attempting to communicate, the researcher will find that the first step he must take in the search for axioms is the classification of the resemblances in nature. As he puts it in *Valerius Terminus*, Cap. 1, "There is no proceeding in invention of knowledge but by similitude" (*Works*, III, 218). Obviously, those sciences in which "knowledge" grows from opinion and common sense—the law, ethics, and business, for example—will depend heavily in the new philosophy on their advocates' powers of comparison. The metaphor becomes one of the principal cornerstones in Bacon's theory of the philosophical style.

As for the maxim, also recommended strongly by Cicero, it too is of great significance to Bacon's conception of a new style for learned discourse. In its highest form it becomes the aphorism, which Bacon preserves for the last significant steps in the "progressive stages of certainty." Maxims, which Aristotle describes in the *Rhetoric* as general statements about particular things, serve Bacon as building blocks in the foundation of the new science. Once he has established a rule, it will reappear constantly in short form to stand for all the experiences and reasoning that led to its formulation. It cuts in half what the author must say, while making it possible to receive the details under discussion in terms of the larger questions involved. The reader is able simultaneously to comprehend and to penetrate with his mind, which Bacon regards as essential to discourse on high levels of thought. Bacon defends maxims and their many uses in his Preface to the *Maxims of the Law*: they express what the "wisest and deepest" of men have in judgment but have been unable to express; they make it possible for a man to limit and define the bounds of his inquiry. Generalizations on particular subjects, Bacon says, "are not to be contemned, if they be well derived and deduced into particulars, and their limits and exclusions duly assigned" (*Works*, VII, 320). Like the metaphor, however, the maxim becomes for Bacon far more than a device of style or method of delivery. It is very much a part of Bacon's scheme for the reform of discovery itself.

Cicero is responding in the *Orator* to attacks on his own manner of speaking; he attempts to show that he does recognize at least three different manners of discourse which may be appropriate for the same man to employ. In stressing the appearance of intense concentration on thought, with a corresponding lack of interest in style, he is saying what many had already said. Reliance on metaphorical language, because of its simplicity and clarity, and the use of condensed expressions of general knowledge, were also recommended by most writers on the plain style. In discussing this threefold classification of rhetorical modes of address, J. F. D'Alton notes that Aristotle's recognition of the inherent perversity of most audiences is probably what first encouraged theorists to distinguish between methods of adornment. Though Aristotle implies that style is unworthy of the rhetor's concern, he devotes, as do Cicero and Bacon, a very large part of his work on rhetoric to that subject. The importance of Aristotle's real opinion of style

> lies in the fact that it had influence on his pupil Theophrastus, and on the Stoics, who held that the true function of the orator was to instruct (*docere*) and to argue from the facts of his case without any appeal to the emotions. It was in turn through Stoic influence that an ideal of the philosophic style was developed, as something essentially plain, contemptuous of the graces of rhetoric, aiming at logical acumen, and concerned more with the matter than with the manner.[7]

While Cicero describes the grand manner as the height of eloquence and the man who employs it as "the first of orators," the Stoic rhetoricians and their followers in the Renaissance scorn any mode of presentation which seeks chiefly to influence the passions. Bacon, who found much in general to draw him to Stoic philosophers, objects strongly both to their modes of reasoning and to the unworkable and idealistic conceptions of rhetoric which they express. They will tend to remain unknown and unread, he felt, and their influence over those who need it will be minimal.

We can see clearly why the Renaissance was confused by competing rhetorical doctrines, and why Bacon takes his stand against them all, by looking briefly at Cicero's conflicts with two formidable contemporary adversaries—the Atticists and the Stoics. Cicero and the Atticists were constantly at odds during the golden period of Cicero's reputation, and it is Attic rhetoric which was most instrumental in accomplishing the complete eclipse which Cicero's reputation suffered for more than a century after his death. Quintilian, who restored his name, summarized the Attic charges against Cicero, which used the terms "bombastic, Asiatic, redundant, and given to excessive repetition."[8] Cicero was pointedly denounced by his detractors as a sophist and was often compared to Isocrates, whose ideal of culture was literally rhetorical and thus brought attacks from Plato and the Socratic circle.[9] The term "Asiatic" was employed to describe Cicero's style, denoting all that is gaudy, common, and tasteless.

As Bacon must have seen, neither the Atticists nor the Stoics were able to make satisfactory cases for their versions of an anti-Ciceronian rhetoric. The contradictions inherent in their arguments are no less obvious than those in Cicero's defenses of his own theory and practice. The differences between the idealism of philosophy and the reality of practice are apparent and numerous in all three schools.

For example, Calvus and Brutus, the chief spokesmen for Roman Atticism, attack Cicero's *De Oratore* and its brief for the grand style on the grounds that such a style is foreign to the Attic tradition. Yet, as R. G. M. Nisbet has said, no Roman style was less in the tradition of Demosthenes than that of the Atticists, whose work lacks "variety and color, blood and juice."[10] The term "Attic" seems to lose meaning if applied to works of no vitality. Even Demosthenes, Cicero notes, freely employed the grand style on suitable occasions. By insisting above all on polish and restraint, Calvus and Brutus would have reduced the effectiveness of rhetoric except in cases where refinement counts for more than persuasive power. No error in rhetorical theory is as dangerous as the intellectuals' tendency to discount the importance of persuasion on all levels of discourse.

Cicero, in spite of his faults, seems wiser than the Atticists. In the *Brutus*, a series of lectures to his friend and pupil, the great rhetorician clarifies his objections to Attic rhetoric. Bacon may have read the *Brutus*, one of Cicero's major works of controversy. It is certain that he had absorbed the arguments put forth there against the plain style and its philosophical justification. In the work, the style of Cotta, an early Roman orator whose manner was imitated by the Atticists, is attacked as the only style which could have been affected by a man of no physical vigor.[11] Calvus, to whom Cicero attributes the misused term "Attic," is criticized for promoting a false version of the Greek ideal. Calvus "was in error and caused others to err with him." Every orator seeks like him to create a wholesome and appropriate style,

> but if meagreness and dryness and general poverty is put down as Attic, with of course the proviso that it must have finish and urbanity,. . . that is good so far as it goes. But because there are in the category of Attic other qualities better than these, one must beware not to overlook the gradations and dissimilarities, the force and variety of Attic orators. (*Brutus*, LXXXII.)

Cicero's association with the grand style derives largely from the nature of his orations. Testimony both ancient and modern is unanimous in its estimate of the superior quality of the late speeches. Tacitus commends them as significant advances in the history of style, and Quintilian says truthfully that, by his time, the name Cicero had "come to be regarded not as the name of a man but of eloquence itself" (*Institutio*, X, i). Most modern critics praise Cicero for a highly wrought style and passionate eloquence, some maintaining that he excelled Demosthenes, the orator who is named by both Cicero and Bacon as the greatest speaker who ever lived. R. G. M. Nisbet, on the other hand, provides a balanced study of the speeches which is more to Bacon's point and which outlines the major arguments in the Stoic rebuttal. Cicero is surpassed as a prose stylist by no one but Plato. His "supreme intellectual gifts" and "vast energies" made it possible for him to achieve more than most public men hope to achieve.

> Yet most of his speeches fail to satisfy. Though both eloquent and serious, he was seldom both at once. He championed unworthy causes for short-term results in front of audiences that he despised. He turned on spurious emotion so often it is difficult to know when he is being sincere. He used his outstanding talents to frustrate rather than to promote action. Except at the beginning and the end of his career, the moral authority of a Demosthenes or a Lincoln or a Churchill eluded him.[12]

All the qualities for which the Atticists attacked Cicero—his floridity, his inappropriate humor, his excessive interest in style, his manipulation of rhetorical devices for false effects, and his lack of *urbanitas*—become traditional complaints lodged against the "full-bodied" rhetoric. Above all these faults, however, it is Cicero's failure to use his powers to effect moral ends that becomes the crucial issue in his feud with the Stoics.

While the Atticists argue primarily the question of whether the plain style can replace the grand style, the Stoic adversaries argue simply that no rhetorical manner, even that which Cicero would describe as plain, is congenial to either philosophy or the truth. Though no philosopher himself, Cicero does call for a distinction to be made between the manners of serious written works and persuasive orations. He recommends that his son Marcus, for example, "read carefully not only my orations but also these books of mine on philosophy" (*De Officiis*, I, i).[13] Then he explains the primary stylistic differences: "For while the orations exhibit a more vigorous style, yet the unimpassioned, unrestrained style of my philosophical productions is also worth cultivating." It was one of Cicero's main goals in life to improve Roman education and surpass the Greeks by preparing young men to be efficient in both thought and action, a goal which required the cultivation of various styles of discourse for various occasions. As he notes, neither Plato nor Demosthenes achieved all he could, because the one was a poor orator and the other an inadequate philosopher. Nevertheless, it must be said, neither of Cicero's styles was acceptable to the Stoic thinkers, who cultivated a barer and more subtle manner than Cicero's most subdued attempts at philosophic discourse. As one editor of the *De Officiis* notes, even that philosophic work "is full of repetitions and rhetorical flourishes, and it fails often in logical order and power."[14] A style such as that of the *De Officiis*, one which affects intellectuality and exclusive concentration on thought, seemed most immoral and unphilosophical to the Stoics.

The Stoic manner, to cite another complication in the history of the plain style, is more appropriate to written discourse than Cicero's without being any less artificial. Though curt, unrhythmical, and pointedly plain, it appears to be governed by no fewer rules. Regarding themselves as pioneers in rhetoric as well as in thought, the Stoic philosophers make much of their arguments with the Ciceronians. And yet they do not manage to avoid the excesses which Bacon was later to find in both schools. As D'Alton says, even Seneca the Younger, in "his love of short phrases, antitheses, balanced clauses, word-play, and the jingle of similar syllables, shows how closely allied he was to the traditions of the schools."[15] The Stoic writers, of course, claim to create such effects in prose for what they regard as philosophical purposes; they see the epigram, the paradox, and other forms conducing to "pregnant brevity" as their special contributions to rhetoric. Even more blindly than Cicero, Seneca the Younger can analyze brilliantly and condemn the very faults of which he is most guilty. The contradictions which his style offers to his theory are as apparent as Cicero's own. Seneca's popularity grew as Cicero's declined, however, largely because of his style. Just as Bacon was later to respond to Elizabethan excesses initially by retreating as far in the opposite direction as he could, so Seneca responded to Cicero's. The results among educated men were the same. J. F. D'Alton says that

with its abandonment of the periodic style, its taste for paradox
and epigram, its unnatural modes of expression, its allusiveness,
its tendency towards obscurity, and at times towards a studied
asymmetry, the Senecan "manner" made a powerful appeal to the
young man of the day, even though its very defects constituted the
basis of the appeal.[16]

Quintilian, though he praises the Stoic philosophy, forbids that it be
taught to boys in the schools. "For such reading will give them a
harsh and bloodless style, since they will as yet be unable to
understand the force and vigour of these authors" (*Institutio*, II, v).

Seneca the Younger's chief goal as a stylist, as one editor of his
Epistles puts it, is to transcend the "somewhat stiff and Ciceronian
point of view."[17] A "forceful manner of speech, rapid and copious,"
Seneca says in Epistle XL, "is more suited to a mountebank than to
a man who is discussing and teaching an important and serious
subject.... Besides, speech that deals with the truth should be
unadorned and plain." The popular style, he goes on to charge, has
"nothing to do with truth; its aim is to impress the common herd, to
ravish heedless ears by its speed." As a result, he claims, the
Ciceronian style has infected Roman life and philosophy by becoming popular and widely imitated. "Wantonness in speech is proof of
public luxury.... A man's ability cannot possibly be of one sort and
his soul of another. If his soul be wholesome, well-ordered, serious
and restrained, his ability also is sound and sober" (Epistle CXIV).
In the same work, then, Seneca relates the "eloquence of the day" to
the political and philosophical vices which seem also to be flour-
ishing. Only a corrupt age would allow its orators to speak as if
setting their words to music—"so wheedling and soft is their gliding
style."

In his belief that style reveals character and, more specifically, the
moral state of a culture, Seneca anticipated Tacitus, another
exemplar of the subdued and manly mode. In his *Dialogue on
Oratory*, the historian demonstrates a concern as profound as
Quintilian's, whose pupil he may have been, for the decline of
Roman oratory. Tacitus, however, invents a speaker who describes a
bad style in the same terms one might use to describe Stoic
discourse. Messalla explains that oratory has declined as an art
because eloquence is "degraded, like a discrowned queen, to a few
commonplaces and cramped conceits." Men no longer teach rhetoric in the Ciceronian context of broad and humanistic learning, and

she is thus "curtailed and mutilated, shorn of all her state, all her distinction, I had almost said all her freedom, and is learnt like any vulgar handicraft."[18] Tacitus is pleased in one sense, however, that oratory has declined in his time, because that art is not "quiet and peaceable," nor does it find "satisfaction in moral worth and good behavior." It is a "foster-child of license," an "associate of sedition, a goad for the unbridled populace." Oratory, Tacitus charges, is an art which is "Devoid of reverence" and "insulting, off-hand, and overbearing" (ibid., pp. 123–25).

Stoicism produced its own rhetoric for another important reason, of course. It always places the branches of knowledge in a systematic scheme under dialectic or logic and thus emphasizes those patterns of communication at the expense of rhetorical ones. The style of Stoic thinkers and their imitators, largely for this reason, has come to be described as philosophical. Those authors are thought of as pioneers in the new rhetoric, not because they ignore the arts of style—diction, rhythm, imagery—but because they claim to employ them to clarify and explain, not to decorate and amplify the truth. E. K. Arnold, in his book *Roman Stoicism*, describes the Stoic manner as dialectical in form; statements are short and pointed and there is an obvious attempt to use words which "precisely and exclusively correspond to the objects described, and therefore lead up to transparent clearness of speech."[19] Because they hold truth in its pure form to be the only criterion for judging style, they are abrupt and sententious; they even take pleasure in paradoxes which make their auditors think deeply and examine logically. As Arnold says in the same passage, their style is that of men "blind to that whole side of the universe which cannot be reduced to syllogistic shape."

In spite of its faults, therefore, in comparison with the Ciceronians', the Stoics' style did seem to merit a reputation as a mode for profound if generalized moral expression. The Senecan manner is in no sense oratorical and is thus freed from the rigid requirements which govern arrangement and presentation in the rhetorical manuals. The Stoics employed a style which violated every prevailing rule of decorum and by its manner suggested a new approach to things. Though they offended many conservative readers with their *sententiae*, they demanded and received a new freedom which allowed men like Seneca to perfect fresh forms—in his case, the

philosophical essay. While such a style may depend on the same
rhetorical devices as the Ciceronian—especially the figures of paral-
lelism—the aim is to produce crisp and concentrated expression
which eliminates everything extraneous to allow focus on content.
Because the only difference between Stoic and Ciceronian manners
that can be firmly established is the absence in the former of what
might be called emotional appeals, that has become the central
factor in discriminating between rhetorical and philosophical modes
of delivery.

But the presence or absence of emotional appeals provides no
adequate basis for distinctions between the grand and plain, the
rhetorical and philosophical styles, a fact which explains Bacon's
inability to see the rhetorical tradition except as the first hurdle to be
jumped in the progress toward a new philosophy. Erasmus notes in
his *Ciceronianus* that the only Ciceronian was the Roman himself
and that no style can be mastered without practice in modified
Ciceronian forms of style and delivery. We learn the same truths
from Morris W. Croll and George Williamson, modern scholars who
have wrestled with the special problems of applying ancient criteria
of style to English prose. Croll defines anti-Ciceronianism partly in
terms of asymmetrical structures, while Williamson demonstrates
that Senecan stylists employ slightly less conspicuous but still highly
symmetrical forms, much as stylists in the grand manner do.[20]
Williamson's attempt to convince us that Euphuistic prose is as
Senecan as it is Ciceronian, as philosophical as it is rhetorical,
underscores the difficulties which must have faced writers like
Bacon in the late sixteenth century. The only distinction Williamson
can make is between "essential" and "accidental" elements of style.
If Lyly's use of antithesis, for example, can be shown by a reader to
assist primarily in the presentation of thought, it conforms admirably to the Senecan use of that structural pattern.[21] In any such
case the rhetorical mode of delivery is identified by the fact that
many features of a writer's manner do not assist directly in the
communication of meaning. This distinction proves finally to be
unenlightening, for Williamson confuses us even about Bacon,
challenging Croll's assessment and showing that the scholar's earlier
distinctions would not hold even with so obvious a Senecan author.[22]
Williamson finds Croll's analysis of the philosophical style unsatisfactory, as indeed it proves to be, but, as Brian Vickers has said,

Williamson's own "self-imposed classification" of prose styles—into loose, antithetical, and circular—serves only to create a frustrating struggle with material which will not yield.[23]

The disagreements between Croll, Williamson, and Vickers, added to the persuasive demonstration by Robert Adolph that Bacon's style owes few debts to Tacitus,[24] force us to conclude that not many insights will emerge from careful analysis of prose patterns or figures of speech in light of the tradition of the plain style. Critics make it clear that Bacon's work is indebted both to the Ciceronians and to the Senecans, and that it is no less rhetorical than philosophical by ancient standards of stylistic judgment. Since Bacon very rarely talks about the details of adornment, we have nothing to judge him by except his theory of rhetoric's role in the larger context of learning. Just as he sets out to correct the abuses of Ciceronian rhetoricians, he outlines the many ways in which the plain writers use style as an obstacle to progress in philosophy. He hopes to be both eloquent and serious in his philosophical works, to improve upon Cicero's delivery and to enhance the moral authority and logical power of the Senecans. To accomplish both goals, he calls for emphasis on variety in discourse, as well as in research.[25] Bacon also mentions "liveliness," which, like variety, is a quality decidedly lacking in the Stoic style, as an essential attribute of any forceful manner. If the Stoics are more virtuous than most philosophers, they fail to stimulate their audiences to acquire the qualities of virtue, because they will not appeal to the imaginative powers of men "in as lively representation as possible, by ornament of words" (*De augmentis*, VI, 3). Moreover, Bacon attempts to replace the rigid Senecan system of logic and dialectic with a pattern of "multiform method." This pattern too should be applied both to rhetoric and research. The attack is leveled against Ramus, as well as against the fathers of the plain style, for Ramus too is responsible for what Bacon regards as the general and related deterioration of scientific method and the communication process among intellectuals.[26] These and other subjects will be pursued in the next chapter, which assesses Bacon's own views on the relation of science to style.

It was the Stoic writers and their disciples to whom Bacon turned for advice on how to improve upon the delivery of philosophy, and it is the advocates of the plain style, from Plato to Montaigne, whom he discusses in the *De augmentis*, VI, 3. For a popular, if high-minded, rhetoric, they serve admirably, he believes. Since the works of Croll, Williamson, and Vickers contain full descriptions of Bacon's views on all these figures but Aristotle, we need only record here that they offer little to the modern scientist. Plato is impractical and idealistic; his remarks suggest that no philosopher can be a rhetorician.[27] And, while Aristotle rescues the art for learned men, he too confuses the explanation of rhetoric's relation to truth and makes it possible for many generations of well-meaning men to perpetuate the schism between philosophy and communication theory. The Stoics are criticized in the same section of the *De augmentis* for their bloodless methods, and Bacon reminds his reader that, while logic "handles reason in truth and nature," rhetoric "handles it as it is planted in the opinions of the vulgar."

If a man of learning is to make reason at one with opinion, he must become a proficient rhetorician. He must learn to use the syllogism and other false forms of demonstration shrewdly for the philosopher's rhetorical purposes. Though science, properly speaking, is not in need of the rhetorician's art for its acceptance among men, its achievements being real and observable, philosophy in general—that is, as opposed to "natural philosophy"—depends heavily on its translation from the minds of geniuses to those of the "crowd of learners." Too often, the thinker allies himself with the "popular arts" when he attempts to communicate his thoughts. Bacon relegates such philosophers to the category of "wits." In a very frank early piece, *The Masculine Birth of Time*, Seneca is purged from the special circle of dedicated philosophers, accused by Bacon of having settled for "literary renown" at the expense of truth. Seneca's willingness to give authority to "a popular and easily acquired knowledge of nature" made fame as a stylist possible for him, but it seriously damaged the development of philosophy in future years. By compromising the "ideal of a stricter and more thorough investigation of the truth," Seneca lost his chance to reform the ways men learn and placed himself in a class with Cicero and Plutarch, men who purified and revitalized style without contributing to the growth of knowledge.[28] Thus, even as moralists, the plain writers fail Bacon the scientist. His sections on morality and the science of ethics owe more to Aristotle than to Seneca or Tacitus. It is Aristotle, in the end, who solves for Bacon the most difficult theoretical problem facing the philosopher who hopes to communicate: that is, how to combine eloquence with the scientist's accuracy and concern for both definition and analysis.[29]

The Debt to Aristotle

Bacon's pronouncements on communication are concerned with theory rather than with application. He tells us often enough that his own manner of delivery in the major works will provide adequate examples and illustrations of his general principles of communication. Because he sets out in the *Advancement* to improve and augment knowledge already available, we are wise to look to his sources whenever they are acknowledged. It is to Aristotle, the most practical and scientific of the classical rhetoricians, and the one whose larger goals are closest to Bacon's own, that the Englishman goes for guides to the formulation of principles for the new rhetoric of philosophy. The debts are complex and profound. Our understanding of them is complicated by Bacon's indifference to "testimonies," as he calls them, and by his tendency to blame his polymathic rival for all the ills which have befallen science. Yet Bacon sees plainly that Aristotle is the only philosopher who is unquestionably "Attic" in his views on the higher nature of the communication process. Aristotle's genius deserves to be improved upon and augmented by a modern disciple, Bacon believes, and he undertakes the task not unwillingly as his own failures to communicate persuasively multiply. It is the Greek who, more than any other figure from the tradition of either rhetoric or philosophy, helps Bacon to contend with the two obstacles to success which we have been discussing here: audience accommodation and the conventions of Roman and Renaissance rhetoric. Though the *Rhetoric* of Aristotle has had at least indirect influence on the majority of subsequent rhetoricians, Bacon takes a step forward by going back to the source, an original idea for his time.[30]

Croll noticed many years ago that Bacon's remarks on logic and rhetoric reveal a "constant dependence on Aristotle's *Rhetoric*," and he called for an investigation of this unexpected phenomenon.[31] Since an understanding of that reliance provides a convenient bridge between this section and the following ones in the present study, it is examined here.[32]

While the scope of Aristotle's communication theory is both broader and more limited than that of Bacon's, the Englishman owes most of his unformed rhetorical doctrines to his predecessor. Though arrogant in his scorn of documentation, and apt occasionally to plagiarize, he seldom fails to admit to a real debt. The two philosophers agree generally on the nature and function of rhetoric, its role among the arts and sciences, its basis in psychology, and the uses to which it puts logical, ethical, and pathetic proofs. Some of Aristotle's hints for a philosophical style are expanded by Bacon, and what he takes to be inconsistencies and deliberate errors are "corrected" magisterially. Moreover, because he writes only to improve or stimulate the growth of man's knowledge, Bacon does original and important new things to Aristotle's fundamental conceptions as he reworks him for a modern English rhetoric. These alterations involve shifts in emphasis or new positions on the ladder of learning for certain disciplines, apparently minor modifications which nevertheless have great significance for the theorist. They translate, in particular, into new, more useful versions of the three forms of rhetorical proof.

The similarities in the authors' views on the general function of rhetoric should first be outlined. Like Aristotle, Bacon was a man of immense learning and a zeal for reform. His rhetoric grows, as Aristotle's does, from an attack on the "delicate and polished" modes of learning which flourished in his day. Just as Aristotle attacks the Sophists for fostering an art lethal to the arts and sciences, Bacon accuses the Ciceronians and, later, the Senecans of thwarting inquiry and analysis among the learned. Bacon's cultural ideal, like Aristotle's, requires initially the thorough reform of logic and rhetoric, the communication arts. Both begin by associating rhetoric firmly and strategically with logic as its subordinate handmaid. In the *Advancement*, Bacon classifies rhetoric as a subdivision of logic, itself a branch of human philosophy. "Now we descend," he says, "to that part which concerneth the Illustration of Tradition, comprehended in that science which we call Rhetoric" (*Works*, III, 409). In the *De augmentis*, VI, 3, which refines and expands his thoughts on the subject, Bacon clearly reduces rhetoric to the art of illustration, but it is also to be thought of as a logical art. While it is carefully focused in definition, though, Bacon in no way precludes the broader Aristotelian understanding of the scope and function of rhetoric. What he seeks to do is to correct Aristotle's error in reducing style—the only part of the old rhetoric which ever belonged to it exclusively—to a "minor" and "vulgar" accessory. Bacon obviously hopes to restore the working relationship between philosophy and rhetoric by giving rhetoric a philosophical authority it had never before deserved. The way to reform rhetoric in the present age is to grant the importance of style and then rework it as a philosophical doctrine which transcends mere ornament. It is apparent that Bacon hopes to see "illustration of discourse" work as the proofs are meant to do in Aristotle's *Rhetoric*. There are even hints from him that he suspected Aristotle of having seen himself that what he calls "proofs" stand in reality as powerful devices of style.[33]

However it is defined, Bacon and Aristotle agree, rhetoric's first duty is a moral one. The business of rhetoric is to make "pictures of virtue and goodness," Bacon says in the *De augmentis*, VI, 3, echoing the claim in I, 1, of the *Rhetoric* that this art seeks first the triumph of truth and justice over fraud and injustice. Though Aristotle speaks primarily of a popular audience and a popular rhetoric, Bacon has no difficulty translating his mentor's objections into his own terms of outrage against abuses of communication among learned men. And, as both authors shrewdly suggest, trickery and deceit of various kinds are required when the end is worthy and the audience is not. Rhetoric, a part of human philosophy in Bacon's system, is placed in a strategic relation to logic and ethics:

> The end of logic is to teach a form of argument to secure reason, and not to entrap it; the end likewise of moral philosophy is to procure the affections to fight on the side of reason, and not to invade it; the end of rhetoric is to fill the imagination with observations and images to second reason, and not to oppress it. (*De augmentis*, VI, 3.)

The key role of the imagination, only implied strongly by Aristotle, is emphasized by Bacon. Aristotle says simply that rhetoric does part of the duty of logic and part of the duty of ethics, and that rhetoric may thus properly be regarded as an "offshoot" from both (*Rhetoric*, I, 1). Bacon, who sees the art in the same light, notes in VI, 3, of the *De augmentis* that

> Aristotle wisely places rhetoric between logic on the one side, and moral and civil knowledge on the other, as participating of both. For the proofs and demonstrations of logic are the same to all men; but the proofs and persuasions of rhetoric ought to differ according to the auditors.

Bacon then improves Aristotle for a new, more practical rhetoric by firmly dividing audiences into learned and popular ones and by suggesting that the doctrine of audience accommodation, a forgotten doctrine in Renaissance rhetorics, should, "in perfection of idea," yield a separate rhetorical strategy for each individual among the auditors.[34]

It is on the audience, in fact, that Bacon and his mentor show strongest accord. The Englishman accepts Aristotle's implied distinction between rhetorics for philosophers and for popular audiences. Though Aristotle does not mention it directly in the *Rhetoric*, many of the "Attic" rhetoricians of later years have found his opening remarks justification enough for the development of what seemed a rhetoric for the learned.[35] On the nature of audiences, both Bacon and Aristotle note that speakers and audiences are fundamentally reasonable (one must believe this is true or give up in despair, Bacon says). Yet they also agree that the rhetor must exploit what the audience believes is the good. Men are inclined to anything that they can be convinced is the good, and Bacon praises Aristotle highly, at the expense of Roman moralists, for instructing both philosophers and rhetoricians to study concepts of virtue and, especially, to formulate ways and means of acquiring it (*De augmentis*, VII, 3).[36] Both authors believe, as Bacon expressed it, that rhetoric handles not truth itself but truth "as it is planted in the opinions of the vulgar." This forces the art of persuasion, on any level, to become a search, as Aristotle says, for the "available means of persuasion."[37] The rhetor must learn to "discern the genuine means, and also the spurious means" of gaining consent (*Rhetoric*, I, 2). Bacon supplements Aristotle and fills a gap by offering collections of sophisms, spurious means of persuasion, which a writer or speaker may need to convince his audience or to protect himself from becoming the victim of false reasoning. Both recognize, too, that fraud must be perpetrated on occasion if truth or the good is eventually to win the day. The object of rhetoric is to discover the "available means of persuasion," whatever they may be. Bacon and Aristotle try frankly to equip their readers with all possible insights into their audiences, to enable them to move whatever manner of men they might confront.[38]

Though the two views on the character of audiences will be treated in the discussion of *pathos* which follows, it should be noted here that both authors strike the "Attic" pose of superior intelligence and show contempt for man's suggestible nature. Concepts of proof or persuasion depend on a thorough knowledge of humanity, and, though he may more often quote Solomon, Cicero, or Tacitus, for illustration, it is back to Aristotle that Bacon goes for an education in how the philosophy of human nature impinges on the art of rhetoric. Bacon admits as much and says that his only serious objection to the master is his inability to see the true significance of *ethos* and *pathos*. They are sciences in their own right and more than just rhetorical proofs; in a sense, they come to form the foundation of Bacon's strategy for the Great Instauration. In regard to logical proofs, the same is true, since Bacon looks on them as the keys to philosophical reform and supplements them with his new induction.

One final point about the general debt of Bacon to Aristotle and his psychology of rhetoric should be made. For, though they are at one on the nature of man, Bacon finds his rationale for a new rhetoric in Aristotle's perplexing and contradictory treatment of style. The skillful analysis of the passions in Book II of the *Rhetoric* leads Aristotle to admit implicitly that style is a vital component in any philosophy of rhetoric and that it should not be left to the handbooks. The audience, he rationalizes, has such a "sorry nature" that elements superfluous to a true rhetoric become important. Though he urges speakers not to allure the auditors to belief or to stimulate their emotions, though he calls style a thing of "real, if minor, importance," he ends by devoting more space to style in the *Rhetoric* than he had in the *Poetics*. It is apparent early in Book I that Aristotle's hopes for rhetoric will not be realized. Contempt for common audiences is implicit in his advice to employ false maxims and sham enthymemes with suggestible men (II, 21) and in his rather sly explanations of other unscrupulous but effective means to gain consent. Once he even pauses to suggest something special for audiences of unusually blunt mentality. It is clear enough then why Aristotle contributed to the division between philosophy and rhetoric: wise men came to regard books I and II as their guides to a plain style, what Cicero was to describe in the *Orator*, XXIII, as a manner which deliberately avoids giving pleasure. At the same time, the many stylists and pedagogues who were their enemies were finding comfort in the *Rhetoric*, usually Book III, as well.

Such problems do not appear in Bacon. He is clearer about the misunderstood relation of both logic and rhetoric to truth. He allows for dual systems of both forms of argument and does not scruple to adapt the Aristotelian proofs as rhetorical devices. This is done without ambiguity and with the understanding that the goals remain truth, reason, and the good; the audience is the same "sorry" one Aristotle envisioned. For Bacon, rhetoric *is* style, and it seems natural for him to attempt to rework the unstated premise of Book III of Aristotle's *Rhetoric* by adding elements from I and II which seem not to belong there. It is part of his plan for the reform of English style and the correction of both Senecan and Ciceronian abuses that Aristotle be revised. As Croll has noted, Aristotle was the only responsible source left for Bacon to cite in his argument; only he possessed power "as unquestionable and orthodox as that of Cicero."[39] Clearness, brevity, and appropriateness, the cardinal virtues of the manner of delivery which Aristotle recommends, are enhanced as philosophical doctrines of style by Bacon's treatment of the three ancient proofs.

Scholars have demonstrated that Renaissance manuals of style, largely under the influence of Peter Ramus, found it easy to convert logical demonstrations of all kinds into schemes and tropes. Of the two hundred figures analyzed by Sister Miriam Joseph, considerably more than half derive from the topics and forms of logic. Some are the exact equivalents of such techniques of demonstration as division, obversion, enthymematic reasoning, and syllogistic argument. She goes so far as to claim that many of these handbooks (those of Sherry, Peacham, Puttenham, and Day, for example) are governed by a concept of figures "so inclusive as to omit little of what has ever been included in a theory of composition, for the approximately two hundred figures of speech which they distinguish represent an analysis of practically every aspect of grammar, logic, and rhetoric."[40]

Bacon too, in his way, is a child of the times, for he employs both the old logic and the new induction as rhetorical modes of demonstration. Deductive reasoning is reduced in his system to a style of arranging and decorating material from the "soft" sciences for the benefit of the "sorry" audiences for which he writes. Inductive patterns in his system, though more suitable to philosophy, also depend for success on vivid imagery and are thus apt to conform more closely to the demands of rhetoric than to those of the new logic. Because both his philosophical plan as a scientist and his literary strategy as an advocate for science depend on the effect of reader response to the "simple sensuous perception," Bacon generally opens his works with colorful and exact metaphors which are indistinguishable from logical analogies. "There is no proceeding in invention of knowledge but by similitude," Bacon says, justifying his scientific method (*Works*, III, 218). Moreover, a man who would persuade other men to take action and reform their thinking must *"pray in aid of similitudes,"* he says, justifying the most prominent features of his own philosophical style (*Works*, III, 407). The "received logics" serve Bacon as strategies for demonstration in intellectual works and as "illustration of discourse" in rhetorical works intended to persuade. When the two combine, as they often do, style and method are indistinguishable, as they are meant to be. Even as he explains it in his philosophical works, the inductive method proves to be chiefly a rhetorical or "artistic" instrument for bringing science down to the level of most men's understanding. Bacon probably saw it that way himself. It is clear that he looked on Aristotle's logic, which he attacks violently in the *New Organon*, as a useful rhetorical scheme for simplifying knowledge for delivery in small packages to minds less acute than his own.[41] It flatters the understanding and thus invites support. The goal is to reverse a trend by treating style as a logical art of illustration, as an art to be learned by method. As Neal W. Gilbert has remarked, Bacon's method is artistic rather than scientific because his notion of experimentation and the new induction, like the concept of deduction, is the clear result of a demand for improved teaching and communication skills.[42] Aristotle, regarded universally as the father of a truly scientific method of demonstration, is seen by Bacon then as the source for a suitable artistic method. Bacon makes no distinction between logic and dialectic, since all methods should allow for uncertainty and discovery, and he seldom draws a clear Aristotelian line between arts and sciences. What we have from him is an effort to reform all the disciplines by reforming the method of communicating or delivering them. It amounts to a scientific art, or a logic of rhetoric, and it is primarily to Aristotle, who also was apparently unconcerned by such paradoxes, that he goes for insights.

In his treatment of logical proofs for the scientist and rhetorician, Bacon strives to preserve the new induction as the key to discovery. For writers or speakers of any kind, he feels, the arts of logical demonstration must be rescued from the stylists and purified again for the purposes of argument and proof. Bacon returns to Aristotle frequently and, in doing so, works to accomplish three goals: (1) correction of inconsistencies and gaps in Aristotle's logic, (2) revision and enrichment of the system of topics, and (3) preparation of the syllogism and enthymeme for duty in social and moral research. As Gilbert has shown, Renaissance thinkers were in considerable conflict as to the function of logic. Though the methodologists of the arts employed it for teaching and stressed its utility, those in the sciences emphasized that strict demonstration and proof are the keys to invention. "The two purposes clashed in logic because logic could be regarded as an art or as a science, and because its inventor, Aristotle, had found it useful both in speaking and in scientific analysis."[43] Bacon, who decidedly did not find logic useful in scientific analysis, chooses to take it as outlined by Aristotle for a sound guide to rhetorical method, one which offers a kind of "half-knowledge" which often "procures assent."

In correcting inconsistencies that he finds in Aristotle's logic, Bacon concentrates on the theory of sophisms and on two minor methods of detecting fallacies. He recommends and often provides lists of sophisms in each area of learning, including rhetoric, and regards this procedure as an excellent means of improving the state if not the storehouse of knowledge. The first of his proposals under *Elenches* in the *De augmentis* is indebted to Aristotle's *De sophisticis elenchis*, as Bacon acknowledges. In the work, he says, Aristotle handles the sophisms excellently "in the way of precepts," though not so well as Plato does "in the way of examples" (*De augmentis*, V, 4). In Book VI of the *De augmentis* and in the *Colours of Good and Evil* Bacon gives examples to supplement Aristotle's theoretical treatment of these forms of persuasion and dissuasion. Since these are the sophisms of rhetoric, he again takes his source to task and reveals his own more candid approach to deception:

> The honest and principal use of this doctrine is for redargution of sophisms; yet it is manifest that the degenerate and corrupt use is for raising, by means of these very sophisms, captions and contradictions. And this passes for a great faculty, and no doubt is of very great advantage. (*De augmentis*, V, 4.)

The philosopher may resent "captions and contradictions"; the ordinary audience, it is implied, does not. They are therefore "by no means to be neglected."

In a letter to Lord Mountjoy, Bacon reveals two significant points about his opinion of Aristotle's handling of the sophisms—points which do not receive attention in the works intended for posterity. First, he suggests that, while it is sheer hypocrisy to illustrate sophistical reasoning extensively while condemning it as specious,

Aristotle may have had a very good reason for failing to state plainly the rhetorical uses for false logic. Perhaps policy forced him "to keep himself close, as one that had been a challenger of all the world, and had raised infinite contradiction." Aristotle fails "to deliver and unwrap himself well of that he seemeth to conceive," whatever the cause, and this leads Bacon to object to him also on the grounds of style. Bacon claims that he himself treats the sophisms "in a new manner" so as to make them "pleasant and lightsome." He admits as well, however, that these forms of persuasion are "colours" and thus are never to be fully understood; their impact on men is difficult to gauge (*Colours*, in *Works*, VII, 70–71). Put simply, Bacon sees that the sophisms may be employed to produce the truth, to vary or misrepresent it, or to deceive and lead men to error (of which he does not approve). Aristotle's "wisdom and diligence" have been misdirected therefore, because he treats them as part of a philosophical system when they belong principally to rhetoric, especially to communication in business and private intercourse. In Book I of the *Rhetoric*, the author labors in vain to provide an adequate discussion of the colors of good and evil, or "popular signs," Bacon says, and thus he fails to establish a basis for deliberative discourse, which seeks the good. His judgment of Aristotle's efforts is typically harsh:

> But the labours of Aristotle regarding these colours are in three points defective; one, that he recounts a few only out of many; another, that he does not add the answers to them; and, the third, that he seems to have conceived but a part of the use of them. For their use is not more for probation than for affecting and moving. For there are many forms which, though they mean the same, affect differently. (*De augmentis*, VI, 3.)

It is apparent that Bacon's complaints are on rhetorical grounds, and fairly so, since Aristotle calls logical proofs a part of rhetoric. Bacon, unlike his source, though, is unequivocal in his approval of these "points and stings of words," so long as they serve the goal of affecting the audience's ultimate consent to a valid proposition. If the writer's aim is probation, or the stimulation of inquiry rather than belief, they may be out of place. Bacon then adds twelve sophisms and their answers to his appendix to rhetoric, implying that they may be used as the reader chooses. If there is any doubt about his debt to Aristotle on this point, he says himself that "I, that should know best, do freely acknowledge that I had my light from him" (*Works*, VIII, 70).

Bacon's last examples of logical methods for detecting fallacies and filling some gaps left by his authority are proposed briefly in the appendix to the Art of Judging in the *De augmentis*, V, 4.[44] There is first the "doctrine of judgment of judgment," or detection of fallacies in the proofs themselves. "It treats of the application of the differing kinds of proofs to the differing kinds of matters or subjects." This is a point made repeatedly by Aristotle, especially in the *Metaphysics*, II, 3, but "though Aristotle has noticed the thing, he has nowhere followed out the manner of it" (*De augmentis*, V, 4). Bacon hardly develops the doctrine himself, though he tells us that it means simply that a true judgment cannot be obtained in a case where the proof employed is unsuited to its purpose, or, as Bacon quotes Aristotle as saying, "we ought not to require either demonstrations from orators or persuasions from mathematicians" (ibid.). In addition, the appendix contains a brief remark on another Aristotelian mode of proof (*Prior Analytics*, II, 13) which has been neglected, the "demonstration in circle." This calls for logical inference from analogy. It does not require that one make progress toward larger or lesser inferences as in deduction and induction. The demonstration in circle is so clearly more useful in rhetoric than in logic that one critic of Bacon reads his explanation of it as another way of describing the Ciceronian period and Ciceronian discourse in general.[45]

Besides using Aristotle's treatment of logical fallacies for rhetorical purposes, Bacon focuses on the doctrine of topics in his search for a workable style. We will look later at the importance of topics to Bacon's style and his theory of interpretation. Here, however, we note only that Bacon's treatment of the logical errors in interpretation owes an acknowledged debt to Aristotle's *De Interpretatione* (to the "name rather than the sense," he hastens to add). He recommends the collecting of places, not for use as conclusions, but as rhetorical aids to the memory. Not having been tested by logical methods, they belong only to the class of stylistic tricks. Aristotle is quoted as support but denounced as a confusing source in the *De augmentis*, V, 4. Proper topics, on the other hand, are thought to hold a legitimate place in logic and to relate to rhetoric as logical proof and as part of the inventional process that precedes communication. As Hardin Craig notes, Bacon sees a new and profound use for topics; because they direct our inquiry and may lead to inductive conclusions, they are a kind of "half-knowledge."[46] While commonplaces in Bacon's system work as arguments and forms to be stored in the memory for future use, topics are merely facts or places "where a thing is to be looked for . . . and as it were indexed." These are vital to both logic and rhetoric, since the growth of knowledge depends on them. It is perhaps the major feature of Bacon's philosophic style that it never neglects to furnish the reader with memorable "topics" to be pondered. General topics are provided by deductive logic and thus are surely in error, but Bacon recommends their use to develop a "faculty of wise interrogation."[47] Particular topics are "mixtures of logic with the proper matter of science" and thus are helpful to thought as precepts for invention. In Bacon's major works, examples are always given of how they lead to discovery. This procedure, like the formulation of general topics, is a vital rhetorical method to the scientist who would stimulate inquiry.

His many references to general topics in fact suggest that Bacon accepts Aristotle's conception of them as "the forms of argument that are common to all speech" (*Rhetoric*, II, 19).[48] Like Aristotle too he treats general topics as if they were the mutual property of logic and rhetoric. Yet, here again, Bacon revises for a sterner view. Rhetorical invention for him is merely an act of recollection (since "it hath already obtained the name, let it be called invention," he says in the *Advancement*, II, in *Works*, III, 390), and logic, he maintains, "says nothing, no nor takes any thought, about the invention of arts" (*De augmentis*, V, 2). The whole system of logic then in use, including the Platonic method of induction, is shifted by him to the invention of speech and arguments, an art of remembrance. In a key passage, Bacon admits that the general topics impinge on the functions of logic and ethics, but their "true and fruitful" use, he insists, is as "cautions against ambiguities of speech" (*Works*, III, 394). It is against equivocation and the misleading properties of words that Bacon struggles always, and, though they do not belong in logic proper, he thinks it wise to treat topics in the *De augmentis*, V, 3. General ones are helpful in meditations, in thinking of what we might say, and as "promptuaries" to guide us to what we might ask; because Aristotle would deny these uses and limit their employment, he asks us to "change a rich wardrobe for a pair of shears." Thus, in shifting the doctrine of topics to a middle ground between communication and research, Bacon strengthens and modernizes the old forms into something useful for a new age. As Gilbert puts it, Bacon transformed the topics into devices for scientists: He turned "the debating procedure of the *Topics* into a transaction in which Nature replaced the respondent and the challenger became the scientist."[49] Though he charges Aristotle with perverting generations of would-be thinkers, a glance at the *Topics* and the *Prior Analytics* reveals sources for his doctrine of the detection of fallacies of interpretation in logic.

The final and most interesting use of Aristotelian logic in Bacon is his application of deductive techniques to social and moral research. Old-fashioned forms of "invention," he admits, can be useful still. "It is true that in sciences popular," he says in the *Advancement*, "as moralities, laws, and the like, yea and divinity (because it pleaseth God to apply himself to the capacity of the simplest), that form may have use." Even in natural philosophy it can serve "by way of argument or satisfactory reason" (*Works*, III, 388). But Bacon's real opinion is expressed candidly in "The Plan of the Work," his introduction to the Great Instauration, when he says, "I leave to the syllogism and these famous and boasted modes of demonstration their jurisdiction over popular arts and such as are matter of opinion" (*Works*, IV, 24). The syllogism is a method for arriving at something like, but not the same as, truth. The sciences of ethics, politics, poetry, and theology, for example, lend themselves ideally to deduction, because the syllogism and enthymeme, simple but prolix forms, are structured for controlling and communicating abstract matter. The human mind, even if it belongs to a philosopher, is an enchanted glass in Bacon's famous figure, a mirror receiving and reflecting rays of thought and opinion irregularly. The syllogism will give the mind that employs it and the mind that receives it an illusion of regularity. Bacon notes in the Preface to the *New Organon* that logicians are forced to distort and color reality because men's minds are "occupied with unsound doctrine and beset on all sides by vain imaginations." He reacts to a very strong demand in his time for a logic that is suited to social and moral research on a high level. This very complicated question of how Bacon restores the methods of research outlined in Aristotle's *Topics* and the *Rhetoric* is treated with clarity by Paolo Rossi.[50] Here we note only that it is to effect a rhetorical end that Bacon admits deduction into his scheme for the reform of learning, that it is under rhetoric that this faulty mode of demonstration is treated. In discussing the invention of speech and arts, Bacon tells how deduction can be used to the advantage of the philosopher. In the Preface to the *New Organon*, however, he is quick to say that "the logic which is received, though it be very properly applied to civil business and to those arts which rest in discourse and opinion, is not nearly subtle enough to deal with nature; and in offering at what it cannot master, has done more to establish and perpetuate error than to open the way to truth." Some subjects, notably the sciences of ethics and politics, thrive on combinations of words and images, which together create new "knowledge," however. For the same reason that it is banned from natural philosophy, the syllogism is offered up as a scheme for regularizing the "soft" sciences. Because the syllogism consists entirely of words and symbols, it is ideal for research in such fields. It is one of Bacon's primary objectives to rescue logic from the rhetoric of style, but he also cautions philosophers who would persuade and at the same time increase man's knowledge not to neglect to provide "sensible and plausible elocution." This is especially important if they hope to increase information and stimulate further inquiry in fields where opinion rather than observable truth counts as knowledge. The syllogism "procures assent but can do no work." In ethics, politics, poetry, theology, and law, of course, all the work is done if assent is procured. It is true then, if somewhat paradoxical, that in Bacon's own works exposition, proof, and refutation are the same as argument, persuasion, and rhetoric. He wrote nothing that does not attempt in some way to do important work by procuring assent to its value and credibility. He cleans up an abusive rhetorical system by going, as always, straight to the point, perceiving the truth, and, in a few words, causing us to perceive it. His job is to argue for science and the new induction. In doing so, as a look at the *Advancement*, the *New Organon*, *The Wisdom of the Ancients*, and the *De augmentis* would show, he employs deductive patterns continually as strategies of arrangement and style. It is part of his carefully conceived plan for achieving "quiet entry" into the minds of his readers, a plan we will examine in the next chapter. The old and outdated logic is employed for what seems a fresh new purpose.

Precisely the same procedure is applied to Aristotle's other two modes of rhetorical proof, *ethos* and *pathos*. Like *logos* these concepts are transformed by Elizabethan stylists into mere figures of speech. Bacon understands why and sees that Aristotle himself sanctions this disservice to rhetoric by describing the art in idealistic and contradictory terms: "This art," he says at the beginning of Book I, "consists of proofs alone—all else is but accessory." Obviously, the interpretation of the *Rhetoric* hinges on what its author means by "proofs." Bacon concludes that he must have intended ethical and pathetic proofs to function as devices of style; no concept of proofs could include the emotional appeals of which Aristotle approves and retain its integrity, yet no rhetoric can have meaning without them. Bacon understands that these proofs work as constituents of an author's manner, just as his manner must be regarded as a function of his proof. They create a personal image that works strongly on the audience, and, at the same time, they provide the kinds of demonstration that are persuasive with every sort of audience. Ethos and pathos are the answers to problems which are posed by the limitations of man's mind, the very difficulties that Bacon cites in the *New Organon* as obstacles to progress in the sciences. Because logos, pathos, and ethos are vital to persuasion on any level, they are sciences in their own right. They must be cultivated by the new philosopher. Had he sought to do so, Bacon could have effected a merger between the stylists' rhetoric of proofs and Aristotle's philosophy of proofs, the one too practical and the other too idealistic. As it is, we must look at a variety of his works.

To begin with ethos, we cite a passage from Hardin Craig's *The Enchanted Glass*:

> How much knowledge of the actual Aristotle the Elizabethans had one does not know; but one feels that the Aristotelian ideal of rhetoric as an instrument in the service of reason, operating upon the passions of men in order to make prevail the wisdom of their superiors, is exactly the Elizabethan conception and desire.[51]

Bacon's sense of his superior wisdom and the license it gives him is nowhere more evident than in his treatment of *ethos*, which is outlined in his system as a science separate from others but, like logic, impinging on or comprehending them all. He is strict in condemning the abuses of learning when they mislead men by simplifying or coloring the facts or by imposing personal impressions on them. But he claims as well that sages ought to be judged by their ends and not by their natures. Because he was a worldly man, much experienced in the practice required for survival at Court, his writing reveals an intelligent, Machiavellian awareness of the means available to the man who would persuade. The morality of persuasion differs from that of scholarship, as Bacon so often observes, but because progress depends on persuasion, he would make a science of ethos and deliver it cautiously to men like himself. In the *Colours of Good and Evil*, for example, he explains that even wise men may, for a number of reasons, need coaxing to reason by methods not entirely scrupulous. The clever adversary, he says, may even use sophisms "to quicken and strengthen the opinions and persuasions which are true." Such "forms and insinuations" sometimes "cause a stronger apprehension ... and many times suddenly win the mind to a resolution" (*Works*, VII, 77). Aristotle saw that this is so, but he would not admit it. Nor would he explain what he did mean in a style that was pleasant and inviting. Bacon undertakes in the *Colours* to correct both flaws in his mentor's work.

In VII, 1, of the *De augmentis*, it is said that "civil knowledge requires only an external goodness; for that suffices for society." Civil knowledge is divided into Conversation, Negotiation, and Government. In developing these sciences for the ambitious man, Bacon supplements his own views by reworking Solomon, Aristotle, Machiavelli, and other sources for new purposes. One part of Negotiation is called the "Doctrine Concerning Scattered Occasions"; it makes the Proverbs of Solomon "politic" by applying them to common situations. Throughout his discussion of ethics, Bacon follows Aristotle closely, until, at this point, he begins to make specific recommendations based on the *Rhetoric*. It is typical of his own ethos that these practical rules are associated with the Christian figure of Solomon rather than with the "anti-Christ" who is his real source. Among the thirty-four observations we find advice on when to give soft answers, how to make the conclusion of a speech reflect well on the speaker, and how to preserve an air of knowing far more than you care to impart ("broken speech" is recommended). In the second doctrine of Negotiation, the "Doctrine Concerning Advancement in Life," Bacon explains how men can be the architects of their own fortunes. Advising from experience, he recommends that we give our own advancement as serious attention as we give our virtue. We ought first to obtain "good information of the particular persons with whom we have to deal," including "their desires and ends," their "weaknesses and disadvantages," and their

special faults and soft spots in character. Then we should take care
to "keep a discrete temper and mediocrity both in liberty of speech
and in secrecy," so that others never know us as well as we know
them. At the same time, it is imperative that each man "take an
accurate and impartial survey" of his own nature. "But it is not
enough for a man only to know himself; for he should consider also
the best way to set himself forth to advantage; to disclose and reveal
himself; and lastly, to turn and shape himself according to
occasion."[52] This advice in the *De augmentis*, VIII, 2, is simple
prudence, Bacon declares. A man must be able to show "with grace
and skill," his "virtues, fortunes, and merits," and to cover his
weaknesses and disgraces by artificial means. Only persons of a
"perhaps too scrupulous morality" will protest when he extends the
doctrine to include advice on how to cover one's defects. Such "evil
arts" may be studied if a man's end is good. He should learn to
"depreciate and despise" whatever is unattainable, and to disguise a
flaw in character by borrowing "the mask and color of the neighbor-
ing virtue," and to "frame and spread abroad some possible reason"
why he fails where success was expected. We can watch Bacon doing
these things himself in his speeches, letters, and occasional pieces.[53]

Nor is ethical proof neglected in his philosophical works.
Attention is given in them all to the development of a style "neither
harsh nor unpleasant." And, as Bacon admits in *The Masculine
Birth of Time*, a pleasant style, even for the "sons of science,"
means one which allures the audience. Because the new philosophy
is a sacred trust he pledges to "come in very truth" and not to defile
it by any fault of style. But he also submits to his readers and agrees
that speakers for the new philosophy shall not "drop all art and
subterfuge." And in the *De augmentis*, VI, 2, he promises to "make
the mind of man by the help of art a match for the nature of
things." The *New Organon*, Book I, as we have seen, is largely
occupied with this problem and with Bacon's first rule for successful
ethical proof: know your audience and exploit what you know.
Moreover, as will become apparent, he experimented with different
ways of presenting himself in his works before he perfected the
humble but immensely strong Moses figure who works so well in the
New Organon. His special problem was one of maintaining "a
discrete temper." As Jonson was to say admiringly, he was "nobly
censorious."[54]

The most important kind of ethical proof, of course, is evidence of a thorough knowledge of audience psychology. Though he found more to admire, and less equivocation, in the Stoics' words on the human passions, Bacon faults their work for merely defining without observing the emotions closely or analyzing them. He praises Aristotle highly for his understanding of the human affections, though only provisionally, as usual:

> And here again I find it strange, that Aristotle should have written divers volumes of ethics, and never handled the affections, as a principal portion thereof; yet in his Rhetoric, where they are considered but collaterally and in a second degree (as they may be moved and excited by speech), he finds a place for them, and handles them acutely and well, for the quantity thereof. (*De augmentis*, VII, 3.)

A study of the passions in Bacon's system is an important science. Because he defines rhetoric as the application of "Reason to Imagination for the better moving of the will" (*Works*, III, 409), however, a careful analysis of the passions, which come under the will in Bacon's scheme of knowledge, is vital to anyone who would persuade. Rhetoric is the only tool, Bacon thinks, which can prevent the passions from forming a confederacy with the imagination, to the everlasting disadvantage of reason and the advancement of learning. Though, like ethos, pathos is broadened and transformed into a science by Bacon, that science quite frequently is treated for the simple Aristotelian purpose of managing men.

In speaking of the human passions, moreover, Bacon usually goes directly to his source and paraphrases his words. The best way to illustrate this kind of debt is to juxtapose passages from both authors:

> 1. Near kinsfolks, and fellows in office, and those that have been bred together, are more apt to envy their equals. (*Of Envy*, in *Works*, VI, 394.)
>
> The persons men envy are persons near them in time, in place, in age, in reputation. And hence the line:
> "Ay, kinsfolk can envy their kin." (*Rhetoric*, II, 10.)

> 2. The causes and motives of anger are chiefly three: First, to be too sensible of hurt; for no man is angry that feels not himself hurt; and therefore tender and delicate persons must needs be oft angry.... The next is, the apprehension and construction of the injury offered to be ... full of contempt; for contempt is that which putteth an edge upon anger, as much or more than

the hurt itself. . . . Lastly, opinion of the touch of a man's
reputation doth multiply and sharpen anger. (*Of Anger*, in
Works, VI, 511.)
There are three species of slight: contempt, spite, and insolence.
(1) Contempt is a form of slight; since men are contemptuous of
what they deem worthless, and what they are contemptuous of,
they slight. (2) The spiteful person, too, shows contempt. . . .
(3) Finally, *hubris* consists in doing or saying things that cause
shame to the victim. (*Rhetoric*, II, 2.)

3. Young men, in the conduct and manage of actions, embrace
more than they can hold; stir more than they can quiet; fly to the
end, without consideration of the means and degrees; pursue
some few principles which they have chanced upon absurdly; care
not to innovate, which draws unknown inconveniences; use ex-
treme remedies at first; and that which doubleth all errors, will
not acknowledge or retract them. (*Of Youth and Age*, in *Works*,
VI, 477–78.)
The young are passionate, quick to anger, and apt to give way to
it. And their angry passions get the better of them . . . they carry
everything too far; they love to excess, they hate to excess—so in
all else. They think they know everything, and are positive about
everything; indeed, this is why they always carry their doings too
far. (*Rhetoric*, II, 12.)

4. Men of age object too much, consult too long, adventure too
little, repent too soon, and seldom drive business home to the full
period, but content themselves with a mediocrity of success.
(*Of Youth and Age*, in *Works*, VI, 478.)
Old men . . . live their lives with too much regard for the expe-
dient, too little for honor. . . . They are slow to hope. . . . Their
fits of passion, though quick, are feeble . . . and their actions are
governed, not by impulse, but by the love of gain. And hence men
in this period of life are thought to be temperate. (*Rhetoric*, II, 13.)

Bacon found the study of human nature deficient in his time and
admits frankly the debt he owes to Aristotle for recommendations
and insights:

These observations and the like I deny not but are touched a little
by Aristotle in his Rhetoric, and here and there in some other
men's writings, but they have never been incorporated into moral
philosophy, to which they principally appertain. (*De augmentis*,
VII, 3.)

As a philosopher and as a rhetorician Bacon seeks honesty and realism. In Aristotle he finds the kind of hypocrisy and lefthanded advice which had preserved for centuries the separation of rhetoric from philosophy. It is apparent that, while he went back to Aristotle more often than not and chose him rather than others to build on, Bacon's primary concern is to make rhetoric respectable as a tool for philosophers in a new age. He tries to give the authority of science to the "illustration of discourse" by limiting it to style and then showing how the "proofs"—logos, ethos, and pathos—may work as devices of style in philosophical discourse. He looks on Aristotle as an original genius who had the misfortune to attract bad disciples, and, as he admits in the letter to Lord Mountjoy, "For where he gave me not matter to perfect, at the least he gave me occasion to invent" (*Works*, VII, 70).

This section of the present study ends on an appropriate note, for neither Aristotle nor anyone else can be described as the acknowledged source for Bacon's theory of the philosophical style, to which we now turn. The two problems—of audience psychology and the rhetorical tradition—which are initial obstacles to the success of the scientist, are, however, largely solved by Bacon's revision of Aristotle.

2   Science and Style

> I find, my son that many men, whether in publishing or concealing the knowledge of nature they think they have won, fall far short of a proper standard of honour or duty. Others again, men of excellent character but poor understanding, produce, through no fault of their own, the same harmful result. What they lack is any art or precepts to guide them in putting their knowledge before the public.
>
> *The Masculine Birth of Time*

Though it may seem unscientific to us, Bacon's theory of style for philosophers is rigorous in its demands on those who apply it. He struggles with the question of a scientist's manner of delivery continually from 1597 to 1625, and both his theoretical and practical works on behalf of the new philosophy employ modified versions of styles which have received some measure of scientific justification from him. The relation of science to style is thus a topic of considerable interest to Bacon, the more so as he moves closer to completion of his grand plan for the Great Instauration. The problems treated in the first chapter of this study—the demand for both intellectual therapy and a new rhetoric—lead him to offer sets of apparently contradictory goals to the intellectual who wishes to communicate.

He determines very early, for example, that the new scientist must perfect a means of achieving "quiet entry" into the minds of his audience. Yet he requires that this strategy somehow work to preserve the truth in its pure form. Philosophy must, in other words, make itself persuasive by containing within it "an inherent power of winning support," yet it must take cognizance of its duty to truth itself and "afford no occasion of error" (*Masculine Birth*, pp. 62-63). Moreover, the scientist must use his manner of delivery powerfully in order to help philosophy "select her followers." If this is the chief goal of a philosophical style, the writer must not fail to see as well that the audience he selects must be "beguiled by art." Bacon puts it clearly in the *Advancement* and *De augmentis* when he urges men to deliver their knowledge in the same manner in which they discovered it, without, of course, failing to observe the rules of "sensible and plausible elocution."

These are ideals—it goes without saying—yet Bacon was able to come reasonably close to realizing them himself in his own work. If he seems to the modern reader to succeed as a rhetorician only to fail as a philosopher, that can be attributed partially to his belief that rhetoric, redefined and employed for high purposes, would prove to be the major weapon on the side of science in the early decades of the age of reason. The advances he made possible for future scientists can hardly be overestimated. Nor was his influence on the style of English intellectuals negligible. While modernized versions of the maxim and the metaphor may be the primary features of the Baconian style for philosophers, it is to the theory which underlies them that we first must look. Three important doctrines of the science of style are treated here. First is the psychology of discovery, which alerts the thinker to his obligations to his audience and to means of fulfilling them without doing violence to content. Then comes the Baconian theory of how style is related to scientific method, a theory which stresses ways of exploiting the human passions and imagination in the interests of reason. Finally, we look at the doctrine of "literate experience," a special and complex approach to the union of philosophy and rhetoric. The three doctrines, repeated continually throughout Bacon's works, are closely intertwined and, in fact, grow from and depend on each other in complicated fashion. Since Bacon trusts his reader to retain what he learns at each level in the "progressive stages of certainty," we should come to his own style with a knowledge of his carefully developed explanations of the general relation of style to science.

The Psychology of Discovery

Bacon's treatment of psychology is derivative. He develops his views on the subject in the *Advancement*, the *De augmentis*, and the *New Organon*, and illustrates them fully in works like the *Essays* and *The Wisdom of the Ancients*. As Karl R. Wallace has shown, the psychological faculties form the foundation of Bacon's program for the advancement of learning.[1] In both the *Advancement* and the *De augmentis*, he names these faculties and distinguishes with some clarity between six of them: Reason, Understanding, Imagination, Memory, Appetite, and Will. Knowledge of how the mind works and of medieval and Renaissance philosophies of human nature seem expected by Bacon of all his readers, and there is no basis for assuming that he found psychology a deficient science. His contribution to it lies in the application of psychology to the communication process, and therefore to the growth of a new mode of learning. Professor Wallace has described this contribution succinctly:

> Bacon tried to show the scientist how to bind the understanding to the senses, to dissect nature, not merely to dissect language. As a result, Bacon invented not a new kind of induction (as induction is understood by logicians), but a psychology of discovery. His unique view of the creative function of imagination made him the first person to formulate a psychological foundation for a rhetoric that by nature had to be reasonable, moral, and appealing.[2]

With Aristotle's help, Bacon finds a way to preserve the "proper standard of honour and duty" in communication on a high level; Professor Wallace's phrase, "the psychology of discovery," exactly describes what the honorable philosopher will seek to instill in those who come to him.

Since the definition in the *De augmentis* describes the function of rhetoric in terms of four of the faculties of the mind, a look at them all in relation to the philosophical style is illuminating. "The duty and office of Rhetoric, if it be deeply looked into," Bacon says, "is no other than to apply and recommend the dictates of reason to imagination, in order to excite the appetite and will" (VI, 3). Together with the even more vital faculties of understanding and memory, these work to produce a new foundation for the reforms necessary in the way men think.

The distinction between reason and understanding, though blurred in most of the texts Bacon may have read, is clear in his works, as are their relations to the art of rhetoric. Generally, the understanding is thought to be man's faculty for assimilating and organizing experience into comprehensible patterns; it is sometimes identified as the intellectual capacity. Wallace's study indicates that reason in the Renaissance was thought to differ from intellect only in that reason was refined to suggest in particular the function of the understanding in its discursive role: that is, its role in communicating and expressing what the understanding has absorbed.[3] Bacon uses the terms "intellect" and "understanding" interchangeably, and "reason" in his work implies the intellectual arts of judgment, method, and delivery. The philosophical style is formulated in a determined move to retrain the human understanding, making it obedient, on the one hand, to the apprehension of the senses, and, on the other, to the demands of reason.

Because the "human understanding is no dry light," the first objective of the scientist who would communicate is to recognize that man's comprehension is subject to "an infusion from the will and affections." On no level of human interaction can this simple psychological truism be ignored. Sciences have so often been reduced by it to pseudo-sciences, in fact, that the new philosophy is challenged by Bacon to take the offensive and perfect a means of controlling the affections strongly enough to provide therapy for the understanding. The first book of the *New Organon* is preoccupied with that goal, for it is the subject of many of its aphorisms and the clear intent of their style. Through a combination of a nobly high method (aphorisms) and a new content (preparation for the new induction), Bacon devises a workable style which achieves the goal and prepares men to enter the kingdom of knowledge intellectually in a "naked" state. In later chapters we will take up the question of style in the *New Organon*. Here we can say that the work clarifies Bacon's view of the understanding as the primary and most abused of the human mental faculties. It has not been allowed, he thought, to realize an existence of actual structures in nature because the arts of logic and rhetoric had conspired to equip it with false forms, more pleasing and more easily grasped than reality itself. The understanding is apt to make simple abstractions and jump to pleasing generalities; formal patterns of thought and presentation encourage it to do so. It is possible, on the other hand, to please the affections by making comprehension of things as they really are an attainable goal for thoughtful men.

Bacon, whose work "does not come down to the apprehension of the vulgar," because it refuses to "flatter the understanding," is particularly interested in replacing the formal demonstrations of deductive reasoning with a new inductive mode. The patterns of deductive logic are attacked on the same grounds as the contrived Ciceronian periods of rhetoric: both depend on words and illusions rather than on observations for their substance. In inductive judgment, however, "the same action of the mind which discovers the thing in question judges it; and the operation is not performed by help of any middle term, but directly, almost in the same manner as by the sense" (*De augmentis*, V, 4). But in the same passage Bacon notes that judgment by syllogism is a product of man's wit, not of his powers of discovery. The syllogism "is a thing most agreeable to the mind of man. For the mind of man is strangely eager to be relieved from suspense, and to have something fixed and immovable, upon which in its wanderings and disquisitions it may securely rest." To prevent the "dizziness of the understanding" which genuine research always causes initially, ancient logicians invented a system of judgment which proceeds, Bacon shrewdly concludes, from fixed principles arrived at in "too great haste to grasp at certainties." This reduces propositions to principles in a middle term, principles "agreed upon and exempted from argument." Thus, in effect, a greater premium is placed on words and language by the syllogism than on experience or observation. While Bacon agrees with other logicians that "the understanding, unless direct and assisted, is a thing unequal, and quite unfit to contend with the obscurity of things," he objects strongly to a procedure which depends on the force of words to order the comprehension (*New Organon*, I, Aph. XXI). The magic of words, though potent, has its primary source in the natural human yearning for clarifying principles of description and judgment. Poetry, for example, is popular because it is facile in accommodating the shows of things to the desire for understanding, "not (like reason and history) buckling and bowing down the mind to the nature of things" (*De augmentis*, II, 13). And, to Bacon's mind, logical demonstrations of the kind fashionable in his time create the same sort of fables as poetry, without its lofty effect on the soul.

> The syllogism consists of propositions, propositions consist of words, words are symbols of notions. Therefore if the notions themselves (which is the root of the matter) are confused and over-hastily abstracted from the facts, there can be no firmness in the superstructure. Our only hope therefore lies in a true induction. (*New Organon*, I, Aph. XIV.)

Words, Bacon says, are not governed as we think, by reason, even though they themselves too often govern the understanding. Because they are "commonly framed and applied according to the capacity of the vulgar," words "follow those lines of division which are most obvious to the vulgar understanding" (ibid., Aph. LIX). These truths, once perceived, place scientists in the awkward position of having to do battle with words themselves in order to enlighten each other and the public. Learned discussions often end in disputes about what words mean. Even strict definitions become unworkable because they too depend on words whose meanings may shift about in the common understanding. It is the ambiguity of language that proves the most formidable obstacle to the progress of the new learning. Bacon's theory of the philosophical style evolves gradually to form a counterattack which will minimize the power of words over man's understanding, imagination, and affections.

Besides the common powers of language to distort and color the meanings of things it ought only to denote, there is its power to give a semblance of reality to things which do not exist. Bacon names "Fortune" and the "Prime Mover" as examples and also points to this phenomenon in the development of words like "humid," where application of it is made to numerous instances which bear no relation to the original observation from which it derived its name. This is done so often that the word loses its roots in experience and is no longer fit for use in the vocabulary of scientists (New Organon, I, Aph. LX). Bacon's search from the beginning of his career as a writer, he admits, is for some power of "signification without the help or intervention of words" (De augmentis, VI, 1). He moves easily in a key passage of philosophical idealism to a conception of language which includes a "philosophical grammar" based on analogy; this science would inquire "not the analogy of words with one another, but the analogy between words and things, or reason." And as a scientist, of course, he has another solution to the problem of words, a problem which, he tells us in the New Organon, I, Aph. LIX, has "rendered philosophy and the sciences sophistical and inactive." This solution is the new induction, the true induction, outlined for learned men as the key to discovery and to communication. Its object, in keeping with the aim of the philosophical style, is to reform the human understanding by grounding it solidly in experience. "The understanding must not therefore be supplied with wings, but rather hung with weights, to keep it from leaping and flying" (ibid., Aph. CIV). Men will be forced to "stay with experience" until it yields a proper conclusion. No further time will be wasted on the "glosses of wit" which the syllogism encourages, and thus words, it is hoped, will also tend to fall in line.

Reason and understanding can never hope to win this struggle, nor will they ever elect to do so, unless their dictates are recommended successfully by rhetoric to the imagination, for it is that faculty of the mind which is most obstreperous. "The end of rhetoric is to fill the imagination with observations and images, to second reason, and not to oppress it," Bacon says in the *De augmentis*, VI, 3. In the same passage, moreover, he notes that it is the business of rhetoric to "make pictures of virtue and goodness," a power dependent on the writer's ability to show these abstractions clearly to man "in as lively representation as possible, by ornament of words." Since rhetoric, classified in Bacon's scheme as a science, is no more than "illustration of discourse," imagination becomes its primary object of concentration. A series of difficulties arises when we recognize, as L. C. Knights has, that "Bacon's use of the word 'imagination' would provide the subject for an 'Exercise in interpretation.'"[4] Though few would willingly accept Knights's argument in regard to Bacon and the "dissociation of sensibility," it is certainly true that imagination figures as one of philosophy's enemies in Bacon. It may be difficult at first to reconcile Bacon's attack on that faculty as one "which may at pleasure make unlawful matches and divorces of things" (*De augmentis*, II, 13), with the obvious fact that his own program depends most heavily on his ability to stimulate the visionary in us all. Because it is that power which allows us to see the future and the past, and that power which gives us the ability both to represent a thought and to "see" another's thought, and that which both fascinates and binds man's mind to things, Bacon comes in later years to take it very seriously indeed and even to respect it as a means to knowledge which is sometimes superior to reason. In the first lines of Book II of the *Advancement*, he describes the imagination as part of the understanding. In his later works it is apparent that, so far as Bacon is concerned, imagination can profitably be exploited by the scientist. It is the faculty which functions creatively to prove and demonstrate the meaning of experience.

It is the scientist's responsibility to recognize also, however, that most men's imaginative powers have been so blunted by false forms and stimulated by phantoms that they now produce only "clouds and vapours," fancies and empty hopes, "hideous and monstrous spectres" (*De augmentis*, III, 5). To restore imagination to its creative best, the scientist will understand first that it does more than take notes from the senses to deliver to reason: it is not, that is, "simply and only a messenger; but it is either invested with or usurps no small authority in itself, besides the simple duty of the message" (*De augmentis*, V, 1). The true scientist will know that, while "imagination hardly produces sciences," it has its seat "in the very citadel of the mind and understanding." Rhetoric, the tool of the scientist as well as of the statesman and poet, is "subservient to imagination," and thus those who hope to communicate on a high level must be on guard against the arts of speech, which may soothe, inflame, and carry the mind away (*De augmentis*, VI, 2). As Bacon explains it in V, 1, of the *De augmentis*, "it is all done by stimulating the imagination till it becomes ungovernable, and not only sets reason at nought, but offers violence to it, partly by blinding, partly by incensing it." In formulating standards for a philosophical style, then, Bacon follows his own advice carefully. He notes that "eloquence and force of persuasion" *can* make "things future and remote appear as present." When this can be accomplished, "then upon the revolt of imagination to reason, reason prevails" (*De augmentis*, VI, 3). The task is simply to engage the imaginative faculties with truth and to turn away the illusions which have worked with words to destroy progress in the sciences. Bacon would no doubt have been pleased to read of Morris W. Croll's claim for the style of the *New Organon*: that, in a comparison, it makes the manners of his contemporaries look "as pallid and ridiculous as ghosts astray in the open daylight."[5]

Still, Bacon is never entirely clear about his attitude toward the imagination. Though we may infer that he looks on it as a faculty which too often transforms the communication process into an irrational function of man's mind, he seldom treats it apart from its role as a function of reason. Imaginative action which results in good is reasonable action. Reason, he says, is likely to employ rhetoric to work on the imagination and correct its abuses. If rhetoric, as it was then defined, frequently seemed not to second reason but to oppress it, that called for renewed emphasis on the subject as a rational science, a branch of logic. Paolo Rossi, in fact, while noting that Bacon strictly classifies rhetoric under the heading "illustration of discourse," claims that a Baconian rhetoric is also a "common logic." Rhetoric works on the imagination in the same way that scientific logic works on the understanding.[6] It is possible, through creative rearrangement and artifice, to bring the logic of science and its discoveries down to a level where it can be appreciated, at least for "its utilities and effects," even by the common man. Bacon does say in the *Advancement*, Book II, that rhetoric is an art "at large"—that is, it handles reason "as it is planted in popular opinions and manners" (*Works*, III, 411). Properly governed, the imagination "performs the office of an agent or messenger or proctor" between reason and the human will:

> For sense sends all kinds of images over to imagination for reason to judge of; and reason again when it has made its judgment and selection, sends them over to imagination, before the decree be put in execution. (*De augmentis*, V, 1.)

For poets and prophets, the imagination of man does an admirable job; for orators, it has functioned as a vital instrument of persuasion. But for the philosopher, it has a function which to the present time has not been performed, Bacon claims. Poetry, after all, is "to be accounted rather as a pleasure or play of wit than a science" (*De augmentis*, V, 1), and eloquence is certainly "inferior to wisdom" (VI, 3). It is clearly time that man's imaginative powers were forced by the scientist to work to their full potential to stimulate inquiry and the growth of reform.

Accordingly, Bacon concentrates not on the first but on the second function of the imagination in the communication process: when it takes reason's decree on sense data to be prepared for execution. Bacon seems satisfied with the behavior of the imaginative faculty when it initially receives images from the sense and delivers them to reason "to judge of." But, somehow, it has failed to encourage men to accept reason's decrees and to act on them with full faith. Somewhere in the complicated process, imagination has managed to usurp reason's authority and send messages itself. At this point the clear duty of the imagination is to work on the human will and appetite to encourage the action desired by reason. While in the moral and civil sciences it has traditionally been a simple matter to persuade men (who, Bacon believes, are naturally inclined to the good anyway) to behave well, the rhetoric of science will have a much more challenging task before it when it undertakes to deliver natural studies to the world. Not only are men likely to become bored and fatigued by the demands which nature makes on their minds, but

n to insist on immediate rewards to make their labor
ile. There must be opportunity for pauses to allow
ation, for limited flights of fancy, and for gratifi-
ual urges. Rhetoric, the science of illustrating, some-
and for the philosopher so that it can meet these
demands without compromising argument or ideas. Every solution
posed by Bacon depends for success on the strict control of the
imagination. It is not his intention to interfere with eloquence, the
"excellently well-laboured" art of Cicero and Quintilian, but to
create a new and complementary theory of rhetoric.

How then can the will and the appetite be excited in a manner
that satisfies a philosopher who hopes to communicate? How can
the dictates of reasons be made palatable by an imaginative power
which does not blunt or alter their essential nature? Two answers
seem to have been formulated by Bacon. The first lies in his analysis
of the will and appetite, faculties for which the scientist has little but
contempt. The second is suggested by his notions of human memory.
These faculties—appetite, will, and memory—are invested with very
special roles in a communication theory which is founded on the
ideals of the *New Organon*: that is, to propound nothing but what is
true, yet to call men to action and belief in a "manner neither harsh
nor unpleasant."

In dividing all knowledge into History, Poetry, and Philosophy,
Bacon associates each branch with one of the faculties of the mind.
History, for example, is "that part of learning which answereth to
one of the cells, domiciles, or offices of the mind of man; which is
that of the Memory" (*Advancement*, II, in *Works*, III, 342-43).
Poetry, of course, is associated with the imagination, and philosophy
with reason. Moreover, philosophy is subdivided into three parts:
divine, natural, and human. When he works his way down to the
human mind, Bacon then makes another distinction, this time
between learning related to the human understanding ("arts
intellectual") and learning related to the human will ("moral
knowledge"). Invention, judgment, memory, and elocution are the
four "arts intellectual," while "moral knowledge" is that "which
considereth of the Appetite and Will of man" (ibid., pp. 417–18).
"The will is governed by right reason, seduced by apparent good, having for its spurs the passions" (*De augmentis*, VII, 1). These three
faculties—memory, will, and appetite—are engaged in obvious ways
by rhetoric to do service in aid of reason. Though the memory is
passive, the others act. Bacon justifies the important role of rhetoric

in his scheme for reform by pointing to its hold over the will. Memory, of course, he promotes to one of the "arts intellectual," while also using it as a substitute for the ancient part of rhetoric called invention—matters to which we will return.

Man's will and appetite are the faculties which convert his knowledge into fruitful action. Once information is discovered by the senses and judged by reason, it is the receiver's option to act by believing it, by using it to inquire for new discoveries, or, even where truth is presented, by rejecting it. In defining rhetoric in the *De augmentis*, Bacon names both the will and the appetite as faculties to be moved. While it is defined in the *Advancement* as the application of "reason to imagination for the better moving of the will," the duty of rhetoric becomes in the translated version of the revision "to apply and recommend the dictates of reason to imagination, in order to excite the appetite and will." It is apparent that Bacon corrected the ethical bias of the phrase "better moving of the will," adding the verb "excite" instead, because his rhetorical standards had changed considerably between 1605 and 1623. Moreover, by adding the appetite as a factor of significance, he finally yields to that faculty's demands on the writer, recognizing that even the scientist must engage man's nonreflective faculties if he hopes to succeed. Bacon always knew that the time to win a point is when you can deal "with men in appetite" (*Of Negotiating*, in *Works*, VI, 493). He hardly expected in 1605, however, to be forced not only to stimulate and satisfy, but literally to create, the appetite for new knowledge and reform. As we move through his subsequent works, however, it becomes clearer that this discovery is forcing him to use imaginative appeals to make reason appealing to the wills and appetites of his readers. Many of the forms of discourse which he rejects in *Valerius Terminus* and the *Advancement* are being employed after 1607. The process of appealing to readers in this way is described in vivid terms of civil strife in the *De augmentis*, VI, 3:

> If the affections themselves were brought to order and pliant and
> obedient to reason, it is true there would be no great use of per-
> suasions and insinuations to give access to the mind, but naked
> and simple propositions and proofs would be enough. But the
> affections do on the contrary make such secessions and raise
> such mutinies and seditions (according to the saying
>> The better course I know and well approve,
>> The worse I follow)
> that reason would become quite captive and servile, if eloquence

of persuasions did not win the imagination from the affections' part, and contract a confederacy between the reason and imagination against them.

The quotation from Ovid expresses Bacon's own belief that men are willfully determined to see nothing for long but what is before them and to act only on the basis of present desires. The charge to rhetoric is that it makes "reason prevail" by rendering it pleasing to the present demands and urges of the receivers. Genuine eloquence makes things "future and remote appear as present." In analyzing the will, Bacon asserts that it is moved by "apparent good":

> For it must be observed that the affections themselves carry ever an appetite to apparent good, and have this in common with reason; but the difference is that affection beholds principally the good which is present; reason looks beyond and beholds likewise the future and sum of all. (*De augmentis*, VI, 3.)

Why Bacon expands his section on rhetoric when he comes to translate the *Advancement* and why he attacks Seneca and even the "sons of science" in the new section become clear enough when we realize the impact which his fear of the influence of the will and appetite was having on his thinking. His emerging understanding of how great an obstacle the nonreflective faculties were posing to the new philosophy led after 1605 to powerful new pleas for the cause: *The Wisdom of the Ancients*, revised and expanded editions of the *Essays*, a new section on poetry in the *De augmentis*, the *New Organon*, and the *New Atlantis*. None of these neglects to employ or to pay tribute to the effects of "art and subterfuge." That certain methods of discourse, dismissed in the *Advancement* and earlier works as "imposture" or mere vaporizing, are later employed to make the future good of the new science appear as present, is also evidence of a change in point of view. The "better moving of the will" is not required or satisfied perhaps by such methods as the acroamatic, mainly because they cater to human weaknesses; but, while Bacon dismisses it as too "enigmatical" in the *Advancement*, he says in the *De augmentis*, II, 13, that wise men of ancient times found that when they had new and strange learning to communicate, and when the audience was reluctant to receive it, they had to resort to "all kinds of fables, parables, enigmas, and similitudes" to quell the seditions of the human will and appetite. Also suggesting that Bacon deliberately moved to a new understanding of this problem is the apparently minor switch he makes in describing the method of probation in the *De augmentis*. Whereas in the *Advancement* that term is used to denote a means of delivering knowledge which seeks to stimulate further inquiry, another term, "initiative," is employed in the *De augmentis*, VI, 2. The initiative method, which is the method Bacon admires most, is said to be named after the "sacred ceremonies," and appropriately so, because it "discloses and lays bare the very mysteries of the sciences." We will meet this method again. Bacon calls it "Handing on of the Lamp," and it becomes one of his chief strategies for the creative management of man's worst instincts. He becomes increasingly more clever in his ability to satisfy the will and appetite of his audience without compromising his goals.

Finally, this survey of Bacon's psychology of discovery must treat the doctrine of memory. It is in terms of memory that all four of the "arts intellectual"—invention, judgment, memory, and elocution—can be understood. As Frances Yates says, the ancient art of mnemotechnics, or the technique of memorizing based on imagery, should have lost its significance after the advent of the printing press. That it did not implies an evolving new theory for the function of that technique in man's intellectual behavior. In her brief remarks on Bacon, Miss Yates notes his passage in the *Advancement* on the reform of the art of custody and suggests that he employs the old principles of order and arrangement for a new system of scientific classification based on memory. Moreover, she suggests, Bacon may even have been affected by the occult and Hermetic texts on memory which she outlines in detail. Though he attacks such systems as useless, Bacon shows appreciation for their power to enchant the mind.[7] Their significance to rhetoric and to the gradually developing sense of the philosophical style, so obvious in his works, has been underestimated. Another study, by Sister Mary Antonia Bowman, concludes that Bacon's whole system of discourse is founded on his doctrine of memory and the attempt to engage his readers' imagination through tricks of retention. Memory, the third of Bacon's four rational arts and the faculty associated with history, would naturally be important to any scientist who planned, like Bacon, to begin the progress to reform with a series of histories based on reason and fact. Memory is also, of course, one of the traditional parts of rhetoric; it acquires greater meaning than that in Bacon's rhetoric, though, because he defines the "invention of speech and argument" as "*Remembrance* or *Suggestion*" (*Advancement*, II, in *Works*, III, 389). The popular style focuses, he thinks, on establishing images and ideas which the memory will store, but the philosopher's style should be designed to stimulate the memory to reproduce on its own what has already been laid up for future use. To these varying purposes we may attribute the obvious differences between Bacon's own styles of discourse. Sister Bowman's analysis of the *Advancement* and the *Essays* provides useful illustrations to prove the point.[8]

Bacon describes the art of memory as a deficient science and says that extant texts are unhelpful because they emphasize the imaginative tricks of retention without giving useful precepts.

> It is certain the art (as it is) may be raised to points of ostentation prodigious: but in use (as it is now managed) it is barren, not burdensome nor dangerous to natural memory, as is imagined, but barren, that is, not dexterous to be applied to the serious use of business and occasions. (*Advancement*, in *Works*, III, 398.)

Though he recommends a "good digest of commonplaces" and the use of ideograms to make words or things visible and thus memorable, he cannot take seriously the ability to repeat long lists or innumerable rhymes. Such talents are no more fit to be listed among the arts and sciences than those of tumbling or rope-dancing; one skill abuses the mind into strange shapes, the other the body.

The very brief sections on memory in the *Advancement* and *De augmentis* conclude with Bacon's statement that "the Art of Memory is built upon two intentions; Prenotion and Emblem" (*De augmentis*, V, 5). Prenotion is compared to hunting a deer in a park:

> By prenotion I mean a kind of cutting off of infinity of search. For when a man desires to recall anything into his memory, if he have no prenotion or perception of that he seeks, he seeks and strives and beats about hither and thither as if in infinite space. But if he have some certain prenotion, this infinity is at once cut off, and the memory ranges in a narrower compass.

This concept emphasizes the ordering of items skillfully so that expectations are created. Emblemizing, on the other hand, is the process of reducing "intellectual conceptions to sensible images." Since a sense impression "strikes the memory more forcibly" than an idea, the philosopher, Bacon believed, will take a lesson from the

rhetoricians and speak whenever possible in pictures. He
"with the simple sensuous impression." This is all Bacor
in his section on memory; yet it is clear that retentio
important function in the rational reform of learning. Nui uː
prenotions and emblems the keys to the inductive-philosophical
style, which leads men through "progressive stages of certainty," but
they work in meaningful ways to make discovery itself possible for the
receiver. In addition, it seems apparent that the three other rational
arts in Bacon's system—invention, judgment, and delivery—are
governed by his conception of memory.

The interrelation of doctrines illustrated by the intellectual arts is
typical of Bacon's system for leading us to conclusions. As he says,

> Man's labour is to invent that which is sought or propounded;
> or to judge that which is invented; or to retain that which is
> judged; or to deliver over that which is retained. So as the arts
> must be four: art of inquiry or invention: art of examination
> or judgment: art of custody or memory: and art of elocution
> or tradition. (*Advancement*, II, in *Works*, III, 384.)

The art of invention in speech or writing is to draw out of our stocks
of knowledge whatever serves the occasion. Rhetoric plays no role in
the discovery of that knowledge. Similarly, the old rhetorical function
of judgment is reduced by Bacon to a question of method, and
method of delivery is determined by audience demand for memorable presentation. The logic he inherited seemed to Bacon more
useful to rhetoricians than scientists. It flatters the understanding
and appeals to the memory, not to the spirit of inquiry. Accordingly,
he recommends that the "crowd of learners" be approached with a
method of delivery whose only object is to communicate knowledge
already delivered, to store up information in the memory rather than
to stimulate a thirst for discovery. In going down the list of available
methods of discourse, in fact, Bacon names them in groups of two,
each group containing one method appropriate to a didactic style
and one best suited to a philosophical style. A magistral method, for
example, is designed to teach, while its opposite, the initiative
method, merely intimates. The exoteric method differs from the
acroamatic in that the one deliberately limits its appeal to the
popular audience, somehow shunning the sensitive or learned, while
the other seeks "by obscurity of delivery to exclude the vulgar from
the secrets of knowledge." Delivery by what Bacon calls "methods"
is also a false and popular way of making difficult matters seem

simple; it makes "out of a few axioms and observations upon any subject, a kind of complete and formal art, filling it up with some discourse, illustrating it with examples, and digesting it into method." Its opposite, the aphoristic method, represents "fragments of knowledge" and invites the receivers to contribute to them (*De augmentis*, VI, 2). These and other methods are employed by Bacon, particularly those which lend themselves to philosophical discourse, and he justifies the diversity by explaining that "uniformity of method is not compatible with multiformity of matter."

Besides invention and judgment, there is the art of transmission or elocution, to which the doctrine of memory is significant as well. Transmission consists of three sciences: grammar (the organ of discourse); disposition (method of discourse); and rhetoric (illustration of discourse). Grammar and illustration, like method, are largely arts of appealing to the memory. In treating the organ of discourse, or grammar, for example, Bacon emphasizes the efficacy of pictures. Just as a true scientific method begins with a "simple sensuous impression" and just as a functional rhetoric "makes pictures," a workable grammar would utilize other pictorial elements as fully as it employs words and letters. Sign language and Chinese characters are cited as examples of communication which are unrestricted in their potential. The use of characters particularly fascinates him:

> Moreover it is now well known that in China and the provinces
> of the furthest East there are in use at this day certain *real*
> *characters*, not nominal; characters, I mean, which represent
> neither letters nor words, but things and notions; insomuch that
> a number of nations whose languages are altogether different, but
> who agree in the use of such characters (which are more widely
> received among them), communicate with each other in writing;
> to such an extent indeed that any book written in characters
> of this kind can be read off by each nation in their own language.
> (*De augmentis*, VI, 1.)

A universal language of pictures appeals greatly to Bacon's imagination as a scientist. All it requires to become a reality is that men agree on the various pictures' meanings and then learn them for use. In the case of natural and observable phenomena, emblems of the data themselves could be employed without any effort. No confusion will be possible with such an organ of discourse, and the idols of the marketplace—"the false appearances that are imposed on us by words"—will suffer a severe blow. The common man's understanding has no defense against the shifts of meaning which most words are continually undergoing. And, when an understanding "of greater acuteness or a more diligent observation would alter those lines to suit the true division of nature, words stand in the way and resist the change" (*New Organon*, I, Aph. LIX). Thus the grammar of the new learning, in an ideal form, would serve both the common audience, by creating pictures which are more memorable than words, and the learned, by solving the most serious problems they face in communicating their findings: the instability of words and their meanings.

More to the point, for the philosopher's purposes, is the language of hieroglyphics, an ancient means of communication which preceded words and letters and which is still "held in a kind of reverence." For the purposes of memory, the language of secret signs appeals to Bacon, whether it communicates through symbolic gestures or in written pictures. They "have always some similitude to the thing signified, and are a kind of emblems" (*De augmentis*, VI, 1). Emblems, pointedly assigned by Bacon to his doctrine of memory, are useful to philosophers because they strike the memory "more forcibly" than ideas. Thus Bacon is true to his scheme when he supplies hints for an organ of discourse limited to didactic purposes and one for philosophical purposes. Characters will be adequate to the needs of the "crowd of learners"; they require no "reading" or interpretation, as emblems do. Emblems, in their true forms, and especially in the form of hieroglyphs, make no attempt to communicate the complexity and variety of what they represent; but, to the learned, they continue indefinitely to yield information the more they are pondered and the more one applies his own learning to them. Hieroglyphs, a special kind of emblem, preserve secret wisdom from the vulgar.

As for common English grammar, there are two kinds: literary and philosophical. The first "is used simply for languages, that they may be learned more quickly or spoken more correctly and purely," but "the other ministers in a certain degree to philosophy." Taking a hint from Julius Caesar, Bacon had the excellent idea of a philosophical grammar based on analogy. It would be interesting perhaps to follow Plato's lead and attempt to discover if words ever did have a basis in reason, but, Bacon says, he prefers to think of "a kind of grammar which should diligently inquire, not the analogy of words with one another, but the analogy between words and things, or reason" (*De augmentis*, VI, 1). This proposal, as we have seen, is part of the dream program for a mode of learning free from the threat of the ambiguity of language. The ordinary man may be satisfied with a grammar easily learned and encouraging to the understanding; the typical grammar of Bacon's day emphasizes "precepts for a chaste and perfect style." What the scientist seeks, on the other hand, is a means of learning something from a culture's use and arrangement of words and letters, with the hope that it might be possible to combine the better features of many languages in a new and superior philosophical form. Is it not of interest, Bacon asks, "that the ancient languages were full of declensions, cases, conjugations, tenses, and the like, while the modern are nearly stripped of them, and perform most of their work lazily by prepositions and verbs auxiliary?" Such an observation forces us to conjecture "that the wits of the early ages were much acuter and subtler than our own" (ibid.). Bacon always felt more admiration for the ancient arts of communication than for the modern, most of which are diluted versions of their older sources.

Still distinguishing between common and uncommon men, still lamenting the loss of control over learning which wise men suffer in the modern age, Bacon ends his section on grammar with a somewhat whimsical treatment of alphabets, which prove also to be designed for two purposes: didactic and philosophical. Most of us employ a greatly restrictive vocabulary and alphabet, but there is a "secret and private" alphabet of ciphers, which may be employed by learned men to pass information without arousing suspicion. Bacon contrives a formula for simultaneous use of two alphabets, one "of true letters, the other of non-significants." By having one stand for the other in secret communication, the writer may hoodwink the most observant readers.[9] The psychology of discovery depends on the existence in discourse of stimuli which send the reader to other sources. In most of his major works, Bacon employs not a secret alphabet but a symbolic code that only the learned among his readers can break.

After grammar and method under tradition comes "illustration of discourse," or rhetoric. This too relates to the doctrine of memory—to prenotions and emblems—and it is an appropriate subject with which to end the discussion of Bacon's psychology of communication. Here again he depends on distinctions between the simple, easily retained aids to the "crowd of learners" and the more challenging devices for philosophers. The didactic function of rhetoric has been neglected, he claims, and its philosophical role entirely misunderstood. Modern men seem to think that, because eloquence supersedes wisdom "in action and common life," it ought to provide the model for teaching and communication among the learned. But eloquence in academic and scientific endeavors should differ from that in the forum or court. It was Bacon's hope that men could communicate on a higher level than the rhetoricians would allow when the preservation and development of knowledge were at stake. He soon realized, of course, that the techniques of persuasion were needed just to make truth acceptable as truth. In a real sense, truth does not prevail until it is accepted as such. By the time the *Advancement* is translated in 1623, Bacon is concentrating closely on establishing the claim of rhetoric to the status of a logical art. His section on illustration of discourse is expanded in order to show that this art has been "excellently well-laboured" only from the common man's point of view. To complement his logic, then, he adds several appendices to rhetoric which correct its imbalance toward the merely stylish and oratorical aspects of the art. Each of these stresses the importance of memory, and each is said to be useful to both the philosopher and the rhetorician.

As we have seen, Bacon adds a list of common sophisms, twelve of which are illustrated and refuted. These generalizations carry the show of logical conclusions and are very useful to the speaker who hopes to persuade. Bacon recommends them for business and private discourse, but warns his readers to take them for no more than words and to see that they do nothing to advance our understanding. A philosopher should learn them and their refutations. Since they are dangerous, Bacon feels that the sophisms deserve more attention. A good rhetoric will also provide refutations. Therefore his efforts on behalf of philosophers include advice on how to meet and expose the "captions and contradictions" which so often pass for wisdom.

Moreover, he recommends that a "preparatory store" of forty-seven antitheses, which he provides, be studied by conscientious writers. In the *De augmentis*, VI, 3, he says that a knowledge of the "antitheses of things" will prove useful in any situation where commonplaces on both sides of a question are needed. These forms are "acute and concise sentences," created, as Bacon advised in his section on memory, to enhance the collector's understanding, to encourage the use of his knowledge, and not simply to provide the common audience or speaker with witty "grains of salt" to aid the retentive powers. Commonplaces are "of great use and support in studying" because they supply matter for invention and they contract "the sight of the judgment to a point" (*De augmentis*, V, 5). To these, Bacon adds a third collection to his "promptuaries," which he calls "lesser forms." These are prefaces, conclusions, transitions, and other small amenities of rhetoric which may be memorized and used with all subjects and on all occasions. They are developed briefly in the *De augmentis*, VI, 3, and in the *Promus of Formularies and Elegancies*. Even the plain style of philosophy may employ such lesser forms with profit for "special ornament and effect." Further hints for the memory of the writer or speaker are given in *Apophthegms: New and Old*, where Bacon offers lively sayings of well-known men and recommends that they be memorized and sprinkled like salt over a bland style. They engage the reader without interfering with the material at hand. Bacon offers nearly three hundred of these apophthegms and says that we may enjoy reciting them alone on occasion. All three of these devices— antitheses, "lesser forms," and apophthegms—are employed by Bacon himself, even in the most advanced of his scientific works. One feature of his style which never alters is the presence throughout a work of half-accurate quotations from a wide range of sources.

Of greater significance to the faculty of memory and to the advancement of learning is Bacon's doctrine of topics, already treated in connection with his debt to Aristotle. He shifts this subject to logic from rhetoric and denies that rhetoric has anything to do with the invention of knowledge. Lane Cooper explains the ancient doctrine of topics clearly in his introduction to Aristotle's *Rhetoric*:

> The common translation, "topic," suggests a rubric or category, a general heading under which specific details are collected or things are said. So to us "topic" often comes to mean a theme, a subject under discussion, the matter of a paragraph or the like. To Aristotle *topos* means a place, and when with him it is a live metaphor, he thinks of a place in which the hunter will hunt for game. If you wish to hunt rabbits, you go to a place where rabbits are. . . . And similarly with arguments. They are of different kinds, and the different kinds are found in different

places, from which they may be drawn. There are the commonplaces in which are found the universal forms of argument used
by all men, and in every science. And, again there are special
places where you naturally seek a particular argument, or an
argument on some point in a more special branch of knowledge.[10]

Bacon, who in the *De augmentis*, V, 5, compares the inventor of
speech and arguments to a hunter pursuing a hare, dedicates much
of his work to the collection and explanation of topics. He repeatedly
emphasizes his role in the new scientific movement as one of
guidance, never pretending actually to be founding a new school of
philosophy. As he sees it, his function is to lead men to the "places"
where the keys to a new learning are to be discovered and away from
the roads to illusion, superstition, and falsehood. Each of his
branches of learning and nearly all of their subbranches are
furnished with topics of inquiry. Bacon seeks to provide pleasing,
accurate, well arranged and classified, and thus memorable, items
for consideration by intelligent readers. In the *Advancement*, we are
told that there are two kinds of topics: those for preparation and
those for suggestion. The former are stored up in the memory for
future use; they concern common subjects which are often discussed. Suggestion, on the other hand, "doth assign and direct us to
certain marks or places, which may excite our mind to return and
produce such knowledge as it hath formerly collected, to the end
that we may make use thereof" (*Advancement*, II, in *Works*, III,
391). This is the primary function of a genuinely learned rhetoric,
and it is "suggestion," he notes, that corresponds to the ancient
topoi. Suggestion is divided into general and particular topics, and
Bacon's study of both, as we have seen, is illuminating, especially so
when we recall that he is discussing the invention of speech and
arguments, which "is no *Invention*, but *Remembrance* or *Suggestion*, with an application" (ibid., 389). The purpose of topics is to
provide what Bacon calls "readiness and present use of our knowledge," but even here there are implications of different uses for
philosophers and other men.

General topics, Bacon says, are to be employed in logic as
convenient stimuli and as handles by which to take hold of a
question. They are helpful in argument, of course, but, beyond that,
they work well in meditation. The philosopher should know as well

that general topics serve not just to "prompt and suggest what we should affirm or assert, but also what we should inquire or ask," which means that they are part of a scientist's rhetorical equipment (*De augmentis*, V, 3). Though topics are not to be confused with knowledge then, "a faculty of wise interrogating is half a knowledge."

Particular topics, on the other hand, are very important to Bacon's scheme for the reform of learning. This subject, he feels, has been neglected.

> But leaving the humour which has reigned too long in the
> schools,—which is to pursue with infinite subtlety the things
> which are near at hand, and never to go near those which lie a
> little further off,—I for my part receive particular Topics (that is,
> places of invention and inquiry appropriated to particular subjects
> and sciences) as things of prime use. They are a kind of mixture of
> logic with the proper matter of each science. (*De augmentis*, V, 3.)

Unlike the ancient rhetoricians, who see particular topics as premises for arguments, Bacon elevates them to a position midway between discovery and communication. The scientist needs an adequate supply of such specific "places" of inquiry just as the speaker does for the purposes of persuasion. Any treatment of the subject, Bacon says, should invest it with the dignity it deserves, for the philosopher employs particular topics constantly in his search for axioms. The method based on topics is thus central to Bacon's procedure both as a writer and as a thinker. The psychology of discovery depends on it.

We have seen that Bacon's analysis of human nature grows from his version of Renaissance faculty psychology, and that it led him to incorporate the Aristotelian doctrine of audience accommodation into his masterplan for philosophical reform. So basic to this plan is the distinction between popular and philosophical modes of discourse that it informs everything he writes. The primary factors of discrimination are psychological. By his standards, most of the forms of discourse available to Bacon were to be described as popular, including what then passed as plain discourse for academics and philosophers. Bacon's only ambition after initial failure to get the new science accepted is to perfect a mode of delivery which would stimulate inquiry and enthusiasm among intellectuals. In order to restore man's authority over the world he inhabits and to create inventors rather than scholars, actors on rather than passive recipients of knowledge, it seemed necessary to persuade men to enter the kingdom of discovery as children again. At the same time, this is impossible, Bacon realizes, unless man's guide or priest of nature can balance hope against the fears of consequences and the promise of adventure against the certainty of disaffection and fatigue. How to achieve such a balance without offending those in power, yet also without yielding a single major article of reform, is the problem for the creator of a new philosophical style. The obvious beginning, made in the *Advancement of Learning*, is to turn style into a science and to ground it in audience psychology. The science of style may then evolve as other sciences do, through trial and error, inductive research, and experimental application of various methods. Bacon's original effort to clean up the popular style and its manuals of theory is dropped altogether, though his own speeches, letters, and occasional pieces did much to improve the state of argument and oratory in his time. After 1605 there are few changes in Bacon's ideas or goals, but the many variations which his presentation of the new science experiences can be attributed to a clearly developing theory of the philosophical style.

Style and Method: Early Conclusions

Bacon's views on the relation of style to method, and on the relation of both to scientific method, are not difficult to summarize. Nevertheless, they reveal the depth and subtlety of his thinking in regard to this central problem of communication on the high levels of philosophical discourse. Since they are best appreciated when they are traced chronologically through the works, from the tentative efforts to express what seemed inexpressible to the final metaphorical triumphs, we will follow their development in Bacon's own mind.

But first a summary of what we will find. Though Bacon wrote many passages on the subject of method in communication, some of them rambling, at least five major principles clearly emerge and continue to dictate his views. The first is simply that the philosopher should strive to present his discoveries and experiences in the same way in which they developed or occurred. Bacon says this because he knows that readers are apt to take a rhetorical method as a paradigm of an author's content and its arrangement in his mind. Philosophy is often equated with the demonstrations employed to present it, and thus demonstrations are "potentially things themselves." Moreover, demonstrations are undoubtedly "philosophy in the making," and whether it is productive depends on the quality of those presentations. The shrewd thinker will lead his readers to his discoveries just as he himself was led to them.

On the other hand, of course, the philosopher must make a realistic assessment of the state of learning in his own time, determining as intelligently as he can what he must do in order to gain an audience. A second principle to which he must adhere then is the one outlined in Bacon's introduction to the Great Instauration, "The Plan of the Work": lead your reader gradually through the "progressive stages of certainty," training him rigorously along the way to go his own way in the march to truth. Though he may begin quite rhetorically, establishing his credentials and providing all the illustrations and ethical proofs a vulgar audience would demand, this is only to "make me the better listened to." He will end, Bacon warns his readers, by abandoning both artifice and method altogether: "For a good method of demonstration or form of interpreting nature may keep the mind from going astray or stumbling, but it is not any excellence of method that can supply it with the material of knowledge" (*Works*, IV, 28). The philosopher's obligations to his readers diminish as the readers gain information and confidence. Briefly then, the six stages of certainty in Bacon's plan are each accompanied by appropriate methods of discourse. As the scientific method is purified, so too is the rhetorical method. We end by rejecting all "ornaments of speech," "elegant disposition of parts," and "everything philological" (*Works*, IV, 254-55).

This determination to purify communication gradually leads in turn to an effort to use method to help science "select her followers." It is made clear in several of the works that the philosopher must regard it as his duty to weed out by way of his style all those unqualified to make the full journey to the noble heights of learning. Beyond the third stage of inquiry the style will be marked by "chastity and brevity." The scientist will forego the temptation to give pleasure to his readers; he will focus on building the "storehouse" of knowledge and will cease to adorn it and arrange it like articles "in a shop." Readers will not be enticed to attend the presentation but rather will be forced to participate in it.

As a fourth point, in fact, Bacon insists that the method of communication in philosophy be designed to urge readers to

examine what is offered and to inquire further about its implications. After lumping all methods together in his angry diatribe
against the tradition, Bacon comes to distinguish more sensibly
between them, noting that most are quite satisfactory for popular
and academic purposes. Others, of course, will have to be invented
for the good of the new philosophy. While Bacon's earliest works are
filled with petulant complaints about current methods of communication, those after 1605 reveal a new confidence and suggest that the
plan of the work is already in operation.

Finally, and for reasons we have already examined, Bacon moves
naturally to a dependence on figurative language, especially the
analogy presented in concrete metaphorical terms, as a vital part of
the philosopher's method. It will enable the philosopher to gain
"quiet entry" into the minds of the receivers, yet it will also allow
him to maintain the integrity of content by avoiding words and
elaborate explanations in favor of pictures. It will open the way to
truth by freeing the mind of concepts and illusions and forcing the
reader to begin with the "simple sensuous impression." When he
speaks of figurative language and the resemblances in nature, it
becomes obvious that Bacon is equating style with method. Not only
are the terms used interchangeably on occasion, but Bacon tells us
that he regards all previous methods of philosophy as rhetorical
forms. Method and content have suffered from the invasion of
rhetoric; it is part of Bacon's code that style should bend to agree
with matter and with the method through which it came to be
known. Ideally, style will echo and vitalize both content and its mode
of presentation. Pictures work psychologically to make this possible,
especially when the material is abstract or unconventional. When it
is time to recommend and apply "the dictates of reason to
imagination," the philosopher will often resort to the language
of similitudes.

Method, Bacon says, is the "architecture of the sciences." The
philosopher will find it incumbent upon him to aspire to a delivery
of material "in the same method wherein it was originally invented,"
and he will discover no appropriate models among the works of
those who preceded him (*De augmentis*, VI, 2). In the same passage
he complains that "as knowledges have hitherto been delivered, there
is a kind of contract of error between the deliverer and the receiver;
for he who delivers knowledge desires to deliver it in such form as
may be best believed, and not as may be most conveniently

examined." Because of the pedagogues' emphasis on style at the expense of matter, Bacon claims in his Preface to Book II of the *De augmentis*, the arts of logic and rhetoric, so vital to the philosopher, have been reduced in his time to "childish sophistry" and "ridiculous affectation." He recommends that professors learn to represent the "real actions of life" in their lectures and that they make some effort to distinguish between true invention and mere recollection. Method will dictate style and delivery and will make an approximate reconstruction of discovery possible in communication.

The crucial years between 1597 and 1609 saw Bacon experimenting with a number of forms for achieving this end. *The Masculine Birth of Time*, for example, constitutes an all-out attack on the great villains of intellectual history, Plato and Aristotle. Though probably not the work of "an extremely precocious youth," as Professor Anderson suggests, this is, as he says, an arrogant and violent attack which does not succeed in showing us how the Greeks fail the modern philosopher.[11] In a list of contents inserted into the manuscript there is a notation by Bacon to the effect that this work is a companion piece to *Valerius Terminus*, "written in Latin, and destined to be separate and not public." Spedding suggests that its style of "contemptuous invective"—so odd a style for Bacon—is simply in the nature of a test or experiment. "Finding that the simple proposition of his views was not winning converts," Spedding conjectures, "he had a mind to try what effect might be produced by putting them forward in a tone of confidence and superiority, and so threw his argument into the form in which we have it here" (*Works*, III, 526). Whatever the cause, the sledgehammer approach reveals Bacon as a passionate and frustrated man. He takes the role of an old man of learning who is addressing a young acolyte. The auditor, whom he addresses as "son," is instructed on the question of method. What philosophers lack is "any art or precepts to guide them in putting their knowledge before the public" (*Masculine Birth*, Farrington trans., p. 61).[12] Like Bacon himself, they face a tradition of concealment and ignorance which makes a straightforward public statement a frightening risk to take. Style must be blended with content and method in order to soften the impact on the new science and to produce an audience receptive to the proposition put forward.

In *The Masculine Birth of Time* Bacon argues that "a new method must be found," and it must provide "for quiet entry into

minds so choked and overgrown" by centuries of error that they do
not comprehend truth in its pure form. It will not be possible to
"drop all arts and subterfuge." Instead, "frenzied" man must be
beguiled. The new method therefore will "be mild and afford no
occasion of error," yet "It must have in it an inherent power of
winning support." This work thus establishes a literary formula
which will hold through the remainder of Bacon's career. The first
chapter sets a stage and provides an artistic introduction which
prepares the mind for the philosopher's method. It employs vivid
metaphors, like the comparison here of a new scientific tradition to
"some lively vigorous vine." It will further create an *ethos* of
authority for the writer. Once these are achieved, Bacon launches
into the interpretation of nature or the sciences without much
literary ado. He nearly always preserves the aphoristic method for
this part of his treatise. The *Advancement of Learning*, the first part
of which conforms to the pattern of a classical oration, follows this
method of achieving "quiet entry." *The Wisdom of the Ancients*
tells thirty-one stories, each of which is promptly followed by a
no-nonsense "interpretation" of moral or philosophical significance. The *New Organon* opens with one of the most persuasive and
moving arguments in English literature, and then proceeds to
straightforward aphorisms in Book II. Similarly, all the literary
trappings of the first sections of the *New Atlantis* serve chiefly to
prepare us for the aphorisms which conclude the work. Bacon, we
can see, conceived of two scientific or philosophical approaches to
the mind of man. His discussion is not limited to the simple
distinction between popular and philosophical modes but is further
refined by distinctions among various forms in both categories. The
creator of the philosophical style needs a system which will at once
prepare the mind for new experiences and provide the method for
dealing with whatever arises. It is vital also that the writer use it to
help science "select her followers."

The method of lining up all the major figures of tradition and
giving each a sound trouncing proves unsatisfactory, and Bacon tries
another tack in *The Refutation of Philosophies* (1608). That work is
an effort to present the vision which Bacon admits has haunted him
since childhood, but to do so with charm and insinuation. As
Spedding has said, it is "a much improved edition of the same
argument" advanced in the *Masculine Birth*, "as perfect a specimen
as we have of Bacon's power as an artist and as an orator" (*Works*

III, 524).[13] The *Refutation* is a dignified address given by a speaker similar to the one in the *Masculine Birth* but less cantankerous. The auditors are a group of progressive thinkers assembled in Paris to hear him. Bacon's tone is controlled. "I have made a special point about the necessity of a preliminary preparation of the mind," he says, and "must not attempt a direct, abrupt encounter with things themselves, for they need to be approached by opening up and levelling a special path on account of the inveterate prejudices and obsessions of our minds" (Farrington trans., p. 103).[14] Thus the method of approach will be carefully worked out. "First I shall adduce certain 'signs' which will put us in a position to pass judgment on philosophies. Then, with a view to undermining their authority, I shall point out, within the philosophies themselves, certain monstrous errors and intellectual absurdities." Pointedly, then, Bacon rejects the method of satire, "that kind of boastful confidence which rejects opinions without being able to confute them," his own method in *The Masculine Birth of Time*. He makes it clear that his audience is to be the "lofty and resolute minds" of Europe's intellectual community, not men in general. We know that Bacon was contemptuous even of the philosophers' demands on style, and especially of their fears of innovation, but here he wisely agrees that it is incumbent upon him, as one who would change their ways of thinking, to prepare the way for reform by adopting a rhetor's pose:

> A man may earnestly wish to rescue himself from long association with error; the motives which prompt him to join my cause may be generous and noble; but he still needs to know what he ought to think about the ancient and received opinions. It remains true, however, that the human mind is not like a wax tablet. On a tablet you cannot write the new till you rub out the old; on the mind you cannot rub out the old except by writing in the new. (*Refutation*, Farrington trans., p. 103.)

From there, Bacon builds an ideal picture. Fifty mature and dignified men of the world—statesmen, senators, churchmen, and ordinary men, among them several foreigners—have taken valuable time to gather in Paris. Their only purpose for doing so is to hear the stranger, the man of science, "a man of peaceful and serene air, save that his face had become habituated to the expression of pity." His oration, transcribed by a "friend" of the author, is a well-digested survey of the state of science, followed by a proposal for the liberation of all mankind from the dark caves of ignorance and dependence. Men will henceforth proceed on the way of "*literate experience*," which is a true path from sense to intellect (ibid., p. 119). It is a very good plan because only a few men can follow it, and therefore the honor of the ancient thinkers will remain intact with the common "crowd of learners." It is a "middle way between practical experience and unsupported theorizing."

A special effort is also made in the *Refutation* to employ imagery effectively. We see this most vividly in the sections of the oration which deal with method, where Bacon first tries an elaborate picture story to explain imaginatively why science has failed to thrive: it is the same tale of the obelisk which Bacon later uses in his Preface to the *New Organon*, an allegory employed to convince us that there must be two tribes of students in learning and two methods for its cultivation. In the *Refutation*, he adds another image:

> It seems to me that men look down and study nature as from some remote and lofty tower. Nature presents to their gaze a certain picture of herself, or a cloudy semblance of a picture, in which all the minute differences of things, on which the practice and prosperity of men rest, are blurred by distance. So men toil and strive, straining the eyes of the mind, fixing their gaze in prolonged meditation, or shifting it about to get things into better focus. Finally they construct the arts of disputation, like ingenious perspective glasses, in order to seize and master the subtle distances of nature. (Ibid., p. 129.)

The points of the two images are that we will never penetrate nature's secrets by performing a few simple experiments, nor will nature ever come to us unless we petition her insistently on her own ground. Bacon's interest in method is explained most cogently in this passage when he says that "methods of procedure are potentially things themselves" (ibid., p. 128). In his work, as in his theory, method is merged with both style and content. The emblematic quality of the philosophical doctrines in the *Refutation* bear this out. One very good one holds that "Nature must be taken by the forelock, being bald behind" (ibid., p. 130). Too many have tried the assault from behind already. Many of these, of course, are worked into the *New Organon*, the *De augmentis*, and the *New Atlantis*, as primary image patterns. So completely can Bacon blend image and idea with method that a metaphor like "Idols of the Mind" can carry the burden of pages of complex philosophical discussion and even in its own right be added as doctrine to scientific history. By 1608, it is clear, Bacon's method was fully formulated and on the verge of success.

Following the pattern of Julius Caesar, whom he admired, Bacon writes of himself in the third person in another early work, *Thoughts and Conclusions* (1607). Here he experiments with another and even less personal means of presenting the difficult material of the new learning. The work consists of nineteen somewhat aphoristic passages, each containing a central doctrine of Bacon's named the conclusion, and a passage which provides "quiet entry." Their forms differ as the author tries various ways of gaining a point. Discussion of the proper method of philosophical communication is the purpose of several of them. Number ten ends with the line: "Bacon concluded that among the internal sources of error this defect of language [ambiguity] must be reckoned a serious and dangerous one" (Farrington trans.).[15] Number twelve rejects the method of fables as an entrance to men's minds, an apparent irony in a work written two years before *The Wisdom of the Ancients*, and one repeated the next year in the *Refutation*. In number thirteen, Bacon mocks Aristotle's method of teaching by "comparing, contrasting and analyzing popular notions" of nature, as well as Plato's admittedly better system of "loose inductions and abstract forms." Alchemists are attacked in thirteen for their "imaginary ordering of nature"; like the magicians, who sometimes shake "a trifle out of nature's lap," they should be "consigned to oblivion or left to the zeal of common and ordinary minds." The remainder of *Thoughts and Conclusions* focuses on the preparation of our minds for a new system of investigation. This, which we will treat in more detail later, is a combination, he says, "of slow and faithful toil" with a few fail-safe techniques to support it: primarily tables and similar forms of "learned experience." As Bacon says, "demonstrations are philosophy in the making," and no scientist will neglect method as a means both to discovery and to communication. This work and its version in English, *Filum Labyrinthi*, appear to be fragments, since the tables we are prepared for do not follow.

One other fragment among the early pieces deserves a close look, *Valerius Terminus* (c. 1603). If *Thoughts and Conclusions* is a rough first draft for Book I of the *New Organon*, this is probably the trial run for Book II of the *Advancement of Learning*.[16] Written in a style which Ellis calls "undoubtedly obscure," it provides many valuable insights into Bacon's inclinations as a writer. As we have seen, it discusses method and style as a topic worth serious consideration, and, at the same time, experiments with method. The full title, *Valerius Terminus of the Interpretation of Nature: With the Annotations of Hermes Stella*, suggests first that Bacon once considered writing under a pseudonym and, also, that he was willing to test the acroamatic method of delivery, provided a series of annotations, written under another pseudonym, were offered as well. Ellis regards the work as the first indication of a distinction in Bacon's philosophy between the inventory and the interpretation as functions of scientific writing, essentially the distinction between the *Advancement*, which surveys knowledge and names its limitations, and the *New Organon*, which attempts to meet the problems identified. The one is capable of delivery in artistic patterns of style, but the other must be accomplished without "the errors and conjectures of art" (*Valerius Terminus*, Cap. 11).

Why Bacon takes the name "Valerius Terminus" is the first mystery posed by the work. Anderson suggests that it is meant to imply the "limits and end to which investigation may proceed,"[17] while Ellis describes the name as a way of intimating "that the new philosophy would put an end to the wandering of mankind in search of truth."[18] Hermes Stella, the annotator, Ellis says, is the man who throws starlight—not sunlight—on nature, just enough illumination to prevent the serious reader from missing the point. His name also contains Bacon's two symbols for King James: Hermes and the star. As Anderson notes, Bacon was engaged in a serious effort to convert the new monarch to his plans for learning, and this work comes only shortly before the *Advancement*, in which the King is praised as the new Hermes. Only parts of the planned work are ever finished, however, and nothing from Hermes, whoever he is, is forthcoming.

Valerius Terminus makes a number of familiar points in emblems. For example, Bacon explains his fascination with Solomon, Moses, and Adam, who reappear in the later works as primary images. The role of reporter to humanity was filled by Moses, who had secret sources of information, and Bacon formulates a composite image of himself which combines this role as messenger with the more meaningful Mosaic function as a destroyer of idols. Similarly, Solomon wrote a natural history under the influence of divine guidance, and he too reappears often as an image. Adam before the Fall, of course, was a creature of great "power or dominion" over nature, but he lacked knowledge of the divine mysteries and demanded it irrationally. The true scientist is like Adam before he began to meddle: free to probe nature to the utmost (Cap. 1). Following a pattern that becomes clearer in later works, Bacon balances these images with both negative and positive ones from ancient mythology. The pagan contribution to knowledge, such as it is, is suggested by figures like Prometheus, Orpheus, Jove, and, in this work, Hermes and Hercules. Negative results of pagan learning are implied by references to Atalanta, Cassandra, Iambe, Proserpina, and Pandora. Moreover, both Christian and pagan symbols are mingled in image patterns with important historical figures who may be regarded as types of the new scientist. Bacon uses Alexander for this purpose in *Valerius Terminus*.

Finally, the most interesting passages in the work reveal Bacon struggling, not just with the general question of method, but specifically with the question of mysterious knowledge and how to convey it in all its shadowy complexity. In the fifth chapter, a fragment, he rejects the myth of "utter-most antiquity" and the fables it is supposed to have created to convey its learning to posterity; such a method of delivery is of no use to a new world where both wit and access to nature allow us to be clearer than fables. Yet throughout the work he praises the method of the Scriptures, which speak no fictions and still communicate indirectly for the most part. A mystic faith is required by the Bible, which impressed Bacon almost as much as its reliance on a kind of intuitive intelligence in all men. In the eighteenth chapter, in fact, Bacon admits that "no man can give a just account of how he came to that knowledge which he hath received." It would be dishonest to pretend to do so. Moreover, in one of his conclusions, he commends the style of delivery which excludes the vulgar:

> That the discretion anciently observed, though by the precedent of many vain persons and deceivers disgraced, of publishing part, and reserving part to a private succession, and of publishing in a manner whereby it shall not be to the capacity nor taste of all, but shall as it were single and adopt his reader, is not to be laid aside, both for avoiding of abuse in the excluded, and the strenthening of affection in the admitted. (Cap. 18.)

Thus Bacon does not lay the acroamatic method aside, but rather embellishes it with a system of annotations, as in the revised *Essays* or *The Wisdom of the Ancients*. Nor does he reject the method of "fragments of knowledge," which he says makes no pretense to completion or connection in the standard sense, serving as it does to reveal the true state of learning and encourage both research and reexamination. Both methods depend on intuition and the reader's prior experience. Both provide a reasonably clear path for the mind to proceed in, but they are paths illuminated by starlight. Neither attempts formal rhetorical guidance, but both depend to some extent on the vital operation of prenotion and emblem, the two parts of the doctrine of memory. As a result, the aphoristic and acroamatic methods serve Bacon's purposes admirably.

To conclude, we may say that Bacon's reform of style and method for philosophical writing has two general purposes: to shift the emphasis in theory from the author and his manner to the content of discourse; and to provide a method of delivery which is both unpretentious and somewhat veiled. He intends to stimulate hope and enthusiasm by substituting starlight for what seemed the utter darkness created by most philosophers' styles. At the same time, a strenuous effort will be made to deliver knowledge in a method very close to that which led to discovery. When it is not possible to be so accurate, no attempt to decorate, organize, or otherwise disguise the failure will be made. The author, whenever he can, will "revisit and descend into the foundations of his knowledge and consent; and so transplant it into another, as it grew in his own mind" (*Advancement*, II, in *Works*, III, 404). This idealism persisted through 1605, but Bacon soon learned that the "art and subterfuge" which he expected all along to employ for "quiet entry" was to be of increasing significance to his success. He had underestimated the strength of tradition and overestimated the flexibility of the intellectual community to whom his work was addressed. By 1623, he is forced to speak clearly and in some detail about the science of rhetoric.

The Doctrine of Literate Experience

"Literate experience" is the term Bacon first uses to describe a kind of invention or discovery which is inferior to the interpretation of nature but also a part of it. It serves as "a degree and rudiment" of the higher invention, and it must be mastered by all those who aspire to follow Bacon into the chambers of true learning. There are few philosophical works written after the *Masculine Birth* which fail to offer still another attempt to explain the author's interest in this concept and its significance to the new philosophy. Bacon himself was never able to provide examples of the interpretation of nature, but he admits to having relied entirely on his skills of literate experience to present the case for a new learning. To understand his views of the philosophical style we must understand the doctrine of literate experience.

Bacon clearly conceived of two legitimate approaches to the mind of man. His discussions of style do not limit themselves to facile distinctions between popular and learned manners of address; they offer instead a number of alternatives in both categories. Philosophical discourse may be simply didactic or it may strive to encourage inquiry and research. The method of presentation will dictate the style, and it too may conform to the demands of the "crowd of learners" or to those of the "sons of science." The scientist may find himself employing both forms of discourse in the same work, in fact, as Bacon himself does in nearly everything he writes after 1605. This is likely to be the case when the writer must deal with unknown or unknowable material. Even when the audience is composed of the followers of science, the writer will be forced to use methods which allow for "quiet entry" into the minds of reluctant receivers, methods such as fables, parables, illustrations, similitudes, and others mainly literary. The wise philosopher will do this before launching into the interpretation of nature, not only because his audience will not respond to him unless he does, but because he will find that he is himself making no progress until his own mind is trained in the methods of "literate experience."

Bacon labors over the explanation of this doctrine for many years. Since it underlines more clearly than anything else in his works the essential relation of style to science, he is determined to make it function as a vital force in the Great Instauration. We can follow its development and judge for ourselves the role it plays in Bacon's larger plan for reform in both the way men think and the way they communicate.

In *The Masculine Birth of Time*, written sometime around 1603, Bacon says very simply that the new philosopher must develop a method which overcomes the barriers put up by the human mind.[19] It must preserve truth in its pure form, offering "no occasion of error"; yet it must also be mild enough to "win support" as an oration or poem would. Bacon asserts that the scientist must beguile his audience with art. What he must do is "provide the favourable conditions required for the legitimate passing on of knowledge." In short, he must transform artistic methods of discourse into scientific procedures which form the basis for the highest kind of inquiry, the interpretation of nature. If he is successful, he will also be training the minds of his readers quite painlessly for the new induction and thus he will help science "to select her followers" (Farrington trans., p. 62).

By 1605 Bacon has formulated two theories about the nature of invention. First, he says in the *Advancement*, there is the invention of speech and arguments, the province of rhetoric. Since invention "is to discover what we know not, and not to recover or resummon that which we already know," the term as used in rhetoric is a misnomer. "It is no *Invention*, but a *Remembrance* or *Suggestion*, with an application" (II; *Works*, III, 389). True invention, on the other hand, consists of two parts: *Experientia literata* and *Interpretatio Naturae*, the one preceding the other in mental operations. While the interpretation of nature is reserved for the *New Organon*, which comes at the second point in the "progressive stages of certainty," literate experience is a mode of discovery which must be apprehended by all aspiring intellectuals before they may proceed. Though he says nothing else in the *Advancement* about the nature of literate experience, he does make it clear that its function will be to create "some effect comprehensible by the sense." That is, this form of invention brings new knowledge to both the writer and his audience (or the scientist and his students) by using comparison and other techniques to explain things which are "too subtle for the sense."

In *The Refutation of Philosophies* (1608) Bacon goes still further with his definition of literate experience by explaining that it is both an art and a scientific method. He promises that "My system and method of research is of such a nature that it tends to equalise men's wits and capacities." It will follow the way of "*literate experience, the art or plan for an honest interpretation of nature, a true path from sense to intellect*" (Farrington trans., pp. 118-19).[20] It will provide "helps and support for the human mind in studying nature and sifting the experience thus acquired." Without details the concept is proposed as a substitute in human experience for "the obscurity of tradition, the giddy whirl of argument, the billows of chance, and the devious course of mere experience." The role of the communication arts is merged with that of initial research to create a viable "middle way between practical experience and unsupported theorising" (ibid., p. 120). Bacon goes on to suggest that all forms commonly used by teachers, including Aristotelian logic and the devices of poetry, may be abandoned by the intellectual in pursuit of new information and new disciples. Literate experience provides a superior means of gaining "quiet entry."

Finally, in the Preface to the *New Organon* (1620), Bacon makes some effort to explain his own method of moving from "mere experience" to true philosophy. Here he uses the phrases "anticipation of the mind" and "interpretation of nature" to describe the forms of genuine invention as he conceives them. Anticipation takes us one step beyond experience because it records and organizes that experience for understanding. And, as Bacon says, the art of literate or learned experience is vital to progress in philosophy. Philosophy needs to have "ready at hand" all the details available to it, and, since "the understanding is by no means competent to deal with it off hand and by memory alone," an art of writing is an absolute necessity. Bacon complains in Aphorism CI of Book I that "experience has not yet learned her letters," and that this forces the new philosopher to teach them to her. He must devote time and effort in the preliminary stages of research to outlining new modes of delivery. "Now no course of invention," he concludes, "can be satisfactory unless it be carried on in writing. But when this is brought into use, and experience has been taught to read and write, better things may be hoped." The striking point in Aphorism CI, of course, is that invention is thought to be literally "carried on" in writing, not simply organized and adorned for understanding.

This explanation, though illuminating, does imply a contradiction in Bacon's philosophy, one which he recognizes and is at great pains to minimize in both Book I of the *New Organon* and *Parasceve*. If we are to begin our research with the "simple sensuous impression" and move directly to interpretation without pausing to draw conclusions or leap to unsupported theories, how can the practice of organizing experience in written form for readers be anything but self-defeating? The primary reply, of course, is that Bacon does allow pauses for conclusions and summary in his system, stipulating only that the understanding be encouraged to penetrate and be prevented by this process from "leaping and flying." Bacon, in fact, wants his reader to take advantage of such "waysides" on the road to interpretation, as the scientist does, and to use them as opportunities to develop hypotheses and tentative theories. So long as axioms are not prematurely formulated, this procedure will provide intellectual therapy.[21] What is produced during these pauses, moreover, will serve as an admirable substitute for the false demonstrations of logic, the "delicacies and affectations" of rhetoric, and the citations from authorities, which form the content in the initial stages of most philosophical systems. A scientist must write down his conclusions and the data on which they are based, and he must do so in a manner which passes on the torch to the next man; otherwise, the sciences can hardly flourish. If the point is not entirely clear, Bacon clarifies and expands his explanation in the *De augmentis*, as we have seen, by insisting that the philosopher present his conclusions and discoveries in "the same method wherein they were invented."

The goal of the philosopher who writes is to "make the mind of man by help of art a match for the nature of things; to discover an art of Indication and Direction, whereby all other arts with their axioms and works may be detected and brought to light." This remark precedes Bacon's long passage in the *De augmentis*, V, 2, on the nature of literate experience. There he offers a practical and specific substitute for the arts of logical and rhetorical invention. Learned or literate experience is something more than the arrangement of experience in patterns which appeal to the understanding and stimulate inquiry: "Learned experience, or the Hunt of Pan, treats of the methods of experimenting." It is called the "Hunt of Pan" because it does no more than organize the search for axioms. As Bacon says, it is a kind of "sagacity" and may not be regarded as a genuine "art or a part of philosophy." It is extremely useful nevertheless, since initial research is conducted in one of three ways. The scientist

> may grope his way for himself in the dark; he may be led by the hand of another, without himself seeing anything; or lastly, he may get a light, and so direct his steps; in like manner when a man tries all kinds of experiments without order or method, this is but groping in the dark; but when he uses some direction and order in experimenting, it is as if he were led by the hand; and this is what I mean by Learned Experience. (*De augmentis*, V, 2.)

Though this technique is inferior to interpretation, it prepares the mind for it.[22] Literate experience is another way of saying learned experimentation.

It might also be described as literary experience, since the directions and indications which are essential to science are delivered in writing and preserved in that form for those who are capable of following them to axioms. Bacon regards this as his primary achievement. He admits to being himself unable to complete the journey to the heights of discovery—it "is a thing both above my strength and beyond my hopes"—but he remains satisfied with the powers of "wit" which allowed him to make a "beginning" in writing (*Works*, IV, 32). The "inherent power of winning support" for the new science lay almost entirely in his ability to make maximum use of learned experience.

In the *De augmentis*, V, 2, then, Bacon explains what he means by literate experimentation. As he explains it there, true experimentation "proceeds principally either by the Variation, or the Production, or the Translation, or the Inversion, or the Compulsion, or the Application, or the Conjunction, or finally the Chances of experiment." Since the aim of the thinker is to transport the knowledge gained from these arts to the minds of others "in the same method wherein it was invented," the implications for a philosophical style in this passage are obvious. We shall see in the next chapters how these experiences affected Bacon's own style. First, however, it should be noted that the passage on Learned Experience in the *De augmentis* has many parallels in those which deal directly with the question of style. The unity of his philosophical system can be illustrated by juxtaposing his remarks on the manner and method of delivery with those on true invention of the "literate" kind in the *De augmentis*, V, 2. We understand finally that Bacon means just what he implies when he describes rhetoric as the "illustration of discourse": that rhetoric for scientific purposes is a blend of the ancient parts of invention, method, and style in a new and logical art of ornamentation. It provides the "quiet entry" so vital to the realization of the philosopher's goals.

Of variety of experiment, Bacon says that it is the key to discovery in any endeavor. Variation in scientific experimentation is as important as variation in discourse, because the human mind, particularly the acute one, wearies of sameness. The features of variety which he outlines in the chapter on invention are easily translated into principles which govern delivery. For example, Bacon chides scientists in the *De augmentis*, V, 2, for neglecting the small and in themselves unrewarding experiments in favor of grand schemes, while in the *Advancement* he chides poets for exactly the same fault. Poets refuse to vary their material by treating the "Georgics of the mind." Writers should take a lesson from Virgil and note that he "got as much glory of eloquence, wit, and learning in the expressing of the observations of husbandry, as of the heroical acts of Aeneas." The "husbandry and tillage of the mind" is no less worthy an occupation than "heroical descriptions of virtue, duty, and felicity" (*Advancement*, II, in *Works*, III, 419). Moreover, just as he recommends variety of experiment to scientists as a way to discovery, he names "multiformity" of method as the way to communicate those findings. What is needed in both cases is material and not quantitative variation, however. Invention is never enhanced by mere increase or proportionate multiplication. Style does not profit from unnecessary addition. "As a rule then," he says to philosophers in the *De augmentis*, V, 2, "it will not be safe to rely on any experiment in nature, unless it has been tried both in greater and lesser quantities."

The second valuable principle of learned experience discussed by Bacon is "production of experiment." This too applies to method and manner. Two productions, repetition and extension, are named for scientists. Repetition is a subtle method because, in both invention and delivery, it threatens to cause a relapse in nature or the reader. "Judgment therefore is to be exercised in this matter." Bacon takes his own advice in the expanded *Essays*. Some undergo what Sister Bowman has called "internal expansion"; they are expanded by artistic repetition of the central idea, not by invented arguments or new ornaments.[23] The *Essays* remain philosophical and aphoristic in the 1612 and 1625 editions, even after revision, because Bacon simply corrects his Senecan tendency to be too curt and cryptic. *Of Studies*, for example, is only refined and clarified by the addition in 1625 of several concrete analogies. To the famous aphorism that studies "perfect *nature*, and are perfected by experience," he adds the following illuminating passage: "For natural abilities are like natural plants, that need pruning by study; and studies themselves do give forth directions too much at large, except they be bounded in by experience." This example outlines the "production" of repetition and expansion, while at the same time showing that by 1625 Bacon has found a way to express the meaning of his important conception of learned experience. Sister Bowman also shows how the principle of extension is applied to Bacon's revised *Essays* to increase information and clarity rather than to decorate the works for a popular readership, as is often charged.[24] Both repetition and expansion "help the memory" and work in Bacon's many revisions to provide the quieter entry he was continually seeking.[25] Comparisons of the more lengthy and artistic *De augmentis* and *New Organon* with the *Advancement* and *Valerius Terminus* would reveal the seriousness with which Bacon applied his own principles of scientific inquiry to his style.

Translation, a third form of learned experience, is described in the *De augmentis*, V, 2, as being of three kinds: "either from nature or chance into art; or from one art or practice into another; or from one art into a different part of the same." Bacon's illustrations include both scientific and literary examples. The observation in nature that grapes or apples ripen faster when they are left to do so with their own kind, he says, is often translated into a similar principle of moral science concerning men and their friendships. Bacon does this himself, using a number of analogies from nature, in his essay *Of Friendship*. The man without friends is as "the savage beast," and the world to him "is but a wilderness." The possession of a friend discharges "the fulness and swellings of the heart." Loss of one, like loss of blood, causes "stoppings and suffocations." Friendship is a "fruit" of life, and, as Bacon says in the *De augmentis*, V, 2, it ripens most fully when allowed to flourish among its own kind. This simple scientific procedure of translation shows how we learn things ("invent") by applying learned experience metaphorically to other experiences: that is, translating from nature to art. In application to style, of course, this means that the philosopher uses analogies to explain what he does, "For nature meets everybody everywhere." He can take Bacon's advice in *Parasceve* and do away with all the "emptinesses" of speech, relying instead on translations to provide his illustrations.

Another rule to remember is that "the more plentiful the examples ... the fewer need be adduced." One or two translations should serve the purpose. A good scientist will realize that the translation from one art into another, on the other hand, could yield infinitely those translations which keep science in a state of growth. He will see that, if spectacles can be invented to solve eye problems, there must be a solution for ear problems. Bacon relates this to style when he notes that, just as painting revives the memory by planting images in the mind, the philosopher will use delivery to create pictures of his points. These emblems will lodge in the memory and be reproduced by the recipient on call. Since it is a rule *"that whatsoever science is not consonant to presuppositions, must pray in aid of similitudes,"* the new scientist will practice translation for more reasons than one. Bacon the writer is an acknowledged master of the art of translation.

Inversion, compulsion and conjunction are "practices" which have only general application to style, though they are central to Bacon's idea of invention by experiment. Inversion is the process of trying "the contrary of that which has been proved." It contributes, if nothing else, the negative evidence without which a science cannot flourish. Compulsion, on the other hand, pushes an experiment to the point where its power is destroyed, as when a magnetic pull is tested to the limits of its endurance. Bacon recommends such experiments, "For whenever a case is established of negation, privation, or exclusion, there is some light given towards the invention of Forms." In his own early works he does exactly that as he searches for the correct method of presenting his material. In the *Masculine Birth* he pushes tradition as far as he can and defeats his own purpose, discovering in the process, of course, what will not work. One cannot get away with denouncing the major figures of tradition, calling Plato a "deluded theologian" and Aristotle the "cheap dupe of words." Recognizing this fact, Bacon then proposes in *The Refutation of Philosophies* a milder method which will preserve the "honour" of the ancients and yet make it possible for modern men to free themselves from tradition. Compulsion is thus useful to both scientist and rhetorician, and Bacon urges the latter to store up common topics in his memory and to practice with them by exaggerating on both sides "with the utmost force of the wit, and urged unfairly, as it were, and quite beyond the truth" (*De augmentis*, VI, 3). The trick is to avoid the alienation of the audience which antithesis or compulsion can cause. Both can be lethal to content.

Similarly, conjunction is an experiment to be done with care. Application of experiment is the "ingenious translation" of one practice into "some other useful experiment," as when the knowledge of the weight of water and wine is employed to determine how much water or wine exists in a mixture of the two. Conjunction of experiment is simply a "link or chain of applications." If you know, from application, of two ways of accomplishing something, it goes without saying that the thing will be achieved more quickly and easily if both methods are used. Yet it also goes without saying that you may fail in your purpose altogether if the two applications "operate in different and contrary ways." Bacon's own experiments in conjunction, both in nature and in writing, sometimes fail for just this reason. The *New Atlantis* and *The Wisdom of the Ancients*, for example, employ two different and workable methods of philosophy, but they work in such contrary ways that they fail to achieve Bacon's purpose for him. He was working on them both, trying to perfect and explain their methods, shortly before he died. The urge to revise can be partially attributed to Bacon's sense of failure in his efforts at conjunction. Still, as he says, "though a successful experiment may be more agreeable, yet an unsuccessful one is oftentimes no less instructive." Since "experiments of Light are even more to be sought after than experiments of Fruit," failure is no occasion for regret (*De augmentis*, V, 2).

It is very clear that Bacon took the question of philosophical delivery seriously enough to devote most of his time to formulating new definitions of invention, method, and style, definitions which would apply to research as well as writing. He treats the problem of delivery in terms which suggest its almost divine significance. Translation of the great truths of nature, the "second Scripture," into agreeable and persuasive invitations to further inquiry was the task Bacon set for himself. The old man in the *Masculine Birth* speaks just as the priest was to do in the *New Organon* many years later:

> My intention is to impart to you, not the figments of my own
> brain, nor the shadows thrown by words, nor a mixture of religion
> and science, nor a few commonplace observations or notorious
> experiments tricked out to make a composition as fanciful as a
> stage-play. No; I am come in very truth leading to you Nature
> with all her children to bind her to your service and make her
> your slave. (*Masculine Birth*, Farrington trans., p. 62.)

In order to succeed in gaining a new audience for philosophy, the writer must be particularly careful about his method of delivery and its effect on the minds of the receivers.

> Does it seem to you then that I bear in my hands a subject of
> instruction which I can risk defiling by any fault in my handling
> of it, whether springing from pretence or incompetence? So may it

go with me, my son; so may I succeed in my only earthly wish,
namely to stretch the deplorably narrow limits of man's dominion
over the universe to their promised bound; as I shall hand on to
you, with the most loyal faith, out of the profoundest care for the
future of which I am capable, after prolonged examination both
of the state of nature and the state of the human mind, by the
most legitimate method, the instruction I have to convey. (Ibid.)

This passage, in 1603, establishes the motives and themes which will
dominate Bacon's career and his writing for the rest of his life.

We have arrived at this point with as much inductive consistency
as Bacon himself could manage. With the doctrine of learned
experience, the principal and carefully developed foundation for
Bacon's theory of the philosophical style is completed. The elements
which make it up have been outlined as they were formulated,
beginning with the early complaints against the effects of logic and
rhetoric on the human understanding, and ending, as Bacon did,
with a reasonably clear view of how style should relate to science in
works of high intellectual purpose. We turn now to the works
themselves and to an assessment of his application of those
principles which he devoted his life to expressing.

3   A Theory of the Philosophical Style

The Aphorism

From the preceding chapters a list of Bacon's requirements for a new philosophical style could be compiled. It will subtly separate common readers from the learned without offending either group. It will imitate nature and the process of discovery as closely as possible, but, rather than deny the powers of "art" and wit to engage the intelligent reader, it will manage those gifts of nature in wiser, psychologically more effective ways to facilitate the advancement of learning among those capable of bringing it about. It will employ negative material whenever it agrees with reality, but it will not be either dark in mood or quibbling in argument, as the current rhetorics of wisdom tend to be. Instead, it will inspire hope and a sense of adventure by artful manipulation of the reader's imagination. Each participant will feel as though he were being ushered into the secret chambers of true knowledge; his understanding will be enhanced by concrete illustrations, not confused by forms or abstractions, and the arrangement of details will allow for the kind of occasional summaries which create the impression that progress is being made. Finally, for many reasons, it will communicate as much as possible through verbal pictures, avoiding words and their false versions of the nature of things in favor of emblematic images which communicate on many levels.

In this and the following chapter we will examine the modes of philosophical delivery which Bacon perfected to meet these demands. Using his own terms, we could call the two primary methods the aphoristic and the acroamatic; that is, the method of fragments and the method of emblems and hieroglyphs. They merge at many points in Bacon's work, of course, and they have similar advantages. Both are related to distinguished traditions of philosophical delivery, traditions which exerted a powerful influence even in

Maxims Fables

Bacon's time. By then, however, both the maxim and the myth had been debased to popular forms of discourse and were being employed most successfully in political writing and poetry. It was shrewd of Bacon to employ scientific versions of methods he claimed to despise in order to gain "quiet entry" into minds still in their grip. And since their power lies chiefly in their mysterious and compelling qualities, their ability to make the author seem wonderfully wise and his material almost biblical in significance, he writes skillfully to preserve these effects in works on nature, science, and philosophy. Both styles of discourse, moreover, lend themselves to Bacon's purposes, because they are demanding of author and audience alike, requiring from both unusual knowledge, concentration, and attention to detail. Each is flexible enough to appeal to most levels of intelligence and to meet even the brightest, most learned reader on his own ground, because they succeed in direct proportion to the reader's knowledge and experience. They do not teach, they intimate. They require, not that the reader believe the argument, but that he examine it. In their Baconian forms, then, the aphorism and the fable break the "contract of error" between the deliverer and the receiver of knowledge by abandoning the adversary relationship in favor of an invitation to join in great work.

It is apparent, on the other hand, that the two methods were devised by Bacon for different reasons and enjoy different relationships with their creator. He never lost his contempt for the fable and other methods of imposture; there is a tendency to treat even his own fable-making whimsically and to suggest in embarrassed tones that his audience forced him to descend to this level. Though the hieroglyph and the emblem enchant him, he admits, he also says that the modern mind has all the advantages of wit, reason, and knowledge to enable it to supplant mythmaking with some more natural and productive method of delivery. Early in his career Bacon rejects the fable as unsuited to any but ignorant audiences, yet he later comes almost naturally to it as a vehicle for both the presentation and the preservation of knowledge. Fortunately, the poet in Bacon responds enthusiastically in later years to his new understanding of how the human imagination works. Like the aphorism, the fable can be used to describe memorably and accurately the findings of the philosopher, and it is even more subtle than "fragments" in its ability to vitalize and color theory so that it remains with readers to be examined. The fable is especially useful also in the delivery of sciences which rest on opinion rather than fact; because the scientist who engages in discussion of moral or civil knowledge must argue, persuasive pictures in narrative form can perform many services for him. Because they require a minimum of words and are susceptible to as many interpretations as there are readers, fables come to occupy an important, if reluctantly-granted spot in Bacon's theory of the philosophical style. Exerting a remarkable and mysterious power over the minds of all men, fables work in every age, Bacon realizes, to enchant and persuade. As early as *The Refutation of Philosophies* and the *Advancement of Learning* he is experimenting with the use of the "dark" method to inspire readers both with interest in his program and admiration for the author.

The aphorism, on the other hand, is a straightforward method of presenting material as it is, and it is the method of delivery which Bacon always admired above all others. It outlines the mysteries of nature without embellishment, so that the real puzzle lies in content. It is not subtle or tempting as the fable is, but Bacon tends to use it in its pure form only when the natural sciences are providing his material. That is, the aphorism works only when the "simple sensuous impression" with which all communication must begin is inherent in content. While the acroamatic method reduces abstractions to sensuous impressions and converts the impressions into aphorisms, the method of "fragments" is employed subtly to arrange these impressions, now in aphoristic form, in true relation to each other. More often than not, abstract material will not yield to a method of delivery in which everything but a "good quantity of observations" is superfluous. Thus the method of aphorisms proves most useful in the natural sciences, while the acroamatic works best in moral and civil sciences and in all discussions of theory; when the passions and the imagination are being worked upon in order to gain "quiet entry," the acroamatic method and its variations are appropriate, but once entry has been achieved it is the scientist's duty to revert to aphorisms as the truest form of delivery.

Bacon's reliance on the aphoristic style is the clear result of the demands of content. Interested chiefly in the advancement of learning and determined to overcome educational and social barriers to the new science, he seeks to reduce man's "knowledge" to that which is genuine and productive. He finds Renaissance Ciceronianism so great an obstacle to these goals that it is described in 1605 as the first disease of learning. In perfecting for the English language a style notable for directness and precision of observation, he answers for himself the two most compelling questions facing the philosopher who would communicate: how best to transmit knowledge without inviting error and how to preserve the imaginative appeal vital to its full acceptance. Though the aphorism may aspire to the profound suggestiveness of poetry, without its studied artifice, and to the persuasive force of the Ciceronian style, without its amplitude, it functions first as a vehicle for the discovery and communication of truth or possibility in its barest form. It is designed to make men think and, if possible, to add to their inherited knowledge. The true aphorism is reserved for communication among the "sons of science." Bacon sees it as a key to the reform of learning and employs it brilliantly to that end. Underlying the literary appeal of his philosophical works is a strong theoretical justification of the aphoristic style. It bears analysis and greatly enhances our understanding of this complex, and admittedly confusing, genius.

Bacon's theory of the philosophical style grows from four fundamental principles of communication outlined in previous chapters. The aphorism is the fruit of each principle applied separately to the demands of content and of their combined effect as well. The first two of these constitute little more than updated classical doctrines. They are, first, the psychology of style, emphasized continually in Bacon's works as the basis for a new mode of discourse, and, second, the doctrine of audience accommodation, which refines the first principle by distinguishing between types of material and receivers. A third and more important principle derives from the first two and from Bacon's special interests and methods. It requires the fusion of style and content in a method which approximates the new induction. This feature of the theory focuses specifically on a manner of delivery appropriate to philosophers in works of high intellectual purpose. It holds that argument and ornament should be indistinguishable in such works and is developed most effectively in Bacon by example. As Vickers has said, Bacon's style may be based on his theories, but it "far exceeds them in range and subtlety."[1] Because even philosophers require imaginative stimulation, however, Bacon goes beyond the consideration of method to propose an aesthetic to govern the inductive-philosophical style. Since words are tenuous and fluid in their meanings, a scientist learns early to avoid them as far as possible. He learns to employ symbolic language, Bacon thinks, and to cultivate a style dependent on the reader's sense of the resemblances between things (rather than notions). Such a manner, if reliant on emblems, hieroglyphs, allegorical symbols, and analogies, may preserve the persuasive charms of art without compromising argument or idea. It is the aphorism which in theory and application answers the demands of the truly philosophical style.

The basic assumption here, that Bacon's idea of style is grounded in psychology, has been treated in some detail in chapter 2. As Wallace has shown in his studies, the faculty psychology which dictates the structure of Bacon's plan for reform accounts for rhetoric's role in philosophy as well. Bacon places the art firmly in a scientific context and provides later theorists with arguments for its authority as an instrument of philosophy.[2] It should again be noted that, for the scientist's purposes, rhetoric is reduced to "illustration of discourse" in Bacon's system, and its traditional parts of invention, judgment, and memory are elevated to the logical "arts intellectual," along with elocution, of which rhetoric proper is a part. Rhetoric is in effect, for the purposes of classification at least, the logical art of style.

As a major element in that art, the aphorism performs for Bacon by acting psychologically on the minds of every kind of reader and by satisfying both rhetorical and intellectual demands. The science or art of rhetoric, in Bacon's scheme, restructures the four ancient parts and substitutes a stylistic equivalent. In each case, the aphorism is the means both by which the end is reached and the idea itself is illustrated.

Invention, the linchpin in ancient theory, is turned into remembrance or suggestion by Bacon. Arguments or philosophies, even whole systems of knowledge, are built slowly by accretion, which compels the writer to develop his particular points in the most memorable forms possible, so that the reader may accumulate them and build with them. Bacon's own style, of course, illustrates how this may be accomplished, for many of his aphorisms have attained the status of proverbs in our language. Men who know nothing of him or his philosophy cite his words as the best possible expressions of difficult truths. Few schoolchildren forget the famous line that "some books are to be tasted, others to be swallowed, and some few to be chewed and digested" (*Works*, VI, 498). Three and a half centuries later, married people continue to smile wryly at the well-known

Baconian observation, which seemed so cynical in their youth, that "Wives are young men's mistresses; companions for middle age; and old men's nurses" (*Works*, VI, 392). That "Revenge is a kind of wild justice" (*Works*, VI, 384), that death "openeth the gate to good fame" (*Works*, VI, 380), that "Virtue is like a rich stone, best plain set" (*Works*, VI, 478), are memorable and much-cited assertions in our life and literature. The *Oxford Dictionary of Quotations*, second edition, contains more than 190 choice passages from Bacon, and the OED finds occasion to cite at least once every work he published and some that were still in manuscript when he died. It is astonishing to discover how often such writers as Milton, Blake, Wordsworth, Coleridge, Hazlitt, and Emerson, not to mention most modern scientists and philosophers, find something in Bacon which says for them what they themselves cannot quite express. Bacon clearly became a *topos* in the literature of our language, and in French, German, and Italian as well. He is used just as he himself used Seneca and Caesar. It is not merely the beauty of his aphoristic style that ensures his survival, but the clarity and invincibility of the ideas from which that style cannot be separated.

Judgment, the second part of ancient rhetoric, is reduced to method by Bacon and also equated with style. The aphoristic style, that is, is a method of both delivery and discovery as well. *A Confession of Faith* is a superb example of how a series of straightforward, particular statements add up finally to a discovery of great significance. If one follows Bacon's example and simply tallies up his beliefs about creation, the deity, and man's place in the cosmic scheme, he may find that he is a deeply religious person despite his sins and his doubts about the established church. Another work, *The Characters of a Believing Christian*, expresses frankly in aphoristic paradoxes the negative evidence, and does so to strengthen and not to impair belief. Though they seem satirical, these paradoxes provide light, if not fruit, and are thus valuable evidence of the truth of Christian doctrine. The first two are good illustrations of the method:

1. A Christian is one that believes things his reason cannot comprehend; he hopes for things which neither he nor any man alive ever saw; he labours for that which he knoweth he shall never obtain; yet, in the issue, his belief appears not to be false; his hope makes him not ashamed; his labour is not in vain.
2. He believes three to be one, and one to be three; a father not to be elder than his son; a son to be equal with his father; and one

proceeding from both to be equal with both; he believes three persons in one nature, and two natures in one person. (*Works*, VII, 292.)

This form of reasoning is employed throughout Bacon's works, both literary and scientific; it finds its parallel in the new method of induction, which is as rhetorical as it is scientific. The third part of ancient rhetoric which affects written works is memory, which Bacon equates with invention; emblems and prenotions are the two parts of memory and the two principal qualities of Bacon's various styles.

Finally, Bacon moves forcefully to alter the ancient conception of style, the fourth part of rhetoric, from "mere accessory" or the wardrobe of content to a science of illustration which controls the imagination and channels its energies in the direction of concreteness, simplicity, and functional beauty. It is style, in all its meanings, that will concern us in the remainder of this study.

By announcing so sternly the duty of rhetoric, then, Bacon recalls for men of learning its traditional value as a power for good and a means of giving strength to truth and reason. He is responding in a natural way to very real abuses of language and learning in his own time and to the disintegration of rhetorical standards. At the same time, he is modernizing the approach to "illustration of discourse" by calling it a science and insisting on its obligation to carry the new learning to the people, especially the intellectual community. The task which rhetoric or style will perform for Bacon and the new world is no minor undertaking, then, for it must somehow meet and overcome all the psychological barriers to complete educational and philosophical reform. These roadblocks are summarized in Aphorism XLIX, Book I, of the *New Organon*:

> The human understanding is no dry light, but receives an infusion from the will and affections whence proceed sciences which may be called "sciences as one would." For what a man had rather were true he more readily believes. Therefore he rejects difficult things from impatience of research; sober things, because they narrow hope; the deeper things of nature, from superstition; the light of experience, from arrogance and pride, lest his mind should seem to be occupied with things mean and transitory; things not commonly believed, out of deference to the opinion of the vulgar. Numberless, in short, are the ways, and sometimes imperceptible, in which the affections color and infect the understanding.

At its most effective, the philosophical style will break the "contract of error" which prevails in rhetoric between deliverer and receiver by contracting a confederacy between all the faculties of the mind. What the affections yearn for, the present good, will be provided imaginatively by subtle presentation of the truth. The deep and frightening subtleties of nature will seem delightful if they are made to echo superstition and vulgar opinion.

The aphorism quoted above illustrates how Bacon uses that method to solve his rhetorical problems, and it suggests the basis of his defense of that form for delivery of scientific conclusions. As a simple construction, it avoids the misleading forms of Ciceronian discourse. Each statement is set apart to be examined; each possesses the power of directing itself to man's reason. At the same time, the picture-making powers of his imagination are encouraged, even forced, to produce from his own experience examples to illustrate the statement's truth. *Copie* is not required here, since the reader is supposed to be able to supply his own. In explaining the function of the aphorism, Bacon classifies it as a method of delivery and compares it with the more popular kind of composition, which makes "out of a few axioms and observations ... a kind of complete and formal art, filling it up with some discourses, illustrating it with examples, and digesting it into method" (*De augmentis*, VI, 2). This procedure appeals to common readers because it gives a false sense of completion to a subject, thus flattering the understanding of the receiver while enhancing the *ethos* of the deliverer. Bacon prefers the aphoristic method of delivery, in which "illustration and excursion are cut off; variety of examples is cut off; deduction and connexion are cut off; descriptions of practice are cut off; so there is nothing left to make the aphorism of but some good quantity of observation." In the same passage, he suggests that an aphorism works well for the writer because it fails in the hands of all but those with substantial information. And, for the receiver, it proves worth receiving because it encourages him to "contribute and add something" in his own turn. Thus two very important-objectives are accomplished for the scientist by the aphorism. It helps science "select her followers" by weeding out all but the best qualified readers; and it fosters the major activity of the scientist, the search for knowledge. Because the aphorism represents "only portions and ... fragments of knowledge," it combines with others like it to show what is known and to suggest what is not. Aphorisms are always ridiculous unless composed entirely of "the pith and heart of sciences," and they are thus formidable weapons against the "idols of the marketplace," the false appearances created by words. Bacon employs them to break the barrier between rhetoric and philosophy. It is a method of aphorisms which causes the reader to examine rather than to believe what he receives, to seek "expectant inquiry" in discourse rather than "present satisfaction."

The aphorism can be employed in the search for axioms, and this means that it appears in its purest form at the second stage of the philosopher's work, the point at which all arts and subterfuges are dropped. The aphorism owes something to classical and Renaissance descriptions of witty forms of discourse, but maxims, *sententiae*, apophthegms, and proverbs are rhetorical devices. Bacon's aphorism is also a method for handing on the lamp, as he calls it; it works to deliver knowledge by stimulating the thirst for it. Though Bacon follows an intellectual tradition of long standing, it is only rarely that his lines are paradoxical or pithy when wisdom counts for more than eloquence. He may have read with approval Cicero's claim in *Orator*, XXVIII, that the brief witty statement "affects a not unpleasant carelessness on the part of a man who is paying more attention to thought than to words." No doubt, he agreed with Seneca and others who see the sententious statement as the essence of a philosophical style. And Aristotle's long discussion of the maxim may have influenced him. But the traditional view of the "saying" or "sentence" does not hold with Bacon in his philosophical works. After achieving the "quiet entry" which the philosopher must work toward, Bacon likes to depend on a form of discourse which is "active and masculine" without being dark and contentious. The aphorism is reserved for the advancement of learning; it becomes a building block in the structure of the next man's intellectual heritage.

A distinction between uses of the aphorism suggests the second of Bacon's principles of the philosophical style, for he employs it in two ways. It is, of course, a primary feature of his theory that it allows for two modes of communication, one for teaching and one for the further progression of learning. Though logic cannot be changed to suit the audience, the proofs of rhetoric should be adjusted according to the nature of the receivers, and Bacon argues persuasively for this reform in the *Advancement* and the *New Organon*. Philosophy has suffered from the dilution of method and content, so that it is difficult to formulate a means of communicating material in its true form without offending audience sensibilities. The only answer to

this problem is to reject readers who are unfit to re
philosophy. Once the proper audience is selected ;
expression suitable for learned discourse are identi
distinctions may be made. In speaking of true invention
to invention of speech and arguments, Bacon describes
literary and philosophical. Outside of his speeches,
occasional works, there is nothing in his work to suggest that style
means anything more to him than an echo of content. If the material
at hand requires "the help of art" to give it that inherent power,
then such help is provided by the various inventive practices
described in the *De augmentis* and *New Organon* as "anticipations
of the mind." Modern scholars have often referred to the differences
between the early and later versions of some of his essays, the two
books of the *Advancement*, and the two sets of aphorisms in the *New
Organon*, as examples of Bacon's two styles.[3] And, in dividing his
works into literary and philosophical efforts, his nineteenth-century
editors thought they were following Bacon's own division. The
tendency has been to see these as representing manners of delivery
suitable for popular and learned audiences, not to regard them as
two versions of learned discourse designed to echo two separate
kinds of true invention. And yet this is the way they must be seen, for
the obvious variations between these works and between different
parts of the same works are accounted for by differences in material.
All the works which reveal such variations are part of the philosophical canon and can be vividly contrasted with the more rhetorical and Ciceronian letters and speeches. Within the philosophical
works, the aphoristic method seems to be dictated not by the
audience, which has determined the method initially, but by the
state of learning in the field under discussion. In these works, it is
the forms taken by the aphorism which indicate the subject's
standing among the sciences. If the material is part of a well-
established body of knowledge or the result of observation and
experimentation, it is treated in the spare prose of announcement.
Questions of theology, ethics, literature, or other matters in which
certainties rarely exist, and questions of theory, call for something
more than method. They demand particular clarity of presentation
and adornment, and because their substance is composed largely of
abstractions, figurative language must be employed to reduce them
to the "simple sensuous impressions" which are most persuasive to
thoughtful men.

In the *Essays*, for example, the aphoristic manner is merged with the metaphorical style of the philosophical writers Bacon most admired. Since his topics are the abstractions and theories of "moral and civil knowledge," he resorts to literary practice to present them. The purpose is to provide a light for his readers to see by. It is to transport his experience and knowledge into the mind of others "in the same method wherein it was invented" that is the goal of the *Essays*. In turn the reader may add to these aphorisms some of his own. Beyond that, he may do original research into subjects as varied as death and gardens, using Bacon's conclusions as points from which to start. The essay *Of Death* strives to present a way of seeing or coping with the fact of mortality, and, though its conclusions may be arguable, they are presented as truths. Some scientific conclusions are mingled with philosophical points of view as well, and this gives the essay the authenticity Bacon seeks. Though it contains quotations, illustrations, analogies, and various figures of speech, all these serve as evidence rather than ornament in the essay. They constitute the only kind of "proof" there is for such claims as that "there is no passion in the mind of man so weak, but it mates and masters the fear of death." This argument is offered to us with quotations from Seneca and references to the deaths of several historical figures. That death is comparatively painless and not to be feared, the central point of the essay, must be accepted as truth only insofar as the aphorisms have within them that "inherent power of winning support" which is the special strength of the philosophical style Bacon envisioned. Two famous ones in *Of Death* compel us to believe because they have the thrust which only truth possesses. No one who has lived for long will deny that "Revenge triumphs over death; Love slights it; Honour aspireth to it; Grief flieth to it; Fear pre-occupateth it." And the logic of Bacon's claim that "It is as natural to die as to be born," is strengthened by the added remark that "to a little infant, perhaps, the one is as painful as the other." All this can be said to disguise unconvincingly the frightening and ugly aspects of death, but that is why the essay was written. Some recognition is given to the facts that physical pain, groans, and the decay of the body are in themselves terrible, but the goal of the writer on moral knowledge is to interpret and humanize the frightening realities. That is why Bacon claims in the *Advancement* that the sciences of "moral and private virtue," the liberal sciences, have as one of their primary duties the mitigation of the fear of death. A moral scientist teaches that death is the most natural event in the scheme of things, that all things are corruptible and subject to decay. Bacon claims that the more men know of nature and the way it works, the more likely they are to deny the power of fate and stand fearless before what Virgil calls "that insatiate gulph that roars below" (*Works*, III, 315).

A brief comparison of the style in *Of Death* with passages which show Bacon the naturalist at work will reveal the differences between the aphoristic manners he employs. Certain observable phenomena of death fascinate him as a scientist, and he reports them simply in Century IV, 400, of *Sylva Sylvarum*. Here the aphoristic passage is structured just as it is in *Of Death*, with a general remark followed by short summaries of the experiments or data which led to the inductive conclusion. The evidence is quite different, however. It is certain he tells us that "an eye upon revenge hath been thrust forth, so as it hanged a pretty distance by the visual nerve; and during that time the eye hath been without any power of sight; and yet after (being replaced) recovered sight." It is also known that a pig's brain can be completely removed, killing the animal, and then replaced, reviving it. Though men without heads tend not to move, decapitated birds will continue moving after the blow. In *The History of Life and Death*, Bacon elaborates on these and other observations. Showing that death is natural and not to be feared, he discusses convulsions, brain fevers, broken bones, festering sores, and so forth, with a scientist's detachment. His claims differ in structure very little from those in *Of Death*. He uses linear addition to describe the signs of impending death, for example: "great restlessness and tossing of the body, fumbling of the hands, hard clutching and grasping, teeth firmly set, a hollow voice, trembling of the lower lip, pallor of the face, a confused memory, loss of speech, cold sweats, elongation of the body" and twelve others. These are followed, not by citations from poets and philosophers, analogies, and other forms of literary practice, but by more aphorisms summing up the findings of scientists, reporting experiments, and seeking hypotheses.

Sylva Sylvarum and *The History of Life and Death* are works that aspire to interpretation, not anticipation. As such, they do not need what Bacon calls the creation of belief. No appeals to imagination or affections are required, because the goal of interpretive works is to create an atmosphere in which reader and writer work together toward the discovery of axioms. Axioms differ greatly from aphorisms, the one being the products of interpretation of nature and the other of literary practice. They merge only in works like the *Sylva* and the *New Organon*, where the search for axioms is the subject or content and must be conducted in aphoristic prose. The distinction between the two kinds of invention is clear in Bacon's discussions of death. Other instructive comparisons can be made between the essay *Of Youth and Age* and the section in *The History of Life and Death* called "The Differences between Youth and Age"; between the essay *Of Gardens* and the various scientific inquiries into gardening in *Sylva Sylvarum* and other works; and between the essay *Of Regiment of Health* with passages in *Life and Death* and other works on the same subject. In the essay on health he purports to be speaking of a "wisdom ... beyond the rules of physic"; he concentrates on intuitive wisdom in giving advice on how to choose a doctor, endure a sudden or seasonal change in diet, or arrive at the table in a mood conducive to good digestion. We are urged to recognize that common sense and intuition are as strong as science when it comes to a personal regimen of health. Each man knows best what agrees with him. Similarly, *Of Gardens* is about the aesthetic and personal delights of horticulture. The sweetness of perfumes, the pleasures of symmetry, and the sheer ecstasy of naming the plants—a joy that Shakespeare and Marvell feel no less strongly—are the subjects of this essay. If one needs advice on germination, fertilization, grafting, and other matters of the kind, he should turn to the descriptions of experiments in Centuries V and VI of the *Sylva Sylvarum*. In recommending histories of both youth and age and gardening, Bacon clarifies his intentions. In the *Catalogue of Particular Histories* he says, "I care little about the mechanical arts themselves: only about those things which they contribute to the equipment of philosophy" (*Works*, IV, 271). The art of gardening, for example, is of significance to the philosopher only insofar as it tells him where to look for scientific evidence for experimentation.

The simplicity of the aphoristic or loose style then mirrors the nature of Bacon's material, and, more specifically, the nature of his audience and his intended uses of content. He believes that it is the resemblances between things that structure man's knowledge. His style is calculated to objectify abstract relationships and ideas, thus to invest readers with perceptions which lead smoothly to a sense of the total context within which the scientist works. The intricate, highly patterned prose of the Ciceronians calls attention to itself, and, what is worse, gives readers a false impression of unity and completion which works against the true aims of science. Any style which is polished and highly dependent on periodic sentences and interlocking subordinate clauses is likely to lure the unsuspecting reader into mindless agreement. The abrupt, sententious aphorism, on the other hand, moves with thought patterns and leads to the particulars on which conclusions are based. An aphorism depends on rhetorical devices for very little of its effect; without the thrust of truth, it appears merely sententious and hollow. Ideally, a philosophical work composed of aphorisms consists of a series of simple sentences, arranged in logical pattern so that the structure speaks as fully of the subject as the words do. The work itself becomes an image of the condition of knowledge in the field under discussion. In short, the method of delivery is nearly identical to the method of philosophy. And, when it is required to clarify or persuade, ornament too is merged with method.

Though style-conscious men have denounced Bacon's manner as convulsive or oracular, what he hopes to do with his aphorisms is apparent. On the one hand, they are straightforward statements of fact or value; on the other, flexible enough to serve strictly rhetorical purposes when they arise. An aphorism can be artfully disguised, as in XLIX from Book I of the *New Organon*, quoted above. There the author employs linear addition and simple coordination to create the impression of a smoothly moving thought. The sense of progression toward a conclusion is achieved by the use of common structural bridges like "therefore," and the plainness of the language easily convinces the reader that the writer is more concerned with matter than manner. Of more significance for Bacon's purposes is the presence in Aphorism XLIX of a good many lesser aphorisms, each of which is the fruit of a process similar to that which produced the conclusion that "The human understanding is no dry light." Each can be found in other forms in one or another of the philosophical works. Book I of the *New Organon* is designed to condense Bacon's thoughts to aphorisms and make them available to the reader before he takes on the task of interpretation. When he arrives at the concrete evidence, he finds the same aphoristic structure and the same flow between the separate parts that is characteristic of Bacon's philosophical style. "Quiet entry" is the goal of Book I, however, and this accounts for the obvious variations in style between it and Book II.

Bacon's plan as a scientific writer is a simple one. His work will fall into six parts, as listed in "The Plan of the Work":

1. The Divisions of the Sciences.
2. The New Organon; or Directions concerning the Interpretation of Nature.
3. The Phenomena of the Universe; or a Natural and Experimental History for the foundation of Philosophy.
4. The Ladder of the Intellect.
5. The Forerunners; or Anticipations of the New Philosophy.
6. The New Philosophy; or Active Science.

The manner in which each of the parts is presented to the reader will differ just as the content differs from that of the other parts. Division of the Sciences, for example, is a very important first step, for it entices readers into the inner circle. Naturally, then, its presentation will be structured in an appealing way. Emphasis will be placed on summary and description. The idea is to "pause upon that which is received; that thereby the old may be more easily made perfect and the new more easily approached." Declaring that an attempt to improve the old while urging acceptance of the new will "make me the better listened to," Bacon promises that in the first part of his work there will be more than simple divisions and lists. He will add discussions of things which have been badly augmented, and so that men will easily understand him, there will be "either directions for the execution" of work that must be done or "a portion of the work itself executed by myself as a sample of the whole." The goal of the *Advancement* then is to provide "assistance in every case either by work or by counsel." The author will be the focus of the work, for it is here that he establishes his credentials and shows that his head is not full of light and vague notions. It is here, in a work which moves like a "coasting voyage along the shores of the arts and sciences," that the author will convince the skeptical readers that he has a realistic plan for the reform of learning and "a clear and detailed conception" of what is possible. Bacon will not write like "an augur taking auspices," but "like a general who means to take possession."

Thus the *Advancement* and the *De augmentis* conform far more closely to the rhetorical demands of the time than do any of the other major philosophical works of the canon. By 1605 Bacon faced the prospect of failure, both as scholar and as public man. He clearly hit upon the idea of appealing to a new monarch who revealed an interest in learning by couching a radical proposal for reform in conventional rhetorical dress. Book I is addressed to the King and is designed to persuade him to the belief that learning is a subject worthy of a ruler's attention. It has been carefully analyzed by many critics and shown to be patterned after a classical oration. Book II follows with the real substance of Bacon's argument: a survey of the gaps and failures in the history of learning. Both are excellent examples of his program for the use of "art and subterfuge," the necessary techniques by which "frenzied man must be beguiled." Like most educated people of his time, King James was committed to traditional pedagogy and the old philosophy; he makes a perfect test case for the new method of presenting science. No attempt is made in either book to suggest what we know to be Bacon's belief: that is, that men must begin over again the construction of knowledge and create a new system of learning founded on reason and modern capabilities. Instead, he convinces the reader of his interest in matters of curriculum and teaching, and he surveys knowledge almost entirely as if he accepted conventional divisions. The work is put together skillfully and is effective in exactly the way Bacon wanted it to be. It engages us with subtle suggestions of more interesting things to come, but it never violates our expectations as readers. The radical proposals are apparent only to those who know what follows. It works as what Bacon calls a key to the greater reform of science and philosophy.

It is not then quite correct to call the style of the *Advancement* aphoristic, especially if we take Bacon's own description of that style as the best one. In Book II, however, he does insist that the method of presentation in the sciences should echo insofar as possible the method of invention. Such agreement is possible, he suggests, only with "knowledge induced," though "anticipated knowledge" may be brought forth the same way if the author carefully descends into the foundation of his consent and discovers how he allowed it to grow in his mind. "For it is in knowledges as it is in plants: if you mean to use the plant, it is no matter for the roots; but if you mean to remove it to grow, then it is more assured to rest upon roots than slips" (*Works*, III, 404). The aphorism is then named as one form of communication of material in the sciences which is superior to conventional delivery. Its "many excellent virtues" cannot be found in the *Advancement*, which is above all a work designed to equip men with the right perceptions, that is, to teach them. For, as he says in the *New Organon*, men must first be told what they should think. This is the initial stage in the "progressive stages of certainty" which the new scientist strives to establish. Though the aphoristic method eliminates formality and ceremony, these are to be found both in the structure and the message of the *Advancement*. Though the aphorism contains no illustrations or descriptions, no discourses "of connection and order," and no demonstrations, the *Advancement* is full of these attributes. The work seems, in fact, to conform very closely with Bacon's own earliest experience. It presents knowledge very much as it was presented to him in the schools. As Bacon descends into the foundations of his commitment to a new order, he sees and makes us see how conventional teaching and learning failed him. This effort leads naturally to Book II and a less than revolutionary suggestion that much more is possible than has yet been accomplished. Thus the *Advancement* constitutes the vital first step in the reformation of philosophy, a tentative effort to inspire interest in change. It very effectively separates the potential audience into the "crowd of learners" and the "sons of science" by looking on tradition only to make it more perfect and to allow the new learning to be "more easily approached."

The second in the "progressive stages of certainty" is illustrated by the *Valerius Terminus* and the *New Organon*. It is the introduction of a new logic together with directions for the interpretation of nature. The purpose here is to "equip the intellect for passing beyond" inherited learning into "the better and more perfect use of human reason in the inquisition of things." There are three primary distinctions between the old and the new logics: the new logic proposes "the invention not of arguments but of arts"; it uses "induction throughout," leaving the "syllogism and these famous and boasted modes of demonstration their jurisdiction over popular arts and such as are matter of opinion"; and it introduces a new form of delivery in which the scientist proceeds "regularly and gradually from one axiom to another, so that the most general are not reached till the last." This latter rule means that writer and reader will be forced on all occasions to begin by examining closely the validity of the logic in use; unlike traditional philosophers, Bacon will not begin with the assumption that any method is workable.

The first eleven chapters of *Valerius Terminus* and Book I of the *New Organon* are designed to provide the therapy for the intellect which the new logic offers. Both are succinctly written, divided into brief sections labeled as chapters or aphorisms, but both are witty, learned, and persuasive as well. The attempt to entice us with "art and subterfuge" is somewhat heavy-handed in the *Valerius*, since the fragmented pieces and the "dark" title do little to stimulate interest, but the first book of the *New Organon* is a brilliantly executed invitation to the interpretation of nature. It sweeps us into the fold not just with compelling logic but by the power of its vision and the poetry of its style. All this is accomplished by a kind of mythopoesis which we shall look at in the next chapter. Here the point is that the aphorism begins to come into its own as the method of style Bacon has been seeking to perfect for many years: it is "active and masculine, without digressing or dilating," which is the ideal of style expressed in the *Advancement*, yet it is also capable of adhering entirely to the truth and doing so in a "manner neither harsh nor unpleasant," the twin goals expressed in the Preface to the *New Organon*. After considerable practice, Bacon has learned to eliminate connections and other confusing "interstices" of prose by the simple substitution of symbolic numbers for them. Illustrations and demonstrations appear very infrequently, which has the intended effect of forcing readers to inquire rather than to believe. We who have followed the hints of the *Advancement* are prepared. The simple purpose of Book I is to strip us of all preconceptions, so that we may enter the kingdom of knowledge as children again. We are asked to do no more than accept the basic claim that axioms may not be reached until sufficient particulars are assembled. Of course, it is a matter of opinion whether the aphorisms of Book I are genuine aphorisms as Bacon conceived of them. A conclusion depends on the way figurative language works, a subject which requires a discussion in itself.

The last sections of the *Valerius* and Book II of the *New Organon*, on the other hand, are written in pure aphoristic prose. Few readers pretend to enjoy or to fully understand everything Bacon is doing in these sections, and the only guidance he gives us is to say that his purpose is to provide directions for interpretations. No pretense of coherence in the whole is maintained, fortunately, and all is deliberately fragmented. Since interpretation itself is not his purpose, we learn most here about the form interpretation should take. Reasonably clear definitions of key terms like "doctrine," "hypothesis," "axiom," and "forms" are given. It is here also that a "just division" between philosophy and science is made, the former differing in that it is concerned with forms alone. True causes and material realities are the business of science.[4] Much of the book is given up to the discussion of how to conduct the next four moves in the advancement of a new philosophy. Since Bacon was unable to complete his plan, it is not right to judge his presentation of the second step as if it were his model for scientific writing, which is a recent trend to develop in Bacon studies.[5] All he pretends to do in Book II is to set down what he knows and has concluded so that others (perhaps more capable, he hints) may take direction from it.[6]

There can be no quarrel with his development of the third step in the plan of the work, which is to provide some natural and experimental histories as a preparation for the new philosophy. They will serve as its foundation. In dedicating the Great Instauration to King James, Bacon calls for a "Natural and Experimental History, true and severe (unencumbered with literature and book-learning)" to be created so that "sciences may no longer float in air." Such a history will provide a "solid foundation of experience," and this will make it possible for what is known to be examined and analyzed objectively. We are then told in the "Plan of the Work" that not only the ornaments of style but the methods of discourse will be abandoned in this third stage. "For a good method of demonstration or form of interpreting nature may keep the mind from going astray or stumbling, but it is not any excellence of method that can supply it with the material of knowledge." It is at this point that the differences between interpretation and anticipation as modes of invention result in very different structures of arrangement in prose. We must turn to the *Parasceve*, "Aphorisms on the Composition of the Primary History," for a clear explanation of the way a would-be interpreter should write up his findings. Preparation for genuine invention requires, first, the elimination of "things superfluous," or matter which "will immensely increase the mass of the work, and add little or nothing to its worth." These include "everything . . . which is philological." Moreover, he will reject "ornaments of speech," elegant disposition of parts, ("as in a Shop") and unproductive controversies. As Bacon puts it, the scientist must "let all those things which are admitted be themselves set down briefly and concisely, so that they be nothing less than words." He will see that his materials are arranged, not to delight, entice, or persuade, like products in a store, but "to take up as little room as possible in the warehouse." After removing all things extraneous, including superstitious stories and descriptions of species, he will write succinctly in spite of himself. "Though no doubt this kind of chastity and brevity will give less pleasure both to the reader and the writer," the content supersedes author and audience. The goal is to build a foundation for philosophy (*Works*, IV, 254–55).

Among those things to be included in a natural history, Bacon lists several items which help to explain the apparent vagaries of his own philosophical manner. A history shall deal with nature's monsters and the inventions of man, as well as phenomena which occur as a part of the scheme of things. Bacon, of course, discusses many things which are not strictly a part of science, but this is done in order to present a complete picture of what passes for science in his age. As a historian he has the further obligation of taking "the mask and veil from natural objects" by reducing them to their constituent parts and rejecting the fables that so often surround them. Whenever necessary he will pause to "make note" of nonsense and explain how it came to be accepted as truth. For example, the belief that "the power of exciting Venus is ascribed to the herb Satyrion, because its root takes the shape of testicles" is explained away by the fact that the herb grows a fresh bulb on the side of the older one each year. Other dilations and digressions of this kind are justified by the author's claim that a scientist must admit into his histories any facts or observations which "turn up anyhow by the way." That crabs and bricks both turn red when heated deserves to be noted, though such information "is nothing to the table." Interesting as they are, however, these items create the impression that we are dealing with a dabbler in natural studies, not a serious researcher. The same impression grows from Bacon's willingness to include in his histories "things the most ordinary." This means that the historian will record "things mean, illiberal, filthy," "things trifling and childish," and "things which seem oversubtle," because they bear indirectly on what is important and may thus influence philosophy. Also to be reported are things false or doubtful, so long as the author adds "a qualifying note" like "it is reported." All these features of the philosophical style are common in Bacon's work. They put the reader off, and they suggest a certain whimsical twist to his mind, as well as a flabbiness of method in this late stage of advancement, which are surprising.

Parasceve concludes with some useful additions to the method of scientific writing. Central to the philosophical style are questions, since they "provoke and stimulate inquiry." These often take the form of particular topics, or subjects to be investigated. The scientist should also outline the manner in which new experiments are conducted, for, though demonstrations are not necessary, some explanation of method will encourage readers to look for better modes of investigation. The same motive leads Bacon to call for the inclusion of the negative evidence which experiments provided. Such evidence should be "plainly and perspicuously set down."

> For I want this primary history to be compiled with a most
> religious care, as if every particular were stated upon oath; seeing
> that it is the book of God's works, and (so far as the majesty of
> heavenly may be compared with the humbleness of earthly things)
> a kind of second Scripture. (*Works*, IV, 261.)

Bacon further recommends that the scientist include canons, "which are nothing more than certain general and catholic observations," so that the reader is kept aware of the larger contexts of science, and to take special care in "the enumeration of things which are" to append "an enumeration of things which are not." The final suggestion is that the philosophical writer add in passage "a brief review" of current opinion and its variations. This procedure he says is very dangerous in teaching—it proves "The ruin and destruction of the believer"—but it serves in a natural history to "touch and rouse the intellect."

A primary history as Bacon conceived it is a catalogue of experiments and sometimes—as in mathematics—of observations only. *Parasceve* is followed by a list of one hundred thirty histories which must be written before philosophy can be given a proper foundation. Some of these Bacon was able to do himself. The third part of the Instauration consists of an Introduction, a "Rule of the Present History," several histories, one Inquiry, one set of topics, one fragment, and three prefaces to histories. A proper history, he tells us in the "Rule," will contain Titles of Concretes and Titles of Abstract Natures. After each title there will be an immediate proposal of Topics or Articles of Inquiry. There follows a History, a list of Experiments, and, when these fail to illuminate, a Designed History which includes Injunctions for new experiments "to meet the special object of inquiry." Tables are used when the material is easily broken down into a series or an enumeration; otherwise each item is numbered and taken separately. The three histories follow this pattern, with particular topics suggested at the beginning and then developed as far as possible in the texts. The *History of the Winds* is a model of how this third step should be taken, but the *History of Dense and Rare* reflects Bacon's frustration with the subject and his disinclination to treat it. It opens with a table of weights which requires a comparatively lengthy review of the manner in which the experiment was conducted, plus seven numbered observations and three injunctions. The history itself is sprinkled with items described as Speculations and Transitions. *The History of Life and Death*, on the other hand, is as readable as such a work can be. It follows the natural order from plants and animals to men, takes each from birth to numerous varieties of death, and includes hundreds of citations from the ancient authorities. Divided into ten parts, it includes most of the forms of scientific discourse already mentioned: fables, random observations, canons, outlines of demonstrations, reviews of current opinion, catalogues, topics, tables, transitions, and observations. Also included, at the end, are Rules and Explanations. A rule, we are told in the second book, Aphorism IV, of the *New Organon*, is an expression "in the simplest and least abstruse language" of the tentative conclusions which experiments and observations combine to produce. The function of a rule is to cut down the amount of research a scientist must do by providing in aphoristic form a simple statement of what is known. Rules discourage misleading evidence and stimulate action or further investigation. They are "nearer to practice" than any method, because they serve both rhetorical and philosophical functions, contracting into memorable but fragmented form the few facts available.

Thus the items which combine to create a Baconian history of nature constitute a strangely varied group. No one would deny the lack of real information which the histories reveal, but Bacon must be defended from too much criticism on this count by his own words. It is his intention in the first three parts of the Instauration to make a beginning by providing therapy for the intellect in the form of rigidly observed steps of ascending awareness. He serves as a guide. "I do not pronounce upon anything," he claims (*Works*, V, 210). The completion of a genuinely new philosophy he candidly leaves to others; it is a "thing both above my strength and beyond my hopes"

(*Works*, IV, 32). His goal is to engage readers so totally by the wonders and mysteries of natural studies that they will be compelled to go a few steps further. He recognizes that his own talent lies in "literary practice," or wit, and that his service is to suggest a new style for scientists. By setting down all he knows in the histories, he provides a foundation for future research. Like his *Essays* and *The Wisdom of the Ancients*, the *Sylva Sylvarum*, published posthumously, was popular for the wrong reasons. Its encyclopedic collection of nature's "monsters," its simple (and often false) explanations, and its wealth of allusions engaged many of the wrong readers and have served to confuse students of Bacon's philosophy. The real purpose of Part III of the Instauration is to survey "experience of every kind" in order to supply the intellect "with fit matter to work upon." The object is "not so much to delight with variety of matter" as to "give light to the discovery of causes and supply a suckling philosophy with its first food" (*Works*, IV, 28–29).

This food, of course, is largely pablum. The aphorism is employed to expose it as such, on the one hand, and to create the impression of intelligence, mystery, and command of the facts on the other. It uses content exclusively, rather than patently rhetorical devices, to engage readers. The content, though it consists of many tales, myths, superstitions, and false experiments, is superior to "art and subterfuge." In a sense, it is truth because it is accepted as truth. It is included in the histories not merely for examination but to draw readers in. Bacon enjoys, as his contemporaries did, such items as lists of pagan and biblical figures who lived more than a hundred years, reports of animals who moved for minutes after death, and tales of meteorological events in magic lands like Peru and Ethiopia. It is fascinating that Alexander had sweet skin, because he perspired heavily, and we are interested in the Belgian cannon which turned to stone. Bacon's data on the sexual preferences of men and women are as compelling as Kinsey's. Such items encourage further research. Aphorisms work with numbers, symbols, and catalogues to suggest in the histories that nature herself is the marvel and that only a method of "fragments" can capture its essence at the dawn of the age of reason.

Of the last three parts of the Great Instauration we have no examples from Bacon. Guidelines are offered for their presentation in the Plan of the Work. Part IV, "The Ladder of the Intellect," will show how the new logic outlined in II can be applied to the material uncovered in III. It is here for the first time that the new philosophy will make sense, for here models will be constructed "by which the entire process of the mind and the whole fabric and order of invention from the beginning to the end, in certain subjects, and those various and remarkable, should be set as it were before the eyes." And in Part V a temporary allowance will be made for useful but tentative conclusions which have not been established by true interpretation. Such conclusions are "forerunners" to genuine axioms and are not binding. A list of these "wayside inns" was to have been provided. Of the final part of the Instauration, Bacon says:

> The sixth part of my work (to which the rest is subservient and ministrant) discloses and sets forth that philosophy which by the legitimate, chaste, and severe course of inquiry which I have explained and provided is at length developed and established. The completion however of this last part is a thing both above my strength and beyond my hopes. I have made a beginning of the work—a beginning, as I hope, not unimportant: the fortune of the human race will give the issue.

In summary, then, Bacon clearly conceives of the aphorism as an ideal method of delivery in philosophy because it mirrors knowledge as it actually exists. It is employed to lead the reader from the confines of his own mental world into a new experience of invention. Though the risk of confusing the reader is present, the aphorism compels the more curious and competent readers to unravel the mystery and fill in the gaps. Since knowledge exists only in portions and fragments, an abrupt and bare style of delivery is most appropriate to it. It works best in the second and third stages of the Instauration. Though more rhetorical than either scientific or logical, the aphorism is nevertheless a higher and psychologically more effective means of blunting the art of rhetoric and minimizing its subterfuge. It proves an admirable method for presenting inductively the facts, fables, and possibilities that must be accumulated for interpretation.

An Aesthetic for the Philosophical Style

The tables and citations and other paraphernalia of the natural histories do not begin to answer the requirements of one who takes all knowledge as his province. It is the fourth principle in his theory of the philosophical style which is formulated to meet the most difficult demands Bacon makes on style. The term "aesthetic" is perhaps the best we can choose to describe his doctrine of adornment, for it implies that he recognized the need for beauty in order to enchant the imagination and thus the minds of his readers. As it then stood, language offered to Bacon little more than a collection of words which represented notions and were themselves abstractions (Aphorism XIV, Book I, *New Organon*). This point is made in scientific terms in the *New Organon* and in rhetorical-linguistic terms in the *De augmentis*. The possibility of arriving at the true state of a matter is reduced proportionately by the number of words one is forced to employ or to read. The "simple sensuous impression" is left behind as the words accumulate. Bacon begins to move toward the philosophical aphorism as a new style for himself by refusing to limit language to words and by making every effort to replace them with signs and symbols. Anything which transmits knowledge without unnecessary connotations or adornment is language fit for philosophers, Bacon believes. Accordingly, he includes gestures, characters (thought to be used in China to stand for things rather than notions), and hieroglyphs among the most powerful devices for communication and urges them on readers as ideals to emulate. Language in these forms functions in one of two effective ways, either by analogy or by accepted convention. Bacon compares gestures and hieroglyphs to the emblem, because they work analogically and always have "some similitude to the things signified." In this section of the *De augmentis*, VI, 1, he also explains that characters work very well because they are simply established as meaning one thing or another and are preserved in that form by custom. Bacon's profound distrust of language and his inability to correct the errors it had perpetuated lead him to develop a style of his own dependent on verbal pictures, analogies, and established convention. Such characteristic forms are apparent in the language of all the philosophical works, but most particularly in those which treat subjects in which the state of knowledge is doubtful and thus specially vulnerable to the abuse of words. Successful efforts to explain theory or to persuade others to accept an analysis or interpretation depend heavily on these forms of language too. Because he is determined to make scientific the philosopher's approach to such disciplines as civil and moral history, theology, poetry, and rhetoric, he formulates a means of reducing their essentials to simple sensuous impressions and thus delivering them in a method and style as scientific as literature could then be. In dealing with those matters, he is careful to employ an aphoristic style notable for its efforts to establish the resemblances between things and to provide for the faithful reader aphoristic conclusions which will play major roles in the inductive process leading to interpretation. Bacon's philosophical style is founded on analogy and accepted convention.

On the simplest level of meaning, his verbal pictures, whether they work as hieroglyphs, emblems, analogies, or metaphors, enhance understanding by clarifying both the object under discussion and its relation to other objects in the framework of philosophy. They are appealing to the psychologist because they work on the reader's memory and imagination as well as his reason. On a higher level, as we shall see in the next section of this study, the pictures combine to do much more complicated tasks for the philosopher. They allow him to employ old myths for new purposes and to invent his own fables to lend coherence and imaginative appeal to his argument. They serve to suggest meanings which may now be inconceivable and to stimulate the full participation of the most learned and creative of readers. They preserve the mystery and beauty of philosophy and, at the same time, soothe the mind's wounds as it encounters a new and more natural world of ideas to replace tradition. Using a tested rhetorical method, especially a myth that has lost its religious foundation but retains its power over the imagination, is one of Bacon's ways of catering to habit only in order to break its hold on man's intellect. Because it is a commonplace in anthologies and surveys to suggest that Bacon is at war against metaphorical language, we shall first establish that such language is the basis of his philosophical style, a point that no Baconian needs to see reiterated. This stylistic feature, plus Bacon's attempts to minimize the abuse of words through established convention, provides preliminary material for the discussion of fable-making in the next section and rounds out the picture of his theory of a philosophical style.

Like most of his contemporaries who were advanced thinkers, Bacon enriched the old chain-of-being metaphor with a conception of the universe as a vast hieroglyph whose secrets could be unlocked gradually, one by one, until the day they are all available and enlightenment comes. In the meantime, man must store these perceptions in his memory and work for knowledge with what is available. Bacon's scientific and moral works are notably as concerned with memory as with discovery, and he never neglects to provide the reader with topics or apophthegms to store for future inquiry. In purely natural studies, elements of the puzzle may be preserved in tables of experiments and in brief, neatly arranged lists of conclusions, but this seldom is enough to strike either the memory or the imagination in works of a moral or philosophical nature. The simple explanation is that the mind requires—both for understanding and for the urge to understand—some sensuous impressions with which to begin the growth to comprehension. Thus for Bacon method, style, and content frequently become fused in an emblem or hieroglyph. The best examples of this are probably *The Wisdom of the Ancients* and the *New Atlantis*, both visionary works which present an ideal of philosophy in traditional but reworked literary form. Written in Latin, a sure sign of its intended audience, the *Wisdom* is a philosophical work which pretends to reveal the hieroglyph as a perfectly logical way for the learned to preserve their knowledge by passing it down only to those who can pierce the veil. Though the method is one he ridicules, he makes the most of it in an effort to entice the intellectual community, still bound by medieval habits of mind, into the chambers of true learning. The *New Atlantis* expresses in superb emblematic form most of Bacon's utopian ideals; it is rich in biblical symbolism and in hieroglyphic wisdom as well. He points more seriously to such methods for their power to delight and claims in the Preface to *Wisdom* that fables and hieroglyphs continue to please common readers who have no notion of their function for philosophers. He suggests the existence once of a supremely wise age which employed these devices as clever means of transmitting knowledge and making it pleasant to receive at the same time. What occurred, unfortunately, was that the basic wisdom was "buried in oblivion" behind a "veil of fiction" and became lost to philosophers of succeeding ages; the hollow shell would survive, even if it made no sense, while the "interpretation" was left to be contrived in each age by the unqualified. As a lesson in how fiction can work lawfully for the advancement of learning, he reads thirty-one classical myths in his own way. In them, he asserts in the Preface, he was inclined to imagine, "lay from the very beginning a mystery and an allegory." Some fables, he says, show "a conformity and connexion with the thing signified, so close and so evident, that one cannot help believing such a signification to have been designed and meditated from the first, and purposely shadowed out" (*Works*, VI, 696).

Though Bacon is fascinated by mythmaking, the evidence does not suggest that he took its secret wisdom seriously, and there is no reason to suppose that he turns his back in 1609 on what he said so emphatically in 1605, 1607, and 1608, about the ponderous and deceptive methods of the fabulists. What he does is to employ their methods strictly in order to undermine them, to thwart their power by draining them of specious appeals and mysterious hints. Everything has a mundane meaning, so Bacon uses old stories to make moral and philosophical knowledge acceptable to a larger audience. The *Wisdom*, in fact, is typical of the way he handles formerly non-scientific subjects. He begins with a form of "quiet entry," a narration, and then ingeniously reduces the best-known fables to aphorisms on these "soft" subjects, so that the reader is forced to accept the argument and admire the author. On the level of metaphor, the myths of Cassandra and Orpheus illustrate his method. Cassandra is said to have extracted promises of clairvoyance from Apollo in exchange for the privileges of love. She reneged after receiving her gift, and the god decreed that she should thereafter speak prophetic truths but never be believed. Each detail of the fable is transformed into one of the aphorisms which Bacon frequently offers in the more straightforward *Essays* or *Advancement of Learning*. This myth, he says, contains a

> reproof of unreasonable and unprofitable liberty in giving advice
> and admonition. For they that are of a forward and rough dis-
> position, and will not submit to learn from Apollo, the god of
> harmony, how to observe time and measure in affairs, flats
> and sharps (so to speak) in discourse, the difference between
> the learned and the vulgar ear, and the times when to speak and
> when to be silent; such persons, though they be wise and free,
> and their counsels sound and wholesome, yet with all their efforts
> to persuade they scarcely can do any good; on the contrary,
> they rather hasten the destruction of those upon whom they
> press their advice.

The myth is deflated, not enhanced, by Bacon's interpretation. The reader interested in Bacon's views on prophecy and the fate of the intuitively wise is disappointed to learn that Cassandra is no more than a figure for the doctrine of "plainness of speech." The story of

Orpheus, on the other hand, is turned into an allegory similar to many in Bacon's works, an allegory of the philosopher and his labors. This is done, he says, by an "easy metaphor," since the myth so clearly presents "philosophy personified." At the same time, persuasive pictures of the philosopher are drawn from the mythical details. The correspondence between these elements and various Baconian ideas is obvious on every level of the stories. Orpheus plays music for the gods in an effort to ransom his wife and, later, music for the beasts of the world, in his melancholy withdrawal from life's great promise. It is easy to conclude that the first music represents natural philosophy and the second moral philosophy. Like natural studies, Orpheus's music seems to succeed and then fails because of "curious and premature meddling and impatience." In looking back to Eurydice, Orpheus commits the same error which had defeated most pre-Baconian scientists: he becomes too anxious too soon to reach conclusions. Orpheus, who turned to the animals in his misery, is like the natural philosopher who abandons his attempt to solve the great mysteries of the cosmos and turns to human affairs.

Like Orpheus, the moral philosopher, despairing of ultimate truths, uses eloquence and persuasions "to insinuate into men's minds the love of virtue and equity and peace." Bacon, who saw that it is the business of rhetoric to "make pictures of virtue and goodness," shows in his study of fables how that may be done. As a scientist, he also justifies the hieroglyphic method as most appropriate to content. He adds in his study of Orpheus interpretations of each detail. Repeating a favorite doctrine of his, for example, he describes Orpheus's aversion to women and children (indeed to humanity) as characteristic of the true philosopher, who recognizes that "the sweets of marriage and the dearness of children commonly draw men away from performing great and lofty services to the commonwealth." Bacon's interest in the literary hieroglyph clearly derives from its function as a vehicle for his own ideas, one which will delight and attract an audience as straightforward counsel will not. He expresses that interest throughout his works, notably in the *De augmentis*, II, xiii, where he demonstrates the uses of poetic method for the philosopher. It is as if he were describing his own method in the *Wisdom* and *New Atlantis*, rather than great works of imaginative literature, when he says there that the ancients communicated new and strange knowledge and resorted to "fables, parables, enigmas, and similitudes" to reach minds unprepared for it. In fact, there is nothing incongruous in the view of Bacon as a poet of rationalism. As will become apparent, he created myths of his own for a new age.

In his admiration for what he thought the mythmakers were doing, Bacon reveals some of his special intentions as a stylist. He hopes to create, where they are necessary, similitudes and analogies which are so close to the things signified that no possibility of error is inherent in them and an absolute minimum of words is required for their full presentation. Having learned from the classical rhetoricians that the metaphor is the one figure really consistent with a plain philosophical style, he attempts to go beyond them by giving scientific authority to metaphorical language. He forces it to function as argument and ornament at the same time; his metaphors are rich, many-faceted, inclusive figures, which contain within them all the lines of development that a well-furnished mind might draw from their original premises. Style is functional in Bacon, not added to but blended with content and method when it is required.

The authority of science is given to such devices of style by the doctrines of invention and method, which are the keys both to science and to communication in Bacon's system. In certain cases, particularly the moral and civil sciences, the psychology of discovery depends almost entirely on the adroit blending of style and content. Though the writer of treatises on the natural sciences must appeal to the imagination of his readers too, he has the advantage of concrete facts, illustrations, experiments, and citations which do the job for him. It is no problem to "apply and recommend the dictates of reason to imagination" here, nor is it difficult to encourage learned readers to assimilate and organize this material in patterns which appeal to the understanding. The content has an inherent logic. And, since tables, numbers, and symbols serve as substitutes for words whenever possible, the greatest obstacle to communication is tempered in its power. But how does the author of theoretical works and works of counsel keep the understanding from leaping and flying? Because "the end of rhetoric is to fill the imagination with observations and images to second reason, and not to oppress it," Bacon strives to send from the senses of his readers images which the reasoning powers can grasp and translate into orders for action. If the imagination is properly governed by the writer, his readers will use it fully in the interests of science. This leaves the second serious problem facing the writer, and that is how to appeal to the will and appetite of his readers by presenting the future or theoretical good as if it were present and personal. Again, in the natural sciences, this task is less difficult than in the softer disciplines, for the naturalist will always stress the present benefits of his experiments and discoveries. As Bacon gradually recognized, however, the theorist must alter the perfect method of induction to allow for imaginative inventions which will clarify, engage, and even haunt. The final difficulty which is solved by the scientific justification of figurative language is the need to perfect a method for storing the philosopher's conclusions in the minds of his readers. The doctrines of invention, method, and memory in Bacon are united by his theoretical treatment of the similitude in all its forms as the scientist's key to success in the first stages of his advance to a new philosophy.

Invention in those early steps is nearly always literary. It is clear that Bacon himself regarded the compilation of what he calls "literate experience" as his own primary talent and that he associates that lesser skill with wit and imaginative genius. It relates to the emblem and hieroglyph, keys to his theory of figurative language, in important respects. Anyone who is attempting to reform radically the way people think must *"pray in aid of similitudes,"* but there is no reason why the figures cannot be expected to work as more than decoration. In his section on literary invention, then, he explains how style and content may be blended. Figurative language is justified by the doctrine of variety, since intelligent audiences demand multiformity of method and weary of sameness. Since variety is also the key to discovery in most endeavors, including scientific experimentation, why not provide material variety in the form of fables and figures which illustrate the point? In the same passage in the *De augmentis*, V, 2, Bacon recommends repetition and extension as "productions" which enhance the art of literary invention; when these are applied to style, as in the *Essays*, analogies and myths inevitably emerge as the best possible devices for extending or summarizing material rather than merely decorating it. Similarly, the inventive practice of translation, or the comparison of phenomena or method in one art or science with that in another, will produce what passes for similitudes. This practice is the most common form of "literary experience" to be found in the composition of Bacon's philosophical works. It is very significant to Bacon and serves in the first stages of philosophical advancement to train the mind for interpretation. As he says in Book II of the *New Organon*,

> Men's labour therefore should be turned to the investigation and observation of the resemblances and analogies of things, as well in wholes as in parts. For these it is that detect the unity of nature, and lay a foundation for the constitution of sciences. (*Works*, IV, 167.)

Quite frequently, as in this part of the *New Organon*, Bacon is to be found comparing plants to men. This is not an "absurd similitude," and it certainly is a more philosophical and progressive method of observation than those used by the ancients, who devote themselves to listing and exclaiming over the variety of things without investigating their similarities.

It is easier to see how Bacon's concepts of method and memory lead naturally to a style dependent on similitudes. As early as *The Masculine Birth of Time*, he speculates on the utility of metaphors to meet all the problems of the philosopher of the new breed: though not untrue to nature, they may provide the "quiet entry" he seeks and at the same time serve the same function as the "art and subterfuge" he knows to be the tools by which "frenzied man" must be beguiled. So long as men do not compare things which do not exist, the method of analogy is helpful to science, he says in the *New Organon*. Moreover, most of the methods of communication which Bacon considers in the *De augmentis*, VI, 2, rely on some form of similitude for success. Even the useless methods do so. And, of course, such forms are vital to the success of Bacon's doctrine of memory, which depends on emblems. The mind is more forcibly gripped by a picture than by an abstraction; the scientist must reduce his theories and conclusions to "simple sensuous impressions" if he is to provide therapy for the intellect.

Perhaps the foregoing fails to explain Bacon's interest in the hieroglyph, even if the similitude in general is accepted as the theoretical and practical basis of his philosophical style. A literary puzzle, or hieroglyph, has many advantages, however, and Bacon recognizes them. It is especially useful in philosophy to engage the learned reader. Though "a kind of emblems," the cryptic picture does not satisfy as a normal emblem does. While any emblem may contain suggestive hints of more to be found and may entice the reader to examine it closely, the hieroglyph is initially meaningless even as a picture. It conforms very closely to the philosophical ideal of style because it does not quench the thirst for knowledge, nor does it discourage further search, as emblems do, by seeming too compendious and inclusive. It preserves the ultimate mysteries of knowledge by foreclosing the satisfaction we all seek and by appearing very difficult to unlock. Thus it does not work as most figures work: that is, to clarify and simplify for initial understanding. For the intelligent reader, the literary hieroglyph inspires hope, a primary goal of the philosophical style.[7] Moreover, it uses the tested technique of analogizing, praised as the key to a new science in the *New Organon*, by doing what Bacon says scientists must do: comparative analysis of things which do not exist in terms of things which do. Interest in the cryptic form of discourse is one of the most obvious of Bacon's obsessions. He speaks with fascination of the ancient practice of hiding wisdom in anagrams (*Works*, I, 86), toys with the possibility of inventing a cipher theory for the same purpose, and even tries unsuccessfully in the third stage of his works to create an "alphabet of nature." The fragment, *Abecedarium Naturae*, is designed to reduce the elements and their behavior to symbols to be learned. This process will simplify the basic knowledge of nature but will also help science "select her followers." In *Filum Labyrinthi*, Bacon also speaks of the philosophical aphorism as part of this effort to preserve wisdom from the vulgar and simultaneously to engage the imagination of the learned.

> Antiquity used to deliver the knowledge which the mind of man had gathered, in observations, aphorisms, or short and dispersed sentences, or small tractates of some parts that they had diligently meditated and laboured; which did invite men, both to ponder that which was invented, and to add and supply further. (*Works*, III, 498.)

Aphorisms, as he says in the *Advancement*, "representing a knowledge broken, do invite men to enquire further" (*Works*, III, 405). Useful as they are to natural science, aphorisms perform well in the more abstract branches of wisdom, for they work smoothly together with fables and parables to produce excellent pictures. Solomon is Bacon's mentor in this art, for his divine writings reveal him as a man "whose heart was as the sands of the sea, encompassing the world and all worldly matters." Citing and commenting upon some of the Proverbs, Bacon is led to conclude that such figurative aphorisms as the "sentences politic of Solomon" are useful because they "offer no violence to the sense, though I know they may be applied to a more divine use." Aphorisms and fables, then, are two versions of the same philosophical ideal. Neither form simplifies experience or limits the boundaries by which it may be interpreted.

Not just the Hebrews but ancient Romans, Greeks, and Egyptians employed a method of delivery superior to those now employed, Bacon says. Whenever they found out any observation worth repeating, they "would gather it and express it in parable, or aphorism or fable." The advantages of these forms include the fact that they provide concrete illustrations or particulars which serve as examples when real life produces none (*Advancement*, in *Works*, III, 453). Bacon does not use them to shroud science in mystery or to equip himself in the garb of a mystic but to preserve the charms of style without violating the sense, to enchant and to explain.

In a larger sense, emblems and hieroglyphs suggest the role that style is to play in Bacon's plan for the reform of philosophy. Such verbal pictures, though sometimes cryptic by themselves, work to reduce the larger concepts on which reform hinges to simple sensuous perceptions. As the reader moves through the *Advancement*, Book I of the *New Organon*, and the *De augmentis*, important works in the first stages of the Instauration, he gradually acquires a complete emblematic view of the relation of the philosophy of science to the details with which it works. At the same time he finds an allegorical and persuasive picture of the scientist himself (namely Bacon) which works subtly on him to argue for reform. Because he believes in empirical observation and, at the same time, in the unity of all man's knowledge, Bacon's most intense metaphorical efforts present these thoughts in pictures. In explaining why he writes a history of learning, he describes the world without one as like "the statue of Polyphemus with his eye out; that part being wanting which doth most show the spirit and life of the person." Like all Bacon's analogies, this one is pure and inclusive. Though the unity of all knowledge is a fact, it cannot be recognized until someone with more comprehensive powers than the average man undertakes to define its character. Such a power depends on the force of style. A few pages later, he contains this concept of interlocking branches in an even more effective analogy:

> The knowledge of man is as the waters, some descending from
> above, and some springing from beneath; the one informed by the

light of nature, the other inspired by divine revelation. The light of nature consisteth in the notions of the mind and the report of the senses; for as for knowledge which man receiveth by teaching: it is cumulative and not original; as in a water that besides his own spring-head is fed with other springs and streams. (*Works*, III, 346.)

An instructive comparison can be made of this image with one revealing Bacon in another capacity; he is a politic man praising his King when he describes James's manner of speaking as "flowing as from a fountain, and yet streaming and branching itself into nature's order, full of facility and felicity, imitating none, and inimitable by any" (Preface, Book I, *Advancement*, in *Works*, III, 262). In addition to assonance, alliteration, devices of point and syntactical symmetry, which call attention to themselves, this image cannot be said to enhance the clarity of content. The first use of the waters image, on the other hand, seems to outline both the method and the program of the advancement of learning without simplifying either. It indicates in 1605 a feature of style which will grow in significance as Bacon's career advances.

In a fragment called *On Principles and Origins*, for example, he intended to use the myths of Cupid and Coelum to color and communicate his theories of the creation. This stylizing is done to invite interest. He reminds us that Cupid, like God, appears in iconography in two forms, an elder and a younger. Also like God, the elder Cupid is not known to have had parents. God's chief concern, like Cupid's, has been to unite bodies, as Cupid does lovers, in order to produce still more bodies. Out of chaos, God, like Cupid, brought order. Bacon here reforms the philosophical style by passing on vital information and ideas in a manner and a method which preserve them but make them pleasant to receive as well. The same is true for his numerous glass and mirror images created to enhance his doctrine for advancement. In undermining virtually all of his age's intellectual inheritance, Bacon has to tread lightly and with accuracy. So he tries to draw pictures that will advance the conclusions for him. He does so in his famous passage on the history of the human mind, in which the subject figures as an "enchanted glass" oppressed by intriguing phantoms and false versions of the nature of things. A similar analogy developed in most of his works compares man's mind to a false mirror which receives and reflects rays irregularly and distorts everything that reaches it or emanates from it. These are but some of a large number of basic figures which are worked and reworked in the philosophical writings.[8]

Many of these primary figures, in fact, work to establish for Bacon certain accepted conventions which will operate throughout his works to enlighten the reader and keep him on the track to interpretation. The integrity of his theory of the philosophical style is revealed by the care he takes to set up certain prenotions which are signposts to the initiated. This is the second ideal of style expressed in the chapter on memory, where Bacon explains that the "art of retaining" is the key to both communication and the growth of knowledge. His use of analogy, as we have seen, supports the contention in the *De augmentis*, V, 5, that the philosopher must reduce doctrines, theories, and propositions to simple sensuous impressions if he is to lead readers from details to valid conclusions. The doctrine of memory is founded on this use of emblems, an umbrella term for all devices which make word pictures and thereby transform "intellectual conceptions to sensible images," and on the use of established convention. Both are central to his aphoristic style and the theory which governs it.

Like the doctrine of emblems, which relates directly to the scientist's search for the resemblances between things, the doctrine of established convention relates to the scientist's determination to avoid the abuse of words by employing clear and figurative definitions. To work around the usual problems with definition—that is, the flexibility of words' meanings—Bacon often uses pictures. These are both clear and memorable. Often, Bacon's readers are misled because they overlook this vital preliminary attempt to equip them with prenotions. He attempts in all his work to begin by explaining with care what he means by a term or phrase and then to capture that meaning in an unlikely but apt analogy like "idols of the mind" or "enchanted glass." The reader, who, naturally, it is assumed, will bring the meaning back on call when a term reappears, must be alert and interested. Those who are neither of these, or who will not read all the extant parts of the Instauration, are likely to be confused. The most obvious error has been the tendency of critics to take the *Advancement* and the *New Organon* as the philosophy itself. Many read the *Wisdom* and assume that Bacon is a mythographer in the medieval tradition, or the *Advancement* and assume he is no more than encyclopedist, or the *Essays* and assume that "little saltpits" or moral wisdom are the keys to his mind. Many examples of his efforts to avoid this sort of misreading have been cited in this study and bear repeating. He tells us with the lengthy comparison of the great obelisk to the rational rebuilding of science that neither wit nor logic alone can work to supplement man's intellectual heritage (*Valerius Terminus* and *New Organon*). The imagination is described as a messenger between reason and the will, though it often usurps authority and substitutes itself for the message (*De augmentis*, VI, 2). The arts of rhetoric are described as a hunter pursuing a hare (Invention), an apothecary arranging his boxes (Disposition), a pedant making a speech (Elocution), a boy repeating verses (Memory), and a player acting on the stage (Delivery) (*De augmentis*, V, 5). These examples provide only hints of the significance of emblems and hieroglyphs in Bacon's attempt to establish customary definitions. More attention to them will be given in the next section of this study.

As a final example of his use of analogy to define, we should look to the important terms in the Great Instauration, the ones on which clarity and persuasion really hinge. Bacon must explain what he means by true invention and the new induction, for example. As he reminds us in the *Valerius Terminus*, "There is no proceeding in invention of knowledge but by similtude" (*Works*, III, 218). Tricky definitions must also be handled largely by pictures. Though the invention of speech and arguments may be compared to a hunter pursuing a hare, true invention, or interpretation, is a procedure like those a general follows when invading a territory occupied by others. After seeing that his soldiers, the instances and observations he has collected, pass "muster," he may proceed through the inductive steps of interpretation. This analogy, developed in the *New Organon*, is joined by numerous others which clarify the nature of interpretation. In the *Advancement*, the scientist is a gardener growing plants, an architect building new temples of learning, a judge bringing knowledge before a new tribunal. Terms like "inquisition" and "inquiry" are employed to define the nature of interpretation, and Bacon speaks often of building through induction a "foundation" for future research. In the *Sylva Sylvarum*, where he recognizes the inadequacy of the present state of knowledge, the new philosophy is described as a suckling child which the new scientist must supply with its "first food." The term "digestion" is often used to define the nature of the second step in invention, when collected data is absorbed and analyzed. In the *Advancement* and *New Organon*, interpretation is sometimes described as a trip down a difficult road, one abandoned and overgrown by years of neglect. It has "wayside inns" for the travelers' comfort and edification, however. This process is also described as the storing of knowledge in a warehouse, after which the bits and pieces are removed one by one and pondered as if for the first time. Like a child, the scientist looks at his facts and experiments as if they were mysteries of the scriptures; then he digests them slowly like food (*De augmentis*, V, 2). Interpretation is finally possible, for it is "the true and natural work of the mind when freed from impediments" (*New Organon*, in *Works*, IV, 115). The worker in the fields of knowledge now has the right seeds for growth and the proper procedures for insuring a harvest. Moreover, he is equipped naturally with the divine desire to augment knowledge for the good of mankind. He has automatically trained his mind to reject false motives. Knowledge for personal satisfaction is "but a courtesan, which is for pleasure and not for fruit or generation"; this dabbling he rejects. Knowledge for profit or glory is like the golden ball tossed before Atalanta, "which while she goeth aside and stoopeth to take up she hindereth the race"; profit and glory are not the scientist's motives, nor does he behave as Atalanta did. The scientist who invents knowledge for special uses rather than universal ones is but as Harmodius "who putteth down one tyrant, and not like Hercules who did perambulate the world to supress tyrants and giants and monsters in every part" (*Valerius Terminus*, in *Works*, III, 222). True interpretation and induction free us all from such errors and make the kingdom of God accessible again.

While Bacon teaches best by example, a conclusion to any study of his theory of style should emphasize the authority granted directly by the author in his admittedly scattered passages on the subject. This investigation has followed the lines Bacon himself suggests in his treatment of the Art of Elocution. Elocution is divided into Organ, Method, and Illustration of discourse. Although the subjects are treated in many other places, hieroglyphs and characters are treated as parts of science in VI, 1, of the *De augmentis*, as is the distinction between philosophical and popular modes of delivery. The section VI, 1, is devoted to the Organ of discourse. In VI, 2, under Method of discourse, he speaks of the differences among audiences and the methods of appealing to them. In VI, 3, he speaks of rhetoric proper in his scheme under Illustration of discourse.

After determining that style is grounded in audience psychology, Bacon naturally concluded that there is a need for two methods of delivery. In focusing on the philosophical style, he devised one for himself which fuses manner with the method and content of discourse. It forces style to follow the thought patterns of the new induction and to create simple sensory data when needed. When figurative language is required to do this, it first serves these purposes, though it also enhances the imaginative power of the "second Scripture" and manages to "touch and rouse the intellect." It is the aphoristic style which Bacon developed to deal with fluid and abstract ideas that best confirms his faith in the doctrine of emblems and prenotions as the most forceful control possible for the whole art of elocution. Designed as the key to his initiative rhetoric, the aphorism works psychologically to sway man's reason and encourage research. It is condensed, memorable, and may, when it is in Bacon's hands, even delight as well.

4   Fable-Making
as a Strategy of Style

The Acroamatic Method

The chain of reasoning which operates to provide philosophical justification for the method of "fragments" also works to give legitimacy to emblems and hieroglyphs. Bacon's scientific method is related to his literary strategy of providing inductively a series of observations from experience which combine throughout to produce still more, until the reader reaches more or less on his own the author's conclusions. The new induction is a process which gradually produces "a certain path for the mind to proceed in, starting directly from the simple sensuous perception." In leading his readers on the paths to interpretation, Bacon attempts to reduce doctrines, theories, ideas, and arguments to concrete impressions which will act on the imagination as pictures do. Though this procedure is philosophical induction, it works best as a rhetorical method for providing the imaginative appeal vital even to a scientist's presentation. Bacon's philosophical works, taken together, as they must be, are carefully integrated, mutually dependent arguments for the new science, arguments which often hinge on the author's success in constructing out of old fables and parables a new myth for the modern world. The new myth, which Bacon takes much more seriously than its ancient analogues, serves as the concrete, sensuous impression on which the new philosophy is built; it is a poetic vehicle for the practical ideals of science. Parables from the Christian tradition yield updated moral philosophy for an age of reason—a Machiavellian look at the world which Bacon admits is only one picture to emerge from so rich a source. And from the details of pagan myths a similar art of transformation draws out doctrines to form a foundation for a new mode of philosophical inquiry. Nor is the presence of the fabulous and parabolical in this rationalist's work limited to ingenious new versions of tradition; there is a mythmaking power about his writing which derives from his determination to provide new fables and a modern creator of them for his world. In seeking converts to science, the "second Scripture," Bacon builds fabulous structures of his own to replace those he destroys. The effects of this strategy of style imply the presence of a rhetorical plan meant to work throughout the philosophical writings. Though he holds the "affectionate study" of rhetoric in contempt and chides himself for spending too much time in the theater, Bacon succeeds brilliantly in exploiting those parts of his intellectual heritage that he most dislikes.

Though the art of fable-making has been continuously abused for centuries, Bacon rejects the notion that the old fables are therefore of no use to the modern thinker. He suggests in his Preface to *The Wisdom of the Ancients* that the creators of those tales merely re-delivered their inherited knowledge in entertaining but carefully drawn stories of gods and goddesses. The relation of the similitudes to the things signified is often too close to ignore, he says. Though such remarks are frequently cited to show that Bacon never could overcome his essentially medieval cast of mind, the *Wisdom*, like his other works on myth, is an essential factor in his plan to rework tradition and extract from it whatever might prove useful to a new age.[1] He seeks to rescue the ancient philosophy, whatever its merits, from "grammarians and schoolboys" and set it up for an examination. In the thirty-one myths which are treated in the *Wisdom*, he finds much evidence to support the doctrines and opinions already sketched in the *Essays* and *Advancement*. The apparent failure of his program with the intellectual community made it necessary by 1609, not to change the program itself, but to enliven the presentation of it. There is little cause to suppose that Bacon's opinion of fables and parables as methods of delivery had changed between 1605 and 1609, though this suggestion has often been made.[2] When such devices must be employed to enhance imaginative appeal they are excellent if ponderous, he always thought. For rhetorical purposes they function well under certain conditions. These opinions account for the increasing interest in myth after 1605. Bacon also had the problem, of course, of somehow fitting this enduringly popular branch of wisdom into his scheme for the reform of knowledge. His powers of persuasion had been so strengthened by 1609 that, as C. W. Lemmi has said, "We are almost ready to believe, as he would have us, that the myths themselves are his subject, and that from them really emerge the ingenious and sagacious ideas which he wishes to convey to us."[3]

Brief glances at the early works will reveal Bacon's less than enthusiastic feeling for the wisdom of ancient fables. Whatever his shortcomings as a philosopher, a sentimental love of old stories and a mystical faith in them are un-Baconian faults. From the beginning of his career, in fact, he recognizes the promise of fables and the mythmaker's art for the purposes of inquiry and delivery. At the same time, he reveals his contempt for the ancient and modern fabulists who have abused the art. In *Valerius Terminus*, for example, he describes the ancient mode of delivery as "utterly unfit and unproper for amplification of knowledge" and admits that he will "not willingly imitate" a form of communication which "muffles her head and tells tales" (*Works*, III, 225). In the same work and in *The Masculine Birth of Time* he clarifies these charges by arguing that it is possible for the fable to be employed by the very learned as a means of protecting both writers and readers. In the *Valerius* he says fable-making is so abused an art that thoughtful men are inclined to reject it out of hand. But a method "of publishing part, and reserving part to a private succession, and of publishing in a manner whereby it shall not be to the capacity nor taste of all ... is not to be laid aside" (p. 248). In the *Masculine Birth*, a figurative method of delivery is justified for another reason. There he says that a tradition of concealment and ignorance in pedagogical and scientific circles forces the man with new messages to adopt some more pleasing and mild manner that will not offend as mere aphorisms do. The necessity for "art and subterfuge" is recognized by the man who would prepare the mind for new experiences.

That none of these early remarks implies acceptance on Bacon's part of either the myths themselves or the pedagogues' false uses of them is demonstrated in the *Advancement*, where "fable" is no more than a synonym for "imposture." The mythmakers are blamed for much of the false knowledge proving so difficult a barrier to the new science and to intellectual therapy. He reports the "history of nature" deficient, largely for lack of "due rejection of fables." In his discussion of man's soul and religious truth, the charge is made that the study of divination tends to produce error, having so far "rather vapoured forth fables than kindled truth." On the use for fables and parables he is specific: they tend "to demonstrate and illustrate that which is taught and delivered" or to "retire and obscure it" (*Works*, III, 344). Bacon approves of the latter effect only in divine poesy, which would not perhaps exclude his own works on the "second

Scripture," but the use of myths in demonstrations and for teaching is sanctioned because "now and at all times they do retain much life and vigour, because reason cannot be so sensible, nor examples so fit." In the same passage, it is noted that divine mythology often seems to invite simple interpretations. In ancient poetry "the exposition of fables doth fall out sometimes with great felicity," and the reader is encouraged to use figures like Jupiter for the obvious purposes. It is doubtful, even in divine works, however, that the moral came before the myth itself or that men like Homer wrote to express cryptically some inward meanings. "I do rather think that the fable was first, and the exposition devised," he says (*Works*, III, 345). Whether they were composed entirely for man's pleasure and not as figurative language is a point on which Bacon has no opinion in 1605, nor does he commit himself on the primary question of whether the ancient poets expressed still older and hidden religious truths of which they themselves were unaware.

The distinction between fables and parables in the *Advancement* is of interest also, though the two terms are often used interchangeably. A parable is "a narration applied only to express some special purpose or conceit" (*Works*, III, 344). It is necessary as a method of instruction, or once was, because men could not, in those primitive times, grasp ideas apart from sense impressions. The genuine fable is a form of communication which holds some secret of "religion, policy, or philosophy" and is employed chiefly to preserve great primary wisdom from the vulgar minds who would certainly abuse it. Wise men penetrate their meanings and continue to preserve them. Later, in his Preface to the *Wisdom*, Bacon refines this distinction by noting that parables often function as parts of fables. Such forms, it is clearly implied in the idealistic mood of 1605, are no longer needed. Men like Bacon, who willingly dedicate their lives and energies to the reform of learning, will succeed in creating a new age in which reason prevails without the assistance of artifice.

Between the *Advancement* and the *Wisdom*, Bacon worked on *The Refutation of Philosophies* and *Thoughts and Conclusions*, both important to our understanding of how he comes in 1609 to muffle his own head and tell tales. The *Refutation* explains in very simple terms that the new philosophy must be preceded by a "preliminary preparation of the mind." The scientist may not "attempt a direct, abrupt, encounter with things themselves, for they need to be approached by opening up and levelling a special path on account of the inveterate prejudices and obsessions of our minds" (Farrington trans., p. 103). It is clear as well that this method of approach is designed for philosophers, the "lofty and resolute minds," and is not offered as a magistral way to deliver knowledge. Instead, the intellectual community forces him to resort to persuasion, and he will obey by becoming a fine rhetorician. The practical advantage to this plan is that it precludes any violence among the "crowd of learners" who will not perceive that the new method calls into question nearly all the ancient philosophers produced. Bacon has by this time, then, expressed both interest in and fear of the acroamatic mode of discourse. Though he sees its value for communication among scholars and appreciates its power to engage two audiences at once and control them both as the philosopher would wish, he resents the need for the modern scientist to resort to such artful methods. The *Essays* and the *Refutation* are tentative efforts in the direction of artifice, using forms of discourse improper to the scientist, but Bacon closes his discussion of this kind of thing in the *Advancement* by remarking that "it is not good to stay too long in the theater."[4]

Thoughts and Conclusions, probably written in 1607, contains two sections on fables which are more illuminating for our purposes than anything we have yet examined. In the eleventh aphorism a detailed explanation of Bacon's rejection of fables reveals that their worst function has been to minimize the acceptance of truth among men. Amadis of Gaul or Arthur of Britain have more power over the imagination than Caesar or Alexander, just as the boasters of alchemy and magic are victorious with the people over the naturalists who would tell the truth. "Everybody knows that those famous captains accomplished greater things in reality than the shadowy heroes of romance are fabled to have done, and that too by modes of action that have nothing fabulous or miraculous about them." The truth loses the battle because "faith has often been outraged by fables," however, and Bacon is forced to conclude that the scientist must avoid the appearance of participating in any tradition so inimical to the mind's best powers as fable-making. He admits that the birth of the centaurs may be compared with those of Hebe and Vulcan in order to clarify the "powers of nature and of art":

Admitting the truth of this interpretation and holding it to be a mark of crass stupidity to reject all tradition without dis-

tinction of kind, Bacon yet concluded that the path to true
knowledge through fictions of this sort has long been closed,
or at least narrowed, and that the excess of such vanities is
destructive of all greatness of mind. (Farrington trans., p. 82.)

In the thirteenth aphorism of the same work this determination is
strengthened by Bacon's conclusion that "truth must be sought
from the light of nature, not recovered from the darkness of
antiquity" (ibid., p. 87).

The reasoning which brings him to such a declaration is not
difficult to follow. In order "to miss no possible path," he admits,
some close study has been made of "that region of cloud and
darkness, the secret recesses of remote antiquity." As part of his
program for the perambulation of learning, he had looked into the
works of the Greek and Roman mythographers and their modern
interpreters. It was certainly conceivable that he could himself
employ their methods of delivery, "if he chose to act with less than
absolute sincerity," and could even convince readers that in utmost
antiquity there existed a science of nature which anticipated all the
findings of the new induction. "He knew well what solemnity it
would add to new discoveries to connect them with remote antiquity," but he rejected the method of fables anyway, because what
the ancients knew and whether that knowledge can be recovered "is
a matter of no moment." Like alchemy and magic, the fables
fascinate Bacon, and he says so, but they do not belong in the
new philosophy.

Nor are they put there by the Preface to the *Wisdom*, in which so
much seems to have changed. This work employs ancient stories as a
method of "quiet entry." No one in the intellectual community to
whom it is principally addressed could possibly mistake these versions for the originals and no one could overlook the deliberate
inconsistencies and omissions which characterize his interpretations.
The *Wisdom* is both a serious examination of a phenomenon in the
human experience, the response to myth, and an effort to stimulate
inquiry into all the fundamental issues raised by the new science.
Bacon's purpose is to engage the nonreflective faculties of his
readers, and he offers a large portion of fancy to those who desire it.
The use of inherited stories conforms, however, to most of the
demands Bacon places on the philosophical style. It denies the
mind's urge to fly to abstractions by precluding the need for too
many words and by reducing the abstractions inherent in the content

to "simple sensuous perceptions" which work powerfully on the imagination to send messages to the reasoning faculties.

The Preface to the *Wisdom* is the best example in the philosophical canon of what Spedding calls Bacon's efforts to "treat popular prejudices of all kinds with the greatest courtesy and tenderness" (*Works*, III, 174). Having already concluded by this time that the Great Instauration must be completed by others, his task has become the laying of a foundation for the new philosophy. It requires presentation at the least risk. As Bacon says in his letter to the Chancellor of Cambridge University, the *Wisdom* is a product of his own wit, written "to give some help towards the difficulties of life and the secrets of science." The method of fables entails little danger to philosophy, he continues, because the "vulgar apprehension" will not be inclined to see anything more in the stories than amusing narratives. Those of "deeper intellect," on the other hand, will not be offended by this method because they will see that it is only a device by which they will be "carried along" to greater things (*Works*, VI, 689-90). The Preface itself makes this point more clearly when Bacon justifies interpretation of ancient myths as an exercise which will succeed, depending on what the reader thinks, in "throwing light" either "upon antiquity or upon nature itself."

Bacon is apologetic and even somewhat ironical throughout the Preface. He explains that a major reason for choosing this method for philosophy is the use to which fables have been put in former times. Employed as toys for leisure and as vehicles for preposterous ideas and arguments, they have become in the modern world the exclusive property of grammarians and schoolboys. No valid means of understanding life deserves to be left to such a fate. Therefore the author rescues them for the intellectual community and gives three good reasons why it should reexamine them. First, as he has noted before, there are fables which seem to demand interpretation; in those Bacon finds "a conformity and connexion with the thing signified, so close and so evident, that one cannot help believing such a signification to have been designed and meditated from the first, and purposely shadowed out." The irony, of course, is obvious here, for the fables Bacon names present few puzzles to be solved and no shadows to speak of. In both the *Advancement* and *Cogitationes de Scientia Humana*, fables of this kind are used for the purposes of explaining both how fables might work for science and how science might bend to admit their methods into its system. In fact, the second reason given in the Preface to the *Wisdom* for another look at the myths is that the names of figures give their secret meanings away; Typhon and Nemesis, for example, have nothing mysterious about them. As Bacon himself admits, fables with obvious meanings "may be thought to have been composed merely for pleasure, in imitation of history." A better reason for reading fables is available, however, and that is simply the "absurd and stupid" face that so many of them have when looked at superficially. Because some stories make no sense at all, they seem "to give notice from afar and cry out that there is a parable below." It is this kind of tale, the one with "further reach," that most entices Bacon, because it can be read as the interpreter chooses. Part of the irony of the Preface is that he criticizes those who "twist the fables" into versions of their own ideas. Anyone who has read the *Wisdom* recognizes Bacon's own genius in doing this same kind of violence to the old myths.

In concluding his apology to fellow scientists for engaging in mythography, Bacon tells them he has concluded that the ancient poets were merely reciting tales they had received. None of them says that they originated with him, which means that the myths may belong to a period of "better times" and should be looked on as "sacred relics and light airs ... that were caught from the traditions of more ancient nations." This possibility extricates Bacon from the difficulty of relying too heavily on the wisdom of the Greeks, whom he despises, and allows him to attach the wisdom of the fables to the Egyptian culture he admired. It gives him great pleasure to study these stories as if they were hieroglyphics, the natural predecessors to letters, "For as hieroglyphics came before letters, so parables came before arguments." Even in the modern age, he continues, the philosopher has learned that the effort to throw new light on any subject requires him to "go the same way and call in aid of similitudes."

Thus the Preface is an excellent illustration of Bacon's ability to hold in poise the desires of the common audience and the aspirations of the new philosophers. Justifying fables as no different from other metaphors in technique, he persuades the scientist to admire their capacity to hold secret wisdom intact for the proper readers and yet also to entertain. Though he does not like to use them for teaching purposes, we are told that fables work well to outline and reduce the subtly involved relationships of the arts and sciences. Even if we reject them for communication among philosophers, we must recognize their value as "a method of teaching, whereby inventions that are new and abstruse and remote from vulgar opinions may find an easier passage to the understanding." Ironically, Bacon implies that even the community of scholars will need this concession to their intellectual weaknesses, and he is right. Spedding is astonished to report that the *Wisdom*, which he lumps together with other "literary and professional works," had in the seventeenth century a reputation among scholars "as a work of learning and authority" (*Works*, VI, 609). Men of primitive times were "rude and impatient of all subtleties that did not address themselves to the sense," and it goes without saying that men now are the same. Even Bacon founds both his literary practice and his scientific method on the initial sensuous impression. The *Wisdom* is a vital part of the foundation for the new philosophy.[5] Though his critique of rhetorical adornment is always biting, Bacon says as early as the *Advancement* that "it is a rule *that whatsoever science is not consonant to presuppositions, must pray in aid of similitudes.*"

Whether he appreciates the ancient fables in themselves is a less important question than what Bacon does with them. Though he converts myths into emblems of his own philosophical concepts, Bacon goes further by reinterpreting them so that they are workable as allegories of the modern scientist at work in his struggle for answers.[6] Subtly read and manipulated they yield excellent arguments for the new philosophy and provide the modern world with images of a new kind of leader. At the same time, they cater to the old habits of thought by conforming superficially with the most popular and effective method of discourse in the Renaissance. One of the great obstacles Bacon faced, for example, was religion, and much of his fable-making is designed to clarify the scientist's relation to God and His world and to convince readers that there is a difference between what man takes on faith and what God has equipped him to discover for himself. Man acquires knowledge of God by learning about His Creation, and the fault of modern philosophy, he says in the *De augmentis*, II, 3, has been a too-frequent application of theological methods, the "superstitious, fabulous, and fantastical," to natural philosophy. The scientist, on the other hand, may be too inquisitive and make the error of Acteon and Pentheus, described in the tenth fable of the *Wisdom* as entering into competition with God. Pentheus, in spying on the secret rituals of Bacchus, violates man's limitations and deserves his punishment of "perpeutal inconstancy and a judgment vacillating and perplexed." This passage and others like it argue well for Bacon's new sense of decorum. In order to separate scientific from religious truths and to obliterate the medieval fear of forbidden knowledge, Bacon meets the theologians on their own ground. By beginning there, he obtains "quiet entry" into the minds of those reluctant to receive his message. So effective is he in this quest that some historians of the present day blame works like the *Wisdom* for the current decline of the arts and humanities. Charles E. Raven, for example, describes Bacon as a "thoroughgoing naturalist who sets aside religion and scripture with a rather hollow show of reverence"; he complains that the *Wisdom* and works of its kind are responsible for the fact that all knowledge except religion is now part of science's province.[7] Similarly, Jean Seznec sees Bacon as part of a modern movement to destroy the real value and meaning of mythology. Though he knows his interpretations of the fables have no value, his "lack of poetic instinct" allows him to "see in mythology only intellectual concepts deliberately transformed into symbols."[8] And Fulton Anderson, when he came to write the first exposition of Bacon's philosophy, remarked that our neglect of the *Wisdom* as a work of philosophy is "among the strangest phenomena in the history of philosophical exegesis." This treatise on myths, "unquestionably one of the most significant contributions to philosophy in the history of English thought," is seen by Anderson as an effective attempt to meet the threat of religion and to subvert its influence by employing its own devices of indirection to present Bacon's unpopular and complex views.[9]

Paolo Rossi answers Anderson's call by examining Bacon's use of myth as a device for science. Though Rossi tends to believe in his claim to faith in the myths themselves, he explains that this is to be expected. He says that "medieval mythological allegory flows in an uninterrupted stream right through the Renaissance," and that, though this method had occasionally been satirized, Bacon knew he lacked the authority and weight to counteract its popularity.[10] The interpretations of fables are divided into "naturalistic, materialistic, methodological, ethical, and political themes." Each signifies an integral relation between the *Wisdom* and the rest of the philosophical works, and it cannot be said that the myths are used simply as a means to an end. In fact, Bacon changed his views on the fable-making of the ancients considerably between 1605 and 1609, Rossi argues, because he came to see that the most vicious of errors in medieval and Renaissance learning was the frivolous uses to which the ancient wisdom was put. He appears to attack the mythographers' habit of using the old fables as vehicles for their own inventions and ideas, saying in the Preface to the *Wisdom* that he will restore their validity by extracting their true meanings for the modern world. Rossi fails to explain why Bacon seeks to correct the abuses of a method by copying it exactly, even to the point of bending the myths to fit his special and sometimes peculiar versions of the nature of things. Nor does he find a reason why the *Wisdom* and Bacon's other works so often contain interpretations which down to the last detail echo those of Renaissance mythographers, especially Boccaccio and Conti.[11]

Through myths of Prometheus, Orpheus, Pan, and Cupid, Bacon gives substance to his case for the new scientist. Distinctions between the philosopher and ordinary men, for example, made throughout the philosophical works, are supported by the story of Prometheus and Epimetheus. Prometheus's story has not yet been understood, he claims, because it has yet to be noted that the ingratitude shown by the human race for the gift of fire represents a positive quality once inherent in man. Though Prometheus created man from clay, he was actively interested in strengthening his product by enabling it to acquire self-assurance. Prometheus, who "clearly and expressly signifies Providence," suggests with his gift that nature provides for nearly all man's needs, if man will but seek the source for help. Men are wrong to see their ancestor's ingratitude as an error, however, for "the accusation and arraignment by men both of their own nature and of art, proceeds from an excellent condition of mind and issues in good" (*Works*, VI, 748). Because he rewarded mankind with new gifts, Jupiter made it plain that the gods are offended by men who are satisfied with what they have and are not willing to admit that much remains to be discovered. Bacon's section on Prometheus, number 26 of the *Wisdom*, creates *ethos* effectively, combining humility with the more often cited pride of mind, and the first part of it reminds us that "a sharp and vehement accusation" brings man more gifts than an "overflow of congratulation and thanksgiving." We are subtly reminded that faith and gratitude are not all that God hopes for from us. He continues in the second part, assuming that he has reached the intellectuals among his readers, by using the story to illustrate a number of principles for the aspiring scientist.

The sluggish ass, entrusted to carry man's gift of eternal youth, for example, is given to man by Jupiter because man complained and by so doing developed a searching spirit. When the ass stops for a drink and is persuaded by a serpent to yield up his burden, we are reminded to "proceed steadily onward by a certain law and method," never giving in to the temptations of profit or fame (*Works*, VI, 750). Man's frustrated reconciliation with Prometheus is an emblem which instructs us never to give up the quest when an experiment fails. Bacon is using Prometheus here, as he does several other times, to provide the example or illustration which life itself fails to offer. He is employed twice in the *De augmentis*, first to illustrate the nature of astronomy and then to illustrate the procedures of true invention. In the essay "Of Sedition and Troubles," he figures as an example of unwise government.

Of more interest are those parts of the fable which contain religious allegory and suggestions for moral behavior. Bacon's favorite doctrines are outlined in the Pandora story, which clearly becomes an emblem of man's fate. Vulcan, god of fire, created Pandora, and the gods filled her vase with all the misfortunes and disasters that now prey on man. Though Prometheus refused to open her vase, his brother Epimetheus gladly did so, closing it only in time to keep hope, which was at the bottom, locked in. The followers of Prometheus are therefore cautious wise men, who forego all the pleasures of life in order to contemplate the future. Such men suffer constantly from thoughts which "prick and gnaw and corrode the liver." Followers of Epimetheus, on the other hand, live for the present and suffer great personal difficulties which prevent their accomplishing anything worthwhile. Their ignorance is a blessing, for they can live on empty hopes and false dreams. True wisdom comes as a gift from God and combines knowledge with pleasure. In closing, Bacon wisely refuses to interpret some features of the myth which correspond to the mysteries of Christianity. This refusal makes it easy for him to disregard inconsistencies and appear to be humble. To attempt an explanation of these things would be to play with fire. It is obvious that the various details of this analysis do not fit together particularly well, for the story is chiefly a device for passing on a philosopher's arguments in a roughly coherent pictorial form. The fable is a vehicle by which we rise to the "nobler heights" beyond.

As Elizabeth Sewell has shown so convincingly, Bacon identifies himself strongly with the mythical figure of Orpheus, whose golden lyre and the music it produces stand for nature and philosophy in the *Wisdom*. Though he is seen in the *Orphic Voice* as "a dark, riddling, emblematic poet, struggling with a metamorphosis of his own thinking and of man's power over the universe, a counterpart of the darkling Orpheus," it is more likely that Bacon uses the mythic figure as a primarily rhetorical device.[12] He is one of the simple sensuous impressions collected to make the philosopher's case more potent. It is "by an easy metaphor" that Orpheus is turned into "philosophy personified" in the eleventh fable of the *Wisdom*. The ideas developed in this analysis are not new with Bacon but they are presented more imaginatively here than in earlier works. As usual, the allegory fails to hold up; Orpheus cannot be both a symbol of the old science (in his haste to see Eurydice) and of the new science. He is employed in the *Advancement* as an emblem of the order learning brings to life and in the *De augmentis* to signify "free and wholesome advice." Yet Miss Sewell is right to note that, even if he is trying to do so, Bacon does not succeed in sterilizing this myth until it is reduced to nothing more than a few concepts. "There is something deep in Bacon which assents to concealment" and hence to the use of the myth both to instruct the common people and to preserve primary wisdom from them.[13] Orpheus is a useful image of the philosopher in the modern world, a figure who suffers and works under the same conditions as Bacon and whose music corresponds to the poetic beauty of the scientist's discovered truth.

Pan and Cupid, to take two very different examples, are used by Bacon as symbols of the creation and preservation of the universe. They are employed to strengthen his arguments for the natural philosopher, engaged in what he calls the primary and divine task of the new age. No brief discussion can do justice to the meticulous way by which Bacon forces Pan to yield his secrets, but the comprehensive treatment of that figure in both the *Wisdom* and the *De augmentis*, II, 13, is the best illustration there is of his ability to render powerful but outdated learning, like the classical myth, useful again. Cupid, too, a figure which struck the fancy of the Renaissance, is eased into the new system with apparent pleasure on Bacon's part.

It seems to be an interpretation of his own method in the *De augmentis*, II, 13, when Bacon explains that poetry can work to the advantage of science by using "fables, parables, enigmas, and similitudes," as the ancients did, to reach minds not subtle enough to comprehend ideas expressed apart from sensory appeals. He goes on to say that even in the modern age philosophers can find no example or arguments that will communicate so clearly as these forms do. Parabolical poetry "appears to be something sacred and venerable," which is a special advantage to the writer with new ideas. The ancient stories he reads help to illustrate this point and to show how faulty the mythographers who preceded him were in their methods. Bacon interprets the fables of Pan, Perseus, and Dionysius, not "for the value of the thing," but because he has promised in the *De augmentis* to provide counsel and examples for the improvement of any discipline which he calls deficient. Each detail in the myth of Pan is interpreted carefully to correspond to Baconian doctrine and to enforce the larger conclusions we are meant to reach. The fable, in all its received forms, is analyzed as an allegory depicting the origin of the universe. An outline reveals the placement of details and the thorough job Bacon does in at once expoding and exploiting the story.

1. Bacon begins with Pan's origins. The three versions hold that he is the son of Mercury, the product of Penelope's intercourse with her suitors, and the son of Jupiter and Hybris. The first two are possibilities, since Mercury clearly signifies God's Word, and since it is also likely that the universe was created by the promiscuous mixture of many different seeds. The third version came down to modern times in the wrong form; the marriage of Jupiter and Hybris (sin) is obviously an allegory of the world's state after the fall of man, and it is Hebrew in origin. Taken together, the three versions of Pan's origins produce a nice allegory of the world's fate: conceived by the Word of God, then filtered through the medium of confused matter, and finally corrupted by sin. It is notable that Bacon rejects both the story of Penelope and the story of Jupiter and Hybris, saying that they could not have been a part of the original fable.

2. The second item of interest is Pan's person. His horns suggest the shape of the universe, broad at the base and pointed at the top, and they also suggest, in their pyramidal structure, the chain of being. His body hair is a figure of "the rays of things." All things reflect and emit rays, a fact most evident in the powers of sight and magnetism in nature. Pan's beard, which is especially long, signifies the sun, which emits the longest and most penetrating rays and even, on a cloudy day, looks as if it has a beard. The upper part of Pan,

which is human, suggests the perfection and beauty of the upper world while the goatish lower half represents the animal and vegetable nature of worldly existence. This arrangement also implies the mixture of divine and bestial in man himself. Everything in nature, in fact, combines inferior and superior qualities prefigured in Pan. Bacon also ingeniously relates the goat's feet to scientific questions of gravity, weight, and magnetism.

The details outlined are by no means the only ones which Bacon collects to enforce his doctrines. He relates Pan's insignia to his own theories of the harmony of all created things and to his belief that God's mysteries can be penetrated only in natural philosophy, where things are laid out to be discovered and understood as they are, but need not be related to any theories of how God did it. Pan's crooked staff implies that "works of Divine Providence in the world are mostly brought about in a mysterious and circuitous manner," and, on the level of politics, that "those who sit at the helm can introduce and insinuate what they desire for the good of the people more successfully by pretexts and indirect ways than directly."

3. Perhaps the most interesting of Bacon's pretexts are those concerning Pan's associates. Because Pan is the nature of things, it is natural that the Fates should be his sisters. Ignorant people, in fact, often confuse events and fortunes with natural laws. The ancients reveal their understanding of the difference when they place Pan in nature and the Fates in caves; nature is open and there to be examined, but the destinies of men are mysteries. It is also natural that Pan should marry Echo, for the only true philosophy is that which exactly echoes the state of nature. Pan's discovery of Ceres is likely too, because the hunter finds useful things, not in abstract philosophies (or, he might have said, fables), but in experience and direct knowledge of the nature of things. Iambe, Pan's putative daughter, is dismissed as a perfect symbol of "vain babbling doctrines about the nature of things." Bacon is further undermining the method of the mythographers when he describes false doctrines as "counterfeit in breed, but by reason of their garrulity sometimes entertaining, and sometimes again troublesome and annoying" (*De augmentis*, II, 13). In leaving this discussion of ancient allegory, Bacon promises to go on to things that really matter and to approach them "with more reverence and attention."

In a short fragment, *On Principles and Origins*, written late in his career, Bacon attempts to employ poetic doctrines again in the search for a viable method of passing on his scientific conclusions. He tells us straightforwardly that he is substituting one kind of oracle for another here, for "it must be understood ... that the things here brought forward are drawn and concluded from the authority of human reason alone, according to the belief of the sense, whose expiring and failing oracles are deservedly rejected since a better and more certain light has been shed upon us from divine revelation" (*Works*, V, 462). Very ingeniously then he manipulates the available versions of the Cupid myth to echo the philosophy of Democritus on the origins of things. At the same time, wherever the myth differs from the philosopher, it gains the author's credence and echoes his own opinion. As he moves into his theory, the myth is almost entirely forgotten, and, as Bacon may have feared, the reader wearies. The fable is employed quite obviously as a device for presenting some very complex truths inherent in the search for knowledge. Cupid, like God, appears in traditionally elder and younger forms; his life and experiences set forth in a small parable "a doctrine concerning the principles of things and the origins of the world," for, in both forms, his function is to unite bodies and create all that exists through his own union with Chaos (*Works*, V, 461). From the facts of the fable Bacon draws these bits of advice for the aspiring scientist: Do not search for origins or speculate about them; Cupid, like God, has no parents and it is surely futile to search for one. Draw conclusions from negative evidence. The belief that Cupid was hatched from an egg laid by Nox (night), though unfounded, laid an egg of its own: that is, new knowledge of Cupid. Most of all, the fable of Cupid tells the scientist of the nature of what is meant to remain unknown; it is designed to stimulate a searching spirit tempered by common sense.

In his use of fables, then, Bacon seems chiefly to be improving his mode of argument. It would be foolish to deny his interest in the fables themselves as curiosities and as material for pleasant games, but we cannot overlook his embarrassment on this point or his serious efforts to make this enduring branch of wisdom somehow consonant with the new philosophy. In a religious world, he hopes to convince men of intelligence that natural philosophy should depend on experience and observation, not superstition, and the classical myth serves as a vehicle for that proposition. At the same time, his own unpopular and Machiavellian views on politics and ethics receive the advantages of "art and subterfuge" by being introduced in the forms of ancient tales. Cassandra's fate is an ironic comment on what happens to men who fail to disguise the truth or play the games of politics in offering advice. The Cyclops are figures of the "ministers of terror" that all rulers employ and discard as expedience requires. Narcissus is an example of the kind of man who fails in business and public life, lacking the ability to combine good and evil traits of character in the special way required for success.[14] Fables and parables dramatize abstractions and give them force. Though Bacon's readings are not always original and are probably not meant to be taken seriously, they color his philosophy in an engaging way and preserve the air of superior knowledge and mystery that he strives to maintain.

Mythmaking

Emphasis should be placed on Bacon's use of the acroamatic method as a moral force in his writing, for it is morally, as well as intellectually and rhetorically, that he argues for the new science and attacks barriers to reform. He knows well that it is the duty of rhetoric at all times to "make pictures of virtue and goodness," and, in establishing himself in his own myths as a physician, a magistrate, a farmer, or an explorer, for example, he creates *ethos* effectively and, at the same time, argues persuasively from a moral basis for modern science. The author is a farmer contemplating a new season, or a doctor confronting unknown symptoms, or a magistrate with a case which must be handled with special delicacy. The implication is that the intellectual community is hostile to this idealist of the new breed, a man who undertakes to change the state of things, rework tradition, and begin again. Man's knowledge, of course, is the field to be cultivated, the disease to be cured, the case to be defended. Man himself is the plaintiff or patient, and it is on his behalf that the author fights. Bacon creates for himself the image of the tough-minded defender and tireless supporter of our right to know. In the *Essays* and the *New Organon* the style is sometimes oracular as the writer expands his image to suggest something holy and godlike in nature. The sciences become a new religion meant to strengthen and not supplant man's heritage. The scientist is God's delegate to the people. His pronouncements on natural and moral philosophy partake of the divine but rest on the logic of the new induction, the powers of thought that God gave even to the brutes. The reader finds it difficult to avoid agreeing with Bacon, so skillfully does he present himself and his case. It is this power of mythmaking which distinguishes and dignifies Bacon's work and convinces us of the integrity of both his philosophy and his theory of communication.

The control and structure of his presentation rests on Bacon's belief in the hieroglyph as an ideal form for the communication of knowledge. His enthusiasm for apparently cryptic figures, explained in the *De augmentis*, VI, 1, stems from his urge to create a "philosophical grammar" based on analogy. Taking Caesar's hint, he "thought of a kind of grammar which should diligently inquire, not the analogy of words with one another, but the analogy between words and things, or reason." After an interesting discussion of ciphers, which he treats whimsically as one of the "smaller and remote islands of learning," Bacon is led to suggest that what is really needed is an art of deciphering so efficient as to be admitted to the new scheme of learning, an art "requiring both labour and ingenuity, and dedicated . . . to the secrets of princes." He engages and entertains readers with nuggets like cipher theories in order to soften them for the significant ideas of the work. In VI, 1, of the *De augmentis*, the most important point is introduced early and is larger than grammar in its implications:

> Before I come to Grammar and the parts thereof . . . I must speak concerning the Organ of Transmission in general. For it seems that the art of transmission has some other children besides Words and Letters. This then may be laid down as a rule: that whatever can be divided into differences sufficiently numerous to explain the variety of notions (provided these differences be perceptible to the sense) may be made a vehicle to convey the thoughts of one man to another.

Feeling that any vehicle for the transference of fact or opinion constitutes language, Bacon suggests the way in which he reads and creates fables. Because they can "be divided into differences sufficiently numerous," classical myths have survived to educate each new age. It requires only an art of deciphering to make them work. In a real sense fables succeed, not through words, but through pictures. They correspond in effect to the gestures of body language and thus constitute an ideal of "signification without the help or intervention of words." This state of communication is naturally perfect and does not apply literally to what Bacon does (he must use words). It merely implies the condition to which his style aspires.

Words, he says, are but "symbols of notions." Too often they create false appearances which have turned philosophy and sciences into dead-end roads. They are "framed and applied" according to the vulgar capacities of the human mind and communicate only to the vulgar understanding. Essential to the growth of reform and the advancement of learning is some near-substitute for words. This alternative is implicitly offered in Bacon's treatment of hieroglyphs, gestures, and characters:

> The Notes of Things then which carry a signification without the help or intervention of words, are of two kinds: one *ex congruo*, where the note has some congruity with the notion, the other *ad placitum*, where it is adopted and agreed upon at pleasure. Of the former kind are Hieroglyphics and Gestures; of the latter the Real Characters ... Gestures are as transitory Hieroglyphics. For as uttered words fly away, but written words stand, so Hieroglyphics expressed in gestures pass, but expressed in pictures remain. (*De augmentis*, VI, 1.)

The advantages to such forms, apart from the reverence in which they have always been held, is that they "have always some similitude to the thing signified, and are a kind of emblems." They bear strong credentials as "the currency (so to speak) of things intellectual." The reader is invited to take this argument or leave it, as he chooses, though "it is not amiss to know that as moneys may be made of other material besides gold and silver, so other Notes of Things may be coined besides words and letters" (ibid.).

We could well choose to take this passage seriously as one of Bacon's few extended discussions of the ideals of a philosophical style. In it he emphasizes the virtues of his own manners: (1) multiplicity of meanings, (2) appeal to the senses and the picture-making powers of the imagination, and (3) the production of clear emblematic relations between the similtudes and things signified. In his philosophical writings, it is fair to say, Bacon even aspires to the strength of communication by gesture and established custom. The first sections are devoted to the construction of pictures or emblems which reappear constantly to speak for the author. They continue throughout and beyond to govern our perceptions of the author's message and to provide our entrance to the more complex and specific findings. The *Essays*, which treat moral and civil subjects, show Bacon reworking his philosophical style with material less important and more tractable than natural philosophy. These little "grains of salt," he says in the Dedicatory Epistle of the 1612 edition, are designed to enhance the appetite for more significant knowledge. The aphoristic manner so appropriate to scientific inquiry is strengthened by the introduction of imaginative appeals to the readers' senses and by the construction of emblematic arguments. That Bacon thought in images is demonstrated by the subtle and almost casual use of them in the *Advancement*, where they are mingled, expanded, and sometimes introduced only to be dropped. Like hieroglyphs or emblems, word-pictures in the *Advancement* communicate their secret meanings to the interested and attentive reader of a certain intelligence, one who participates imaginatively in the author's struggle to recruit others for the task of reform. To other readers the work is merely another tract on education, an encyclopedia. The *New Organon*, on the other hand, reveals Bacon's awareness by 1620 that more color and coherence of metaphor is required if recalcitrant readers are to be drawn into the great adventure. In calling this work a prose poem, various readers from the poet Shelley to Elizabeth Sewell have pointed to its intense and emotional beauty of argument, its tone of spiritual commitment, and the visionary quality of the author's ideas. It is in Book I of the *New Organon* that the aphoristic and acroamatic methods merge to produce Bacon's finest piece on behalf of science. Finally, in the *New Atlantis* he reveals a new power of mythmaking in the old tradition of the hieroglyphic writers and succeeds in creating a vision that would serve as an inspiration to the intellectual community for years to come.

Any study of the development of a philosophical style should begin with the *Essays*. R. S. Crane has demonstrated conclusively their relation to the rest of the canon, and Stanley E. Fish has recently convinced us of their adherence to the rules of inquiry established in the *Advancement* and *New Organon*.[15] Stephen C. Pepper's work has clarified succinctly the process by which the essays use ideas "as material for aesthetic organization and appreciation."[16] The 1625 essays and revisions clearly seek to entice the reader to more meaty stuff by presenting some of the larger bits of moral and civil knowledge in a delightfully appealing and economical way. They encourage thought and further research. One of the major reasons for expansion, moreover, is to allow the figurative presentation of their conclusions and pronouncements:

that is, to communicate through emblem. The obvious purpose of the *Essays* is to clear the foliage away from some of the most sensitive topics in human experience and to provide in its place aphoristic pictures which show things just as they are. The pictures serve all the purposes of a philosophical style. Not only do they minimize the use of words and abstractions, but they plant seeds in the imagination which will grow and pictures in the memory which will be retained. Truth is "a naked and open day-light, that doth not shew the masques and mummeries, and triumphs of the world, half so stately and daintily as candle-lights" (*Of Truth*).[17] Envy is a "gadding passion, and walketh the streets" (*Of Envy*). Boldness is "a child of ignorance and baseness" (*Of Boldness*). "Fortune is like the market; where many times, if you can stay a little, the price will fall" (*Of Delays*). The aid of friends is like the pomegranate, "full of many kernels" (*Of Friendship*). Such pictures reflect Bacon's feeling for similitude as a philosophical form. They contribute to the tone of high and serious purpose and help to build an idea of the moral scientist in the reader's mind as one who "reduces intellectual conceptions to sensible images," which Bacon says in the *De augmentis*, V, 5, is the role of the emblem in discourse. This essential task clears "a certain path for the mind to proceed in, starting directly from the simple sensuous impression," which is Bacon's description of his own scientific method. How closely he identified method with style is apparent in the *De augmentis*, as is the role the *Essays* are to play in his plan for the advancement of learning. The analogies, concrete examples and citations from authority, which account for much of the added bulk in the expanded essays, work in moral philosophy, like the scientist, to derive "axioms from the senses and particulars," the goal Bacon sets for himself in the *New Organon*, I, Aph. XIX. Of more significance is the presence of the author himself in the *Essays*, the controller, contriver, pronouncer. Sensitively and with the weight of personal experience, he appears alternately as benign and angry, wise and willful, but always as the observer of sublime detachment, a man qualified to insist on our attention. He speaks like an oracle and succeeds by saying what thoughtful men know to be the truth. Moral and civil knowledge, like Orpheus's music for the beasts, is of less importance to Bacon than natural philosophy, but writing of it in the *Essays* gives him an opportunity to perfect a style that will carry his greatest contributions to what he hopes will be a receptive audience.

Bacon's attempt, whether a "hollow show" or not, to give moral force and the sanction of religion to science and to his Machiavellian observations on behavior is carefully calculated to succeed in the *Essays*. It is a vital part of the myth he is creating of the scientist as God's delegate on earth, and it functions below the surface so that it speaks chiefly to the perceptive reader Bacon imagines. "The Student's Prayer" and "The Writer's Prayer" tell us clearly what he hopes to do in this respect. The student prays for "new refreshments" of knowledge from the fountains of God's goodness and for the "unlocking of the gates of sense, and the kindling of a greater natural light." These gifts will more perfectly illuminate creation without interfering with divine mysteries. The writer prays for the power to use the "Intellectual Light" bestowed on man to convince others that whatever is natural is good and should be known (*Works*, VII, 259–60). Similarly, the twelve religious meditations, originally published with the *Essays* and *Colours of Good and Evil* in one volume, strive to associate Baconian doctrines with the Bible and God's Word. They tell us that the scientist is a man who labors in God's works and earns his rest on the Sabbath, that he deserves to be ranked with the prophets who accomplished miracles in nature with His help, and that he works in nature, studying God's creatures as well as His Word, as man was instructed to do. The precept for naturalists and philosophers is "*Try all things and hold that which is good*," or "*Be you wise as Serpents and innocent as Doves*" (*Works*, VII, 245). Man must come to his world for study without presuppositions and prepared to enter "*the deeps of Satan*." These rules have the authority of Scripture. The *Essays* themselves, then, or "Counsels, Civil and Moral," freely use the Bible to comment upon or support the frank observations of Bacon's experience. They tell us what we need to know if we are to be fully aware of the nature of God's creatures. This is their only real counsel. Some of the essays are divided into discussions of theological truths on the one hand and social or natural truths on the other, both evidence of the divine intention and where it failed. *Of Death*, *Of Truth*, *Of Envy*, *Of Goodness and Goodness of Nature*, and *Of the Greatness of Kingdoms and Estates*, conform to this pattern. Some make the case for the new philosopher subtly by noting that "depth in philosophy bringeth men's minds about to religion" (*Of Atheism*), or that "inquiry of truth is ... the sovereign good of human nature" (*Of Truth*), or that "in all superstition wise men follow fools" (*Of Superstition*). The "theological virtue" of charity and the moral virtue of goodness are imputed to the new scientist, who describes things exactly as they are so that men may see the truth. Machiavelli is praised in *Of Goodness* for having the courage to say that too much Christian virtue is a fault which contains the seeds of man's own destruction. Epicurus is described as "noble and divine" in *Of Atheism* for his honest remark that "There is no profanity in refusing to believe in the Gods of the vulgar: the profanity is in believing of the Gods what the vulgar believe of them." The volume published in 1597, containing the *Essays*, the *Colours*, and the *Religious Meditations*, sets just the right tone for a philosopher writing in a persuasive manner for other learned men. As Bacon says in *Of Vicissitude of Things*, there are three ways by which a new sect of any kind may be established: he rejects both the sword and what he calls "signs and miracles," choosing instead the way of "eloquence and wisdom of speech and persuasion."

It is in the extended philosophical works that Bacon's style shows to greatest advantage. In the Preface and "Plan of the Work," which introduces his scheme for the Great Instauration, he sets up some of the governing metaphors which will continue to argue for the new science and its leader. He describes his method as initially concrete and sensual; it forces men to use their senses properly as agents of the understanding. "I conceive that I perform the office of a true priest of the sense (from which all knowledge in nature must be sought, unless men mean to go mad), and a not unskillful interpreter of its oracles; and that while others only profess to uphold and cultivate the sense, I do so in fact" (*Works*, IV, 26). After a discussion of the idols and the scientist's commitment to identify and reject them, Bacon moves to a new analogy, the scientist as architect. Since philosophers have traditionally built "mimic and fabulous worlds of their own," the only hope for "greater increase or progress lies in a reconstruction of the sciences." The foundation will be formed by natural history, which has been "squeezed and moulded" by man's art but will be restored by the new science. Bacon then compares the new scientist to a nurse, who, unlike those who "instil into children" the "fables and superstitions and follies" which warp their minds, will cleanse their mental operations. This nurse, "having the management of the childhood as it were of philosophy," will "with a religious care ... eject, repress, and as it were exorcise every kind of phantasm." The "Plan of the Work" closes with a comparison of the philosopher to a farmer who labors in the fields of God, "keeping the eye steadily fixed upon the facts of nature and so receiving their images simply as they are." Unlike former philosophers, who created unpalatable and unnatural fruits made of dreams, the new scientist will merely plant seeds, like a true servant of nature, and will rest on the conviction that "the fortune of the human race will give the issue." In one passage which appears early in his Preface, Bacon shows how these various analogies will work to create a composite myth of the new breed of inquirer. Philosophy and the sciences, he says, stand at the present time like "statues, worshipped and celebrated, but not moved and advanced." In the next line they are said to flourish briefly and then to degenerate; they have not been "growing gradually" to reach "their full stature." The sciences as they then stood were "barren of works" because of lack of cultivation. Throughout the longer works these comparisons of the scientist with priests, farmers, architects, and nurses are mingled with each other to present a case for Bacon and his work. They structure the arguments of the *Advancement*, its Latin translation, and the *New Organon*.

In the *Advancement* the following images of the scientist are developed: farmer, doctor, magistrate, lawyer, soldier, explorer, jeweler, cook, architect, and minter of coins. Some of these images have been identified and dealt with as argument by Brian Vickers in his study of philosophy and image patterns in Bacon.[18] His conclusion that Bacon actually thought in images is supported by a study of the way they work. They are casually introduced and are never the subjects of elaborate expansion or discussion. At the same time, however, most of them reappear repeatedly in different contexts to plant seeds in the reader's mind and to convince him that the material is being delivered "in the same method wherein it was invented." In expanding the agricultural metaphor, for example, he speaks of knowledge as a storehouse, a field to be cultivated, a tree to be pruned. At the beginning of Book II the modern philosopher is compared to a farmer who each season must inspect his fields to determine which parts "lie fresh and waste." Bacon's job is described as "husbandry of the mind," or as the "generating and propogating of sciences," or as a stirring of "the earth a little about the roots." He is a planter of seeds, a curer of canker, a laborer in the fields of learning. References to seeds, stems, plants, transplants, growth and fruition occur often in his evaluations of the various fields of learning. In another steadily building image, Bacon is a physician confronted by symptoms and diseases which must be eliminated before they destroy mankind. "Infest," "decay," "corrupt," and "infect" are common words in his survey of the arts and sciences. The diseases and "peccant humours" of learning threaten to "putrify and corrupt" man's mental health. This "degenerate" knowledge must be attacked by the physician of the mind, whose diagnosis cites "excess" of "delicacy and affectation," "vermiculate questions," the absence of light (and consequent spinning of the "cobwebs of learning"), and, the "foulest" diseases, imposture and credulity, which have rendered the sciences "degenerate and imbased." In one passage Bacon combines the farmer and the doctor to describe the affections of men as a subject for the scientist's interest, just as "the knowledge of the diversity of grounds and moulds" should interest a farmer, or "diversity of complexions and constitutions" the physicians (*Works*, III, 437). The metaphor is indistinguishable from the logical analogy in most of Bacon's similitudes.

In using the images of a magistrate or lawyer to enhance the scientist's *ethos*, Bacon employs throughout the *Advancement* verbs like "prosecute," "judge," "appeal," "amend," and "contract," to suggest the tasks and duties which are his to perform. The philosopher must preserve and add to man's "patrimony," fight against sedition and tumult among the branches of knowledge, and break a "contract of error" whenever he spies one. Bacon continually takes the position of a judge determining the extent to which a would-be science is "lawful." Philosophers of the past have created such havoc that all things tend to "dissolve into anarchy." The common man is prosecuted for allowing poetry to make "unlawful matches and divorces of things," and for giving his passions full reign, in spite of their "mutinies and seditions," which cause reason to remain "captive and servile." In that passage on rhetoric, Bacon urges "eloquence of persuasions" to "contract a confederacy between the reason and imagination" (*Works*, III, 410). That, of course, is what he is trying to do in his use of analogy to create a new myth for the world. In his literal and figurative use of the term "law" he attempts to ally the new science with the natural and divine laws of the cosmos and to create the writer in the image of a qualified judge.

In Book I of the *New Organon* the imagery is strengthened and intensified to create a unity of effect not sought in the *Advancement*. It is organized tightly around the image of the scientist as a

Moses figure, clearing the world of its false idols and preparing man, against powerful opposition, for the promised land and salvation. The idols of the mind form the key image, standing as they do for the barriers to a rule of reason. The tone of the book is deliberately oracular, highly dignified and serious, and tersely declarative. The direct religious imagery is seldom abandoned, though few passages are as expansive as the one in which his purpose in the work is described. The idols, he says, must "be renounced and put away with a fixed and solemn determination, and the understanding thoroughly freed and cleansed; the entrance into the kingdom of man, founded on the sciences, being not much other than the entrance into the kingdom of heaven, where-into none may enter except as a little child" (Aph. LXVIII). Each aphorism forms a picture of some kind which appeals to the simplest of our responses while subtly improving the author's image in our minds and preparing us to move forward to the more complex material of Book II. All preconceptions and prejudices abandoned, we are like children, ready to be received. The effort to release us from the idol's captivity includes an attack on logic as the cause of our fall from grace. It made the world a "boundslave" and thought a slave to words (Aph. LXIX). A return to paradise requires a rejection of old logic and misused words, after which we will discover that axioms will begin to cluster like fruit (Aph. LXX). Learning, unfortunately, has so far been largely an evil influence, producing superstition and idolatry, "enchantment from progress," "a reverence for antiquity." Truth, the "daughter of time," seldom appears now because men are "impotent (like persons bewitched)" (Aph. LXXXIV). These comparisons are continued when Bacon suggests that modern alchemists are like the sons of the father in an old fable. The father left riches buried in the vineyards; the sons plowed them all, found nothing, but learned that "though no gold was found there, yet the vintage by that digging was made more plentiful" (Aph. LXXXV). Most contributions to knowledge in the past then have been accidental. Other fables are employed in a similar way to make a case for the real religion. The legend of King Arthur, for example, is compared to the "vanities" of philosophy, which differ from the true arts as Arthur does from Alexander the Great (Aph. LXXXVII). Lest we miss the point, Bacon compares himself with Alexander in Aphorism XCVII. In XCII, he is like Columbus, whose "wonderful voyage" and theory of new continents were thought laughable, but "were afterwards made good by experience, and were the causes and beginnings of great events." Other philosophers, in the meantime, are being dismissed as figures, who like Atalanta ran childishly "after golden apples" (Aph. CXVII).

The true philosopher (namely the author) is a worker in God's fields. He is a healer of men's souls. He recognizes that "natural philosophy is after the word of God the surest medicine against superstition, and the most approved nourishment for faith, and therefore she is rightly given to religion as her most faithful handmaid" (Aph. LXXXIX). Because knowledge is now so "tainted and corrupted," the new science must hear the "confession" of the old, admit that its "calumny on nature herself" has brought despair to the race and "doomed men to perpetual darkness." Incumbent now upon the modern philosopher is the task of separating "dogmas" from axioms and facing the "worst of all auguries" with courage. He must enter the "wastes and deserts" of time (Aph. LXXV–LXXVIII). Nearly all this is said in the first person, and the author himself emerges as the one true savior. His discoveries are "new creations and imitations of God's works" (Aph. CXXIX). "I hear myself soberly and profitably," he says, "sowing . . . for future ages the seeds of a purer truth" (Aph. CXVI). I "wait for the harvest in its due season" (Aph. CXVII). I do not raise a "capitol or pyramid to the pride of men," but lay "a foundation in the human understanding for a holy temple after the model of the world" (Aph. CXX). I follow "the example of the divine creation" and seek entrance to "all the secrets of nature's workshop" (Aph. CXXI). Up to now "no one has yet been found so firm of mind and purpose as resolutely to compel himself to sweep away all theories and common notions" (Aph. XCVII). In short, Bacon is the man to "let the human race recover that right over nature which belongs to it by divine bequest" (Aph. CXXIX). He is the one to show us all that true science is true religion.

Bacon's is a brilliant argument, dependent on the force of pictures drawn in our minds, planted like seeds, which together form a new fable, much like the old hieroglyphic myths, for a new age. The *New Organon* is Bacon's most effective example of how the philosophical style he devised, though rich in metaphor and symbolism, carries the message of the new science without compromising it or misrepresenting its true meaning. At its best it is colorfully suggestive and figurative; it imitates the serious and mysterious tone of the old fables and asks to be approached with the reverence they have received. At the same time, it exposes those myths as hollow and reworks their elements into useful tools for the rational rebuilding of man's intellectual heritage.

We turn finally to the *New Atlantis*, Bacon's impressive illustration of how the acroamatic method may be employed to teach and to stimulate inquiry. The dark and enigmatic manner, true here to its tradition as a means of philosophical delivery, accomplishes at once the two potentials of the fable as a rhetorical device: instruction in "what to think" and preservation for the learned of the sacred mysteries of science and religion. It provides in concise form and with vivid clarity a complete emblematic picture of the philosopher's ideal world. Written earlier but revised in 1624—and purposely left as a fragment for publication, because "the rest was not perfected"—the *New Atlantis* combines the fable with the aphorism to produce a typically Baconian model for the delivery of really important material.

The first part provides a heavy dose of "art and subterfuge" which allows the writer to make his entry into the readers' minds. Yet it manages to avoid the "excess of such vanities" which can destroy "all greatness of mind." Though we sense his impatience to get beyond the Platonic and Christian symbolism, the travel lore, and the social documentation, so that the Father from Salomon's House may speak his aphorisms on the goals of the new science, Bacon pauses long enough to satisfy the requirements of the two audiences of intelligent readers he envisions. As Judah Bierman has shown, one of these groups consists of reluctant readers who fear the effect of the new learning on their social and religious values.[19] Bacon reassures some of these with a picture of a world in which society and worship flourish under the aegis of the new philosophy. Though we know that he has little concern for the impact on society and religion, that he may hope it will be revolutionary, and that, in any event, it is inconceivable in concrete terms, he is still capable of couching his proposals in references to a golden age of the past. Others among the skeptical are likely to reject this utopia because so many of the details of life and worship are neglected. Anyone who actually studies it, of course, will see that conventional social and religious values are undermined by the *New Atlantis*. Modern Europe, rather than Plato, is the villain of the piece. Bensalem is created as an imaginative appeal to draw in readers and not to satisfy curiosity on every level of concern. Much of the material which a real utopia would present is a mystery anyway, and Bacon simply refers these things, as he does in the *Wisdom*, to the category of sacred mysteries. The *New Atlantis*, though it appeals to a general audience of intelligent readers, no more fits the model of a utopia than the *Wisdom* fits that of mythography. Both mythic and utopian forms of delivery are for Bacon vehicles to the "nobler heights" beyond.

The extra meaning in the first part of the *New Atlantis*, in fact, accounts for Bacon's ability there to draw in another audience, readers of intelligence who have been trained to think by allegory and whose great learning allows them to enjoy difficult literary puzzles. These are thoughtful men who are wise to the ways of the acroamatic style. They expect cryptic symbols and recondite allusions; they like to put the pieces together and emerge with answers. When they succeed, they come up with Baconian doctrines which contradict the conservative visions the *New Atlantis* seems to present. Howard B. White, in a stimulating analysis of the work, shows just how widely a learned reader may range in his interpretation of a Baconian fable. From careful examination of Plato's *Timaeus* and *Critias*, Egyptian and Hermetic lore, some Renaissance travel literature, Giordano Bruno's philosophy, and Bacon's own hints in earlier works, White concludes that within the *New Atlantis* there is a secret doctrine of politics which the author transfers only to the most sensitive and alert of his readers, those who can interpret and combine allusions to the remotest sources with reasonable ease.[20] People who prefer the straightforward text can find all these "secrets" openly expressed in Book VIII of the *De augmentis* and in slightly less direct form in the *Essays* and the interpretations which follow the fables in *The Wisdom of the Ancients*. But Bacon does not discourage those who love hieroglyphs in the *New Atlantis*. He says frankly there that the wise man must wear a mask for society and keep his special knowledge from strangers. There are two kinds of riddles in Bacon's philosophical works: those which have no answers and those whose solutions may exist but are of little importance to the job at hand. His strategy is to engage readers with the second kind of puzzle in order to recruit them for the effort to solve the first. This procedure trains the mind and stimulates its urge to research. The unanswered questions in the

myths of Orpheus, Pan, and Cupid, like the many little riddles in
Part One of the *New Atlantis,* are in themselves "nothing to the
table," but, by focusing on the revered and occult mysteries of the
past, Bacon inspires interest in those which will shape the future.

Part One is marked by most of the attributes of fiction: characters
plot, action, and image. The characters are figures like those in the
Wisdom, simple sensuous impressions, analogical forces for clarity
and argument. They are allegorical symbols like those in Spenser's
set pieces, identified only by the qualities which define their
meaning, whether it be their dress, their speech, their professions or
habitats. The narrator is a wise European mariner without the
education which marks those who pass for wise in the schools. He is
stunned by the great mysteries, and he is clearly a figure of the new
scientist, tied to and representing a backward-looking culture which
has lost its way. Before the story ends, he has emerged as the new
leader of the misplaced westerners; it is he who receives information
on Salomon's House and is allowed to publish it. The Governor of
the Strangers' House is used in a similar way to provide transitional
material, all of it in the form of fables representing the knowledge of
nature, which will qualify the new scientist to enter the chambers of
true learning. The Governor is a Christian priest. At the same time,
Joabin the Jew, who is nothing like European Jews, is the vehicle for
Bacon's doctrines of religious toleration, marriage, and chastity. He
is the character who introduces the mariners to the Father of
Salomon's House, who is himself an allegorical figure of the future
scientist and of the remote past. That is, he is both God and God's
son the scientist. He is a man of great dignity who condescends to
tell the narrator, whom he calls "son," in private of the activities and
goals of the great project.

The action and plot of the fable lead to a dramatic conclusion
centering on this Father. Though plot is functional and barely kept
alive by Bacon, the use of set pieces and flashbacks prepares us for
what is to come. Bacon is very gently leading us from one form of
worship, a mystical Christianity marked by faith, to a kind of
naturalism marked by reason. It is here, in his efforts to suggest that
these are compatible, that many of the mysteries necessarily appear.
We wonder why the lost mariners are greeted with a scroll in four
languages, why Spanish is the only modern language represented on
it, and why the people of Bensalem will not allow themselves to
associate freely with the westerners. There is a question as to why the

Governor must suppress some of the details of Bensalem's founding. And minor problems like the number symbolism and the frequent appearance of the color blue in strategic places (not to mention the Father's peach-colored shoes) are very interesting. They abound in the *New Atlantis* and intensify the atmosphere of expectant inquiry and mystery.[21] The long narration of the Governor, the first major pause in the story, is designed to set Bensalem firmly in a Christian context and has the "secret" purpose perhaps of eliminating modern Europe from that divine circle. The Governor relates the exploration of nature in intricate symbolic ways to the rise of Christianity. The history of the New Atlantis is a story set in the past but obviously referring to a possible future for the western world, one in which the new science brings the New Jerusalem. The second major interruption, in fact, comes when the narrator describes at surprising length the Feast of the Family, "a most natural, pious, and reverend custom" which reveals Bensalem as "compounded of all goodness" (*Works*, III, 147). It is in this set piece that many social doctrines from the *Essays* and elsewhere appear, particularly those regarding love, death, old age, kingship, and law. Bacon tells us that this feast is accorded to any man who has lived to see thirty of his descendents reach the age of three. For two days, the Father, or Tirsan, as he is called, consults others and meditates upon family problems, solving them by fiat. All members obey: "such reverence and obedience they give to the order of nature" (ibid., p. 148). On the third day there is a feast full of symbolic props and ceremonies and suggesting nature worship. Though much of this imagery is mysterious, the use of ivy and clusters of grapes recalls the similar imagery in the early works and the *New Organon*. If the grapes stand for axioms, as they do in the *New Organon*, then the ritual in the *New Atlantis* in which the Tirsan passes his golden fruit to his chosen son, designated "Son of the Vine," has a clear meaning. It seems to signify Bacon's technique of cloaking his message in hieroglyphs which can be read only by those who know his full plan for science, revere it, and thus qualify for the search for true axioms. These are guesses, though it must be admitted that the Tirsan's act anticipates the scene in which the narrator is called "son" by the Father of Salomon's House, who then ushers him into the secret chambers. That the narrator is chosen by his fellows over the group's leader to receive this honor is also very suggestive of Bacon's hopes for the future in Europe.

Some of the images in the *New Atlantis* are more obvious than these. References to Plato's dialogues and to the old Atlantis provide a comparison between the old and the new philosophies. These have been catalogued and studied by White as a refutation of the Platonic argument.[22] Most educated readers of his time would spot Bacon's allusions to Plato. Nor would they miss his exploitation of his contemporaries' romance with travel literature, which is evident in his use of Peru, America, Persia, China, and other interesting nations to add color to the story.[23] The voyagers are on their way from Peru to China and Japan when they lose their way. Like other intellectuals of his time, Bacon is fascinated by Oriental writing, religion, and social customs, as he is by the tropical nations so different from his own.[24] America figures in his works as the continent prophesied by Seneca and as the location of what Plato believed to be the old Atlantis. As a scientist, he disregards both of the ancients and looks to Columbus as a source for knowledge; but in the *New Atlantis* America is the land of the first great kingdom. The Governor's narration includes many of the superstitions and tales that Bacon mocks in the *Sylva Sylvarum* and elsewhere, especially those emanating from Egypt. The former Atlantis was destroyed by a flood one thousand years after the Great Flood, and so the Americans are now a much younger people than those of the rest of the world.

> For the poor remnant of human seed which remained in their mountains peopled the country again slowly, by little and little; and being simple and savage people, (not like Noah and his sons, which was the chief family of the earth,) they were not able to leave letters, arts, and civility to their posterity. (*Works*, III, 143.)

The Christian imagery is most important and most obvious in Part One of the *New Atlantis*, while God is mentioned briefly and only in passing in Part Two. Bacon both strengthens and undermines orthodox Christianity, as he does in Book I of the *New Organon*, by striving to appeal at the same time to those whose loyalties are with religion and to those who are chiefly concerned with philosophy. Bensalem is a Christian nation, but Salomon's House existed there before the nation was converted. The study of nature is man's first obligation; it will lead to the worship of God himself if it is carried out properly. Thus, when a great pillar of light rises up from the sea, it is a wise man from Salomon's House who studies it and the cross of light on top of it. It is he who teaches the people that there are divine laws and natural ones. And, by the mysterious powers of the learned, he is able to discern that this miracle is genuine, not one of the "impostures and illusions" that so many people adore. It is the scientist who has the courage to look mysteries in the face and to request of the new-found God that he answer some of them. He therefore is honored with the Bible and proves to be the one who can interpret it and the letter from God to mankind. The island, it proves, is chosen by God because it has earned "salvation and peace and goodwill" (*Works*, III, 138). In comparison, the European wanderers are lost in a "wilderness of waters," begging for mercy, and unentitled to be admitted to the secrets of Bensalem's success. The people of the New Atlantis are "partakers of the blessing." They live in the "Virgin of the World," like Adam and Eve, where there is a "Spirit of Chastity." While they remain unknown to Europe, they have studied its customs carefully and have rejected them. They repudiate the "preposterous wisdom" symbolized by western sexual mores. When Joabin has finished telling all this to the narrator, the narrator's reply is "that he was come to bring to memory our sins; and that I confess the righteousness of Bensalem was greater than the righteousness of Europe" (ibid., p. 153). The Bensalemites' perfection in the eyes of God is symbolized by Salomon's House, which they think was a configuration of the King of the Hebrews, Solomon, and of his works on natural history (which are unavailable to the western world). The name suggests the power both of Solomon and of the ancient king Solamona, who founded the House. It is dedicated to the study of the "Works and Creatures of God," and is "the very eye" of that Christian kingdom.

In part two of the *New Atlantis* then the Father of Salomon's House delivers in clear, very well organized aphorisms the points Bacon wishes to make. Having seen King James rule for more than twenty years without taking a step in the right direction, and having given up his own hopes for taking them himself, Bacon revises his fable in a last attempt to insure the Instauration's survival.[25] At about this time he is reworking the *Wisdom* and writing *On Principles and Origins*, using the acroamatic methods he usually avoided, but changing them to provide only "quiet entry" and subterfuge which will widen his audience and entertain even the "sons of science." Since the West has finally been chosen to receive the wisdom of Salomon's House, Bacon hopes, it is communicated in simple terms:

> Son, to make you know the true state of Salomon's House, I will keep this order. First, I will set forth unto you the end of our foundation. Secondly, the preparations and instruments we have for our works. Thirdly, the several employments and functions whereto our fellows are assigned. And fourthly, the ordinances and rites which we observe. (*Works*, III, 156.)

What follows is a list of all the experiments, observations, instruments, and men that must be assembled for the interpretation of nature. The Father speaks just as Bacon hopes to in his own most serious work: in fragments which are "plainly and perspicuously set down," so that no occasion for error is afforded where accuracy really counts.

The fate of the *New Atlantis*, though it was influential for some years and though it names some scientific goals that still prevail, has upheld Bacon's belief that the acroamatic method is a very dangerous one to employ. Like most of his other works of fable-making, it has contributed to his reputation as a tradition-bound Renaissance man. Even Sprat, author of the *History of the Royal Society*, fails to see that Bacon is demythologizing natural studies by employing myth itself, or that he is following his own method of inquiry by comparing in the *New Atlantis* things which do not exist with things which do. Less learned readers will see the work as a light on antiquity perhaps, but the "sons of science" will read it for the light it throws on nature. The ancient and revered art of mythologizing will yield its powers to the new maker of myths, and the emphasis for study will henceforth be on the uncharted side of the similitude (the things which are or can be). Thus both the writer and the reader will be protected in this initial stage of the development of the new learning. Bacon understands his role in intellectual history and plays it well: though the path to true knowledge through fables has been "narrowed," there is nothing to prevent science's spokesman from using his wit to create new myths from old ones to serve as vehicles to carry men along to greater things. Because the devices of poetry make content "appear" sacred and venerable, Bacon will use his considerable talent in that direction to provide the new mythology. He will do so, "not for the value of the thing," but in the interests of the advancement of learning and the relief of man's estate. Thus he accomplishes as a stylist what his mentors in ancient Rome and on the Continent fail to accomplish. Instead of thrusting his new ideas at readers with no consideration for their imagination or passions, he employs myth and metaphor to enchant every faculty of his readers' minds. Certainly this is a dangerous risk to take, as subsequent events have demonstrated, yet Bacon remains in favor with both groups to whom the *New Atlantis* is addressed, though, in our own age, those audiences' roles have been reversed. Those who still participate in the romance of science and technology continue to cite Bacon as one of the fathers of the age of reason. Those who regret the losses and compromises entailed by a commitment to naturalism are turning increasingly to a study of Bacon as a poet and fabulist. He was among the last to enjoy the best of both worlds.

Notes

Chapter 1

1. The best guides to this development are W. G. Crane, *Wit and Rhetoric in the Renaissance* (New York: Columbia University Press, 1937); Sr. Miriam Joseph, *Shakespeare's Use of the Arts of Language* (New York: Columbia University Press, 1947); Rosemond Tuve, *Elizabethan and Metaphysical Imagery* (Chicago: University of Chicago Press, 1947); and W. S. Howell, *Logic and Rhetoric in England: 1500-1700* (New York: Russell and Russell, 1961).

2. Sr. Miriam Joseph documents this shift fully in *Shakespeare's Use of the Arts of Language*.

3. Cicero, *Orator*, ed. and trans. H. M. Hubbell (Cambridge: Harvard University Press, 1962).

4. For references to and praise of Cicero, see especially the *De augmentis*, I, 1; VI, 3; and VIII, 2. Cicero is quoted more than forty times in the Spedding edition of Bacon's works and, in the essay *Of Building* (*Works*, VI, 482), there is clear evidence of his familiarity with the *Orator* and *De Oratore*.

5. "The Life of the Honourable Author," *Works*, I, 13. For an entirely different and not uncommon view of Bacon's "practice," see Richard L. Ashhurst, *Some Questions of Legal Ethics Suggested by the Life and Career of Lord Chancellor Bacon* (Philadelphia: George Buchanon and Company, 1906). There Bacon is said to have disgraced the bench by his greed and his lack of compassion, gratitude, and a sense of either justice or duty. We owe this sort of uninformed attack to the influence of Thomas Babington Macauley, a "historian" whose essay on Bacon in the *Edinburgh Review* for July 1837, much read and reprinted, has done untold damage to Bacon's character and reputation among those who do not read Bacon or histories of his period. The essay is a flawless example of all the unscrupulous rhetorical tricks of what Bacon calls the "magistral method" of discourse: quotation out of context, *ad hominem* arguments, selection from the relevant facts, the use of connotative words like "tyranny," employment of small and undemonstrated charges to build the case for major ones, confusion of dates, and even occasional outright misstatements. For clear proof of these charges against Macauley, interested people should consult both Spedding's *Life* and his privately printed *Conversations with a Reviewer, or a Free and Particular Examination of Macauley's Article on Lord Bacon in a Series of Dialogues* (London: Richard and John E. Taylor, 1848). Ralph Waldo Emerson, who has a lot to say about Bacon, is also fair. See especially, "Lord Bacon," *The Early Lectures of Ralph Waldo Emerson*, ed. Stephen E. Whicher and Robert E. Spiller (Cambridge: Harvard University Press, 1959), I, 320-36.

6. *Timber, or Discoveries, Ben Jonson*, ed. C. H. Herford, Percy and Evelyn Simpson (Oxford: Clarendon Press, 1947), VIII, 590-91. Modern studies of Bacon's oratory include Robert Hannah, "Francis Bacon, The Political Orator," in *Studies in Rhetoric and Public Address in Honor of James Albert Winans* (New York: The Century Company, 1925), pp. 91-132; and Karl R. Wallace, "Chief Guides for the Study of Bacon's Speeches," *Studies in the Literary Imagination* 4 (April 1971), 173-88.

7. J. F. D'Alton, *Roman Literary Theory and Criticism: A Study in Tendencies* (New York: Russell and Russell, 1962), p. 70.

8. Quintilian, *Institutio Oratoria*, ed. and trans. H. E. Butler (Cambridge: Harvard University Press, 1963), XII, x-xii.

9. See Werner Jaeger, *Paideia: The Ideals of Greek Culture*, trans. Gilbert Highet (Oxford: Oxford University Press, 1948), especially vol. III.

10. R. G. M. Nisbet, "The Speeches," in *Cicero* (New York: Basic Books, 1965), p. 52.

11. Cicero, *Brutus*, ed. and trans. G. L. Hendrikson (Cambridge: Harvard University Press, 1938).

12. Nisbet, "The Speeches," in *Cicero*, pp. 77-78.

13. Cicero, *De Officiis*, ed. and trans. Walter Miller (Cambridge: Harvard University Press, 1938).

14. Ibid., "Introduction," p. xii.

15. D'Alton, *Roman Literary Theory*, p. 233.

16. Ibid., p. 334.

17. Richard M. Gummere, "Introduction," in *Ad Lucilium Epistolae Morales* (Cambridge: Harvard University Press, 1961), I, xi.

18. Tacitus, *Dialogue on Oratory*, ed. and trans. Sir William Peterson (Cambridge: Harvard University Press, 1946), p. 101. Another useful source is J. Wight Duff, *A Literary History of Rome in the Silver Age* (London: Ernest Benn, 1960), pp. 447-76. Robert Adolph presents a case against the influence of Tacitus on Bacon's style, in *The Rise of Modern Prose Style* (Cambridge: MIT Press, 1968), pp. 26-78.

19. E. K. Arnold, *Roman Stoicism* (New York: The Humanities Press, 1958), p. 149.

20. George Williamson, *The Senecan Amble: Prose Form from Bacon to Collier* (Chicago: University of Chicago Press, 1951), pp. 20-31.

21. Ibid., p. 37.

22. Ibid., p. 117.

23. Brian Vickers, *Francis Bacon and Renaissance Prose* (Cambridge: Cambridge University Press, 1968), pp. 13-14. Croll explains that antithesis, as it is employed by Lyly, works as "purely a 'scheme,' that is, a figure of the arrangement of words for an effect of sound. It is not meant to reveal new and striking relations between things; and it is as different as possible, for instance, from such a use of it as in Bacon's saying that 'revenge is a kind of wild justice.' " "The Sources of Euphuistic Rhetoric," in *Style, Rhetoric, and Rhythm: Essays by Morris W. Croll*, ed. J. Max Patrick and Robert O. Evans (Princeton: Princeton University Press, 1966), p. 243.

24. Adolph, *The Rise of Modern Prose Style*, pp. 26-78.

25. See especially the *Advancement of Learning, Works*, III, 419.

26. Both W. S. Howell and Father Walter J. Ong reject the current notion of Bacon as a disciple of Peter Ramus. Ramus, as Howell has noted in *Logic and Rhetoric in England*, pp. 369-70, "indicates his belief in one system for both science and opinion, and in one theory of invention and arrangement for both logician and rhetorician." Bacon criticizes the Ramistic system in the *De augmentis*, VI, 2; in the *Advancement*, I (in *Works*, III, 292); and in *The Masculine Birth of Time* (pp. 63-64 in Benjamin Farrington, *The Philosophy of Francis Bacon: An Essay on Its Development from 1603, with New Translations of Fundamental Texts* [Chicago: University of Chicago Press, 1966]). He seems to be aware of the superficial resemblances between his own system and Ramus's and to make a special point of calling our attention to the profound differences between them. "In remedying the deficiency which he finds in the theory of method as set forth in the controversy over Ramism," Howell says, "Bacon allows method to stand as a part of judgment in logical theory, and even gives the reasons for his stand, thus obviously implying his agreement with Ramus on this point. But Ramus had thought of method exclusively in terms of the delivery of knowledge from one expert to another or from expert to public, and had therefore committed himself to two divisions of method, the natural and the prudential. It is in respect to these cardinal tenets of Ramism that Bacon expresses disagreement, and his disagreement is made manifest ... by the expression of a theory that urges method to consider how it may contribute to the advancement as well as to the mere delivery of learning" (ibid). In *Ramus, Method and the Decay of Dialogue* (Cambridge: Harvard University Press, 1958), Fr. Walter Ong makes it clear as well that Ramus's ideas on invention were Ciceronian to the core. While both Ramus and Bacon sought to make contact with "things themselves," Ramus was clearly "not interested in observation in the Baconian much less the present day sense" (pp. 60 and 195). Other sources for a comparative study of these two figures are Rosemond Tuve, *Elizabethan and Metaphysical Imagery*, pp. 331 ff., where the Ramistic system's effect on Renaissance style is outlined; Frances Yates, *The Art of Memory* (Chicago: University of Chicago Press, 1966), pp. 231 ff., where the differences between Bacon and Ramus on memory are suggested for the reader; and Paolo Rossi, *Francis Bacon: From Magic to Science*, trans. Sacha Rabinovitch (Chicago: University of Chicago Press, 1968), pp. 65 ff., 142-59, 173 ff., and 198 ff., where the superficial resemblances between the two are analyzed fully. As Benjamin Farrington says, "It is a mistake to look to Luther, Calvin, or Ramus for the moral or mental formation of Francis Bacon." *Francis Bacon* (see earlier, this note), p. 17. Bacon took the twentieth-century view of the Ramistic system, a view which sees it, in the words of Neal W. Gilbert, as "the acme of banality." *Renaissance Concepts of Method* (New York: Columbia University Press, 1960), p. 129.

27. *De augmentis*, VI, 3; see also Vickers's excellent analysis of Bacon's debt to Plato, *Francis Bacon*, pp. 30-59.

28. Farrington's translation of the *Masculine Birth*, in *Francis Bacon*, p. 64.

29. See the *De augmentis*, VII, 3.

30. See Marvin T. Herrick, "The Early History of Aristotle's *Rhetoric* in England," *Philological Quarterly* 5 (1926), 242-57.

31. Croll, "'Attic' Prose: Lipsius, Montaigne, Bacon," in *Style, Rhetoric, and Rhythm*, p. 195, n. 3.

32. This section on Bacon and Aristotle appears in somewhat different form in *Speech Monographs* 39 (1972). Many more details are collected in my dissertation, "The Origins and Influence of Bacon's Rhetorical Theory," University of Wisconsin, 1968.

33. One critic, George Williamson, defines Aristotle's rhetoric in the same terms in which he defines Bacon's, but without making the connection. For the former, everything beyond "the requirements of perspicuity may fall into the category of ornament," while, for the latter, style consists of "all that may be added to bare argument," including even "the turn or shape of the argument itself." *The Senecan Amble*, pp. 41 and 163.

34. Williamson reads this passage as a new theory of private rhetoric or "policy." Ibid., p. 160.

35. D'Alton treats this from Theophrastus to the Senecans in *Roman Literary Theory*, p. 70. Croll's essays remain the best guides to the history of the plain style in the Renaissance. For Bacon, see especially Vickers, *Francis Bacon*, and Adolph, *The Rise of Modern Prose Style*.

36. Cf. *De augmentis*, VI, 3; *Rhetoric*, I, 6.

37. I am using *The Rhetoric of Aristotle*, ed. and trans. Lane Cooper (New York: Appleton-Century-Crofts, 1932).

38. William K. Wimsatt and Cleanth Brooks find a "four-layered mattress" in the *Rhetoric* between the truth and the speaker's version of it, "two of the layers being psychological, that is relating to the character and feelings of speaker and audience, one, the layer of probable cognitive arguments, being at least unscientific, and, the fourth, the layer of apparent arguments, being feathered with actual deception." "The Verbal Medium: Plato and Aristotle," in *Literary Criticism: A Short History* (New York: Alfred A. Knopf, 1957), p. 68.

39. Joseph, *Shakespeare's Use of the Art of Language*, p. 17. See also chapters 7 and 8 for an analysis of the figures.

40. Joseph, *Shakespeare's Use of the Art of Language*, p. 17. See also chapters 7 and 8 for an analysis of the figures.

41. Gilbert, *Concepts of Method*, pp. xxiv and 223. Jonas Barish discusses the "logic" of Bacon's style briefly in *Ben Jonson and the Language of Prose Comedy* (Cambridge: Harvard University Press, 1960), p. 60. See Karl R. Wallace, *Francis Bacon on Communication and Rhetoric* (Chapel Hill: University of North Carolina Press, 1943), and Rossi, *Francis Bacon*, for guides to Bacon's views on deduction. The rhetorical uses for induction are outlined by Margaret Wiley in "Francis Bacon: Induction and/or Rhetoric," *Studies in the Literary Imagination* 4 (April 1971), 65–79.

42. In addition to Gilbert, *Concepts of Method*, pp. xxiv and 223, and the other sources named above, see Fulton Anderson's chapters on Bacon and Aristotle in *The Philosophy of Francis Bacon* (Chicago: University of Chicago Press, 1948).

43. Gilbert, *Concepts of Method*, p. 222.

44. Bacon divides the Doctrine of Fallacies into three parts: detection of "sophistical fallacies"; detection of "fallacies of interpretation"; and detection of "false appearances, or idols." All three of these doctrines, treated in the *De augmentis*, V, 4, owe something to Aristotle, though acknowledgments are sometimes lacking.

45. Williamson, *The Senecan Amble*, p. 157.

46. Hardin Craig, *The Enchanted Glass* (New York: Oxford University Press, 1936), p. 175. See also the *De augmentis*, V, 3.

47. See Rossi's analysis, *Francis Bacon*, pp. 214-23.

48. See Wallace, *Francis Bacon on Communication*, pp. 56-73.

49. Gilbert, *Concepts of Method*, p. 224.

50. Rossi, *Francis Bacon*, pp. 147-63.

51. Craig, *The Enchanted Glass*, pp. 173-74.

52. Cf. the *Rhetoric*, II, 1: an orator must "give the right impression of himself" and be "thought to have" the qualities of intelligence, character, and good will. Most important is that he get his judges into the proper mood—an impossible task unless, through study, he has come to know them well.

53. In the *Essays*, "or Counsels Civil and Moral," Bacon adapts his ethical proof to another audience and another rhetorical purpose by attacking the sort of advice he gives here in the *De augmentis*. Those who hide their faults and ignorance, for example, are ridiculous and "fit for a satire to persons of judgment." *Works*, VI, 436.

54. *Timber, or Discoveries, Ben Jonson*, VIII, 590.

Chapter 2

1. Karl R. Wallace, *Francis Bacon on the Nature of Man* (Urbana: University of Illinois Press, 1967).

2. Ibid., p. 6.

3. Ibid., pp. 96 ff.

4. L. C. Knights, "Bacon and the Dissociation of Sensibility," *Explorations* (New York: New York University Press, 1964), p. 120. See also J. L. Harrison, "Bacon's View of Rhetoric, Poetry, and the Imagination," *Huntington Library Quarterly* 20 (1957), 107-25. Knights is challenged most cogently and persuasively by Jeanne Andrewes in "Bacon and the Dissociation of Sensibility," *Notes and Queries* 199 (1954), 484-86, 530-32.

5. Croll, " 'Attic' Prose," p. 196.

6. Rossi, *Francis Bacon*, p. 179.

7. Yates, *The Art of Memory*, pp. 370-73. Rossi also explores this question in *Francis Bacon*, pp. 207-14. For another central passage see Bacon's *Sylva Sylvarum*, Century X, 956, in *Works*, II, 659.

8. Mary Antonia Bowman, "The English Prose Style of Sir Francis Bacon," Ph.D. Diss., University of Wisconsin, 1964. For a critique of this thesis, see Brian Vickers, *Francis Bacon*, pp. 265-67.

9. The most dependable source for treatment and criticism of the nature of Bacon's influence on cipher theories are William F. and Elizabeth S. Friedman's *The Shakespearean Ciphers Examined* (Cambridge: Cambridge University Press, 1957), which treats the subject from a cryptographer's point of view, and S. Schoenbaum, *Shakespeare's Lives* (Oxford: Clarendon Press, 1970), pp. 529-626, which provides a number of amusing and tragic examples of the effect of Bacon's dabbling with cipher theories. See Ellis's note, *Works*, I, 657, and the Appendix, in *Works*, I, 841-44.

10. Cooper, *The Rhetoric of Aristotle*, p. xxiv.

11. Anderson, *The Philosophy of Francis Bacon*, p. 44. Farrington offers an interesting argument for the year 1604 as the time of composition, in *Francis Bacon*, p. 18. Spedding is "inclined to suspect," on the other hand, that the second part of the work was not written before 1608 and explains himself persuasively. *Works*, III, 524.

12. Farrington's translation of the *Masculine Birth*, in *Francis Bacon*.

13. Spedding's argument for 1608 is of interest here.

14. Farrington's translation of the *Refutation*, in *Francis Bacon*, pp. 103-33.

15. Farrington's translation of *Thoughts and Conclusions*, in *Francis Bacon*, pp. 72-102. Section numbers and their titles are supplied by the translator.

16. Spedding takes exception to this common assumption in a learned note, *Works*, III, 208 ff.

17. Anderson, *Francis Bacon*, p. 16.

18. Ellis, in *Works*, III, 201.

19. See Farrington's argument for this date, *Francis Bacon*, p. 60.

20. Farrington defines this procedure as "the intellectualisation of the industrial process," ibid., p. 119, n. 2.

21. See Spedding's helpful notes, *Works*, I, 623.

22. See Anderson's analysis of this doctrine, *Francis Bacon*, pp. 284-88.

23. Bowman, "The English Prose Style of Sir Francis Bacon," pp. 194 ff.

24. For full discussions of Bacon's audience-oriented changes in style, see Vickers, "Literary Revisions," in *Francis Bacon*, pp. 202-31, and Maurice B. McNamee, S.J., "Literary Decorum in Francis Bacon," *St. Louis University Studies*, Series A, Humanities, I, 3 (1950), 1-52.

25. It is not true, on the other hand, that Bacon ever really abandons his original style for what he called "methods," a charge that has been made by D. C. Allen, "Style and Certitude," *ELH* 15 (1948), 167-75.

Chapter 3

1. Vickers, *Francis Bacon*, p. 215.

2. On the extent of Bacon's influence in the seventeenth century, see especially Richard Foster Jones, *Ancients and Moderns: A Study of the Scientific Movement in Seventeenth-Century England*, 2d ed. (Saint Louis: Washington University Studies, 1961). On Bacon's influence in the eighteenth century, see William P. Sandford, *English Theories of Public Address, 1530-1828* (Columbus, Ohio: H. L. Hedrick, 1931), pp. 90-109; and Vincent Bevilacqua's two articles: "The Philosophical Origins of George Campbell's *Philosophy of Rhetoric*," *Speech Monographs* 32 (1965), 1-12, and "Baconian Influences in the Development of Scottish Rhetorical Theory," *Proceedings of the American Philosophical Society* 111 (1967), 212-18. Another important source is Howell's *Eighteenth Century British Logic and Rhetoric* (Princeton: Princeton University Press, 1971), pp. 584-600. Vickers gives a summary description of Bacon's impact on eighteenth- and nineteenth-century literary figures in *Francis Bacon*, pp. 232-61; some of those judgments are conveniently reprinted in *Seventeenth-Century English Prose*, ed. Mary R. Mahl (New York: J. B. Lippincott Company, 1968), pp. 495 ff. See also Karl R. Wallace, *Bacon on Communication*, chap. 11, and "Aspects of Modern Rhetoric in Francis Bacon," *Quarterly Journal of Speech* 42 (1956), 398-406.

3. See especially McNamee, "Literary Decorum," as well as Williamson, *The Senecan Amble* (especially the chapter "Bacon and Stoic Rhetoric") and Bowman, "Francis Bacon."

4. For the standard criticism of Bacon's doctrine of forms, see Virgil K. Whitaker, *Francis Bacon's Intellectual Milieu* (Los Angeles: Clark Memorial Library, UCLA, 1962), and "Bacon's Doctrine of Forms: A Study of Seventeenth-Century Eclecticism," *Huntington Library Quarterly* 33 (1970), 209-16.

5. See Rossi, "Rhetorical Tradition and the Method of Science," in *Francis Bacon*, pp. 186-223; and Margaret Wiley, "Francis Bacon: Induction and/or Rhetoric," *Studies in the Literary Imagination* 4 (April 1971), 65-79.

6. For an excellent analysis of Bacon's method of inquiry, see Benjamin Farrington, *Francis Bacon: Philosopher of Industrial Science* (New York: Henry Schuman, 1949), pp. 123-31. Other important reading on this subject includes the prefaces by Robert L. Ellis to the philosophical works and the *New Organon*, in *Works*, I.

7. One study that must be made is of Bacon's influence on modern poetry. The natural beginning would be with George Herbert. For suggestive but inconclusive remarks on the relation of Bacon to Herbert, see Joseph Summers, *George'Herbert: His Religion and Art* (Cambridge: Harvard University Press, 1954), pp. 97-99, and Appendix B, "Bacon and Herbert," pp. 195-97. Arnold Stein also treats the subject briefly in his introduction to *George Herbert's Lyrics* (Baltimore: Johns Hopkins University Press, 1968).

8. Oddly, very little has been done on Bacon's style. Vickers comes close to his goal, which he describes as the reinstatement of "Bacon as a writer," *Francis Bacon*, p. 261. Bacon's mythopoesis has been examined by W. R. Davis, in "The Imagery of Bacon's Late Works," *Modern Language Quarterly* 27 (1966), 162-73, and James S. Tillman, in "Mythmaking in the Philosophical Proposals of Francis Bacon," Diss. University of Rochester, 1971. John M. Steadman has examined Hercules as one of Bacon's "heroic topoi," in "Beyond Hercules: Bacon and the Scientist as Hero," *Studies in the Literary Imagination* 4 (April 1971), 3-47.

Chapter 4

1. See Charles W. Lemmi, *The Classic Deities in Bacon* (Baltimore: Johns Hopkins University Press, 1933), pp. 177 ff. and 209-12; Brian Vickers, *Francis Bacon*, p. 173; Tucker Brooke, *A Literary History of England*, ed. Albert C. Baugh (New York: Appleton-Century-Crofts, 1948), p. 596; Douglas Bush, *English Literature in the Earlier Seventeenth Century* (Oxford: Clarendon Press, 1962), p. 190; J. A. K. Thomson, *Classical Influences on English Prose* (New York: Collier Books, 1962), p. 190; and Sidney Warhaft, "The Anomaly of Bacon's Allegorizing," *Papers of the Michigan Academy of Science, Arts, and Letters* 43 (1958), 327-33.

2. The best argument for this point of view is Rossi's in *Francis Bacon*, pp. 73 ff.

3. Lemmi, *Classic Deities*, p. 46.

4. For an exhaustive account of Bacon's use of this image see Brian Vickers, "Bacon's Use of Theatrical Imagery," *Studies in the Literary Imagination* 4 (April 1971), 189-226.

5. Bacon's remark in the Preface that the myths contain hidden wisdom because no man's dreams can be so grotesque as they, is ironical in light of his own treatment of dreams as a naturalist. See *Sylva Sylvarum*, *Works*, II, 650 and 666; the *Advancement*, in *Works*, III, 368; and the *De augmentis*, II, 2, in *Works*, IV, 296, for examples.

6. The originality of Bacon's interpretations of the classical myths is in dispute. Though it is true, as Lemmi says in *The Classic Deities*, that Bacon's details tend always to come from Conti and Boccaccio, or some other well-known mythographer, Farrington is correct to note that he owes only his point of departure to these sources (*Francis Bacon*, p. 49, n. 1). For a discussion of this question, see Mary M. Rush,

"Bacon's *Wisdom of the Ancients*: The Uses of Mythology," Diss. Tulane University 1969. This study argues with some success that the interpretations are either completely original with Bacon in the *Wisdom* or are older versions adapted to new purposes.

7. Charles E. Raven, *Natural Religion and Christian Theology* (Cambridge: Cambridge University Press, 1953), p. 107. See also Basil Willey, *The Seventeenth Century Background* (Garden City, N.Y.: Doubleday and Company, 1953), pp. 208 ff.

8. Jean Seznec, *The Survival of the Pagan Gods*, trans. Barbara F. Sessions (New York: Pantheon Books, Bollingen Series XXXVIII, 1953), p. 250 n.

9. Anderson, *Francis Bacon*, p. 57.

10. Rossi, *Francis Bacon*, pp. 76–77.

11. Lemmi has shown in the *Classic Deities* that comparative analysis will reveal many similarities between Bacon's readings and those of these mythographers. This knowledge does not necessarily convince us that Bacon's purposes are the same.

12. Elizabeth Sewell, *The Orphic Voice: Poetry and Natural History* (New Haven: Yale University Press, 1960), p. 61. For another view, see Howard B. White, *Peace among the Willows: The Political Philosophy of Francis Bacon* (The Hague: Martinus Niehoff, 1968), pp. 208–17. For White, the Baconian Orpheus is a secret figure of "definitive morality."

13. Sewell, *Orphic Voice*, p. 96. I cannot agree with the argument in this passage that there is a struggle in Bacon between the cipherer and the hieroglyphic poet: the philosopher who would instruct and the visionary who would conceal. His interest in both forms of discourse is to provide a method of teaching and inspiring the learned without offending the learners (who may, on a second reading, come to his work as converts). If such a conflict were present in the *Wisdom*, we would have, I think, a very different work.

14. There are informative chapters on Bacon's morality in Rossi, *Francis Bacon*; Rush, "Bacon's *Wisdom*"; and White, *Peace among the Willows*. See also the section on Bacon and Aristotle in chapter 1 of the present study.

15. R. S. Crane, in "The Relation of Bacon's *Essays* to his Program for the Advancement of Learning," *Schelling Anniversary Papers* (New York: Century Company, 1923), pp. 87–105, demonstrates the centrality of the *Essays* to the program for the Great Instauration. Stanley E. Fish, "Georgics of the Mind: The Experience of Bacon's *Essays*," *Self-Consuming Artifacts: The Experience of Seventeenth-Century Literature* (Berkeley: University of California Press, 1972), pp. 78–155.

16. Stephen C. Pepper, "An Essay on the'Essay: An Aesthetic Appreciation," *The New Scholasticism* 41 (1967), 295–311.

17. Though I am using the Spedding edition of the *Essays*, in volume VI of the *Works*, a better edition for comparative purposes is Edward Arber's *A Harmony of the Essays of Francis Bacon* (Westminster: A. Constable and Company, 1895). See Jeanne Andrewes, "Bacon and the Dissociation of Sensibility," pp. 530–31, for an excellent analysis of this image.

18. Vickers, *Francis Bacon*, pp. 174–201.

19. Judah Bierman, "Science and Society in the *New Atlantis* and other Renaissance Utopias," *PMLA* 78 (1963), 492–500. A more recent article by Bierman is *"New Atlantis* Revisited," *Studies in the Literary Imagination* 4 (April 1971), 121–42.

20. White, *Peace among the Willows*, pp. 108-89.

21. White has very interesting answers to all these questions; see especially chapter 10, ibid., where he treats color and number symbolism.

22. Ibid., pp. 109-27.

23. In addition to White, *Peace among the Willows*, pp. 141 ff., see Robert Ralston Cawley, *Unpathed Waters: Studies in the Influence of Voyagers on Elizabethan Literature* (New York: Octagon Books, 1967), pp. 242-47.

24. See, for examples on China: *Works*, I, 651-52; II, 448, 577; III, 240; IV, 237; VI, 516. On Peru: *Works*, V, 158; VII, 21, 22. On Persia: *Works*, II, 458, 532; VII, 49, 50, 53, 63.

25. See Anderson, *Francis Bacon*, p. 26, on this effort, and pp. 295 ff. on the influence of the *New Atlantis*.

Index

Abecedarium Naturae, 130
Abstractions in science and style, 9, 25, 58, 98, 107, 142-43
Accepted conventions in scientific writing, 122, 133-37
Accommodation: rhetorical means of, 13, 68, 76-77, 101; Aristotle's doctrine of, 36-39
Acroamatic method, xi, 69, 85-86, 98, 124-33, 137-53, 156, 165, 169
Acteon, Bacon's interpretation of, 145
Adam, 7, 85-86, 169
Adolph, Robert, 34, 174 n. 18
Adonis, 19
Advancement in Life, the doctrine of, 25, 50-52
Advancement of Learning, 3, 14, 20-22, 25, 37, 46-48, 56-77, 81, 84-85, 87, 89, 93-94, 100, 106, 108-9, 112-15, 125, 130-33, 138-41, 143, 145, 149, 156, 160
Aeneas, 93
Aesthetics in scientific style, 121-36
Alchemy, Bacon's views on, 11, 84, 141-42, 162
Alexander the Great, 86, 120, 141, 162
Allegory, 83, 102, 124-25, 131, 146-50, 165
Alphabets, 72, 130
Ambiguity, 46, 60, 72, 84
America, 168
Anagrams, 130
Analogy, 41, 45, 71, 78, 93-94, 102, 108, 122-23, 127-29, 131-32, 154-57, 159-61, 166
Anderson, Fulton, 80, 85, 146

Anticipations of the mind, 90, 109, 113, 116. *See also* Literate experience
Antithesis, 30, 33, 73-74
Aphorism, x, 10, 58, 70, 81, 84, 86, 93, 98-121, 122, 125, 133-36, 137, 139, 156, 162, 164, 169
Apollo, 125
Apophthegms, 106, 124
Apophthegms: New and Old, 74
Appetite, the human, 64-67, 128
Application, experimental method of, 95-96
Aristotle, x, 13, 22-31, 35, 36-54, 57, 84, 90, 106, 176 n. 44
Arnold, E. K., 32
Ascham, Roger, 19
Asianism, a fault of style, 27
Atalanta, 86, 135, 163
Atticism, Roman, 4, 23, 27-29, 39
Axiom, 9, 25, 70, 76, 91, 106, 109, 115, 121, 162, 167

Bacchus, 145
Bacon, Sir Francis: alters public statements on value of fables, 142-45; analyzes human imagination, 61-64; analyzes nature of memory, 67-76; analyzes understanding, 8-10, 57-58, 104-5; analyzes will and appetite, 64-67; attributes styles to stages of philosophy, 112-21; becomes reluctant disciple of Aristotle, 36-54; defines rhetoric, 57, 61-62, 65, 86, 102-5, 161; develops aesthetic for philosophic style, 121-36; develops doctrine of